THE ECCLESIAL CANOPY

In this third book of his trilogy on ecclesiology Martyn Percy unfolds a vision for the church. Percy's well known gifts as theologian and writer shine through the lively and insightful theological sketches in this volume. The author speaks of a living, breathing church with remarkable capacities for renewing social life. The result is an imaginative, attractive and engaging spirituality of the church in contemporary culture. Faith, hope and charity emerge as key marks of an ecclesial canopy. The book is an engaging, wise and stimulating commentary on the persistence of religion in western society.

The Rt Revd Dr Stephen Pickard, author of *Theological Foundations for Collaborative Ministry* and *In-Between God: Theology, Community and Discipleship*

Seeking to dynamically alter the way that theologians, ecclesiologists, students of religion and ministers look at the relationship between church and society, this book takes religion, politics and society as basic categories and explores how oft-overlooked issues are in fact highly significant for the shaping of theological and ecclesiological horizons. *The Ecclesial Canopy* is not, however, simply about reading meanings into religion, politics and society. Rather, it sets out to faithfully interpret much of the material that surrounds us, yet is often taken for granted or unnoticed. Paying close and patient attention to beliefs, language, artefacts, rituals, practices and other material – all of which are constitutive for ecclesial life and theological identity – this book offers an invitation of engagement to the scholar or minister.

The Ecclesial Canopy makes a significant and important contribution to the field of pastoral and practical theology. Building on the concepts of implicit and invisible religion, Martyn Percy offers a fresh and original interpretative 'take' on contemporary society, appealing to clergy, laity, scholars and all those working in the field of theory and reflective practice in practical and pastoral theology.

Explorations in Practical, Pastoral and Empirical Theology

Series Editors

Leslie J. Francis, University of Warwick, UK,
Jeff Astley, North of England Institute for Christian Education, UK
Martyn Percy, Ripon College Cuddesdon and
King's College, London, UK

Theological reflection on the church's practice is now recognised as a significant element in theological studies in the academy and seminary. Ashgate's series in practical, pastoral and empirical theology seeks to foster this resurgence of interest and encourage new developments in practical and applied aspects of theology worldwide. This timely series draws together a wide range of disciplinary approaches and empirical studies to embrace contemporary developments including: the expansion of research in empirical theology, psychological theology, ministry studies, public theology, Christian education and faith development; key issues of contemporary society such as health, ethics and the environment; and more traditional areas of concern such as pastoral care and counselling.

The Ecclesial Canopy
Faith, Hope, Charity

MARTYN PERCY
Ripon College Cuddesdon, and King's College, London, UK

ASHGATE

Published by
Ashgate Publishing Limited
Wey Court East
Union Road
Farnham
Surrey, GU9 7PT
England

Ashgate Publishing Company
Suite 420
101 Cherry Street
Burlington
VT 05401-4405
USA

www.ashgate.com

British Library Cataloguing in Publication Data
Percy, Martyn.
  The ecclesial canopy : faith, hope, charity. —
  (Explorations in practical, pastoral and empirical theology)
  1. Theology, Practical. 2. Pastoral theology. 3. Church and the world.
  I. Title II. Series
  261.1–dc23

Library of Congress Cataloging-in-Publication Data
Percy, Martyn.
  The ecclesial canopy : faith, hope, charity / Martyn Percy.
    p. cm. — (Explorations in practical, pastoral, and empirical theology)
  Includes bibliographical references and index.
  ISBN 978-1-4094-4119-9 (hardcover : alk. paper) — ISBN 978-1-4094-4120-5
(pbk. : alk. paper) — ISBN 978-1-4094-4121-2 (ebook) 1. Church growth.
2. Mission of the church. 3. Christianity and culture. 4. Pastoral theology.
5. Theology, Practical. I. Title.
  BV652.25.P467 2012
  261–dc23

                                                                    2011041729

ISBN 9781409441199 (hbk)
ISBN 9781409441205 (pbk)
ISBN 9781409441212 (ebk)

Printed and bound in Great Britain by the
MPG Books Group, UK.

For Stewart, Nick and Tim

And so we rise –
We scraps of hope and bone
Are gathered,
Aligned by sinew and desire
To cry for, to breathe our All,
Our Abba.

In this truth we stay,
As Spirit spreads her cloak
Over the bare soul's flesh
And rocks the crib of our content.

The sky is cavernous
And creation sighs,
Its clay also, a bed
For cherishing.

(Roland Riem)

Contents

Acknowledgements

I am grateful to a number of friends and colleagues in the writing of this book. In particular, to staff and students at Ripon College Cuddesdon, who provide an unfailing environment of wisdom, nourishment and support in so many and varied ways. And thanks are also due to those graduate and research students I have been fortunate enough to accompany in their studies – for their ideas and influences they have brought to bear on my own thinking. Particular thanks are also due to Emma Percy, Jenny Gaffin, Ian Markham, Gareth Jones, Stephen Pickard, Paul Kwong and Peter Koon – for many conversations, and for their insightful comments.

This is the third in a trilogy of sketches concerned with ecclesiology, and, like the preceding two volumes, the genesis of this volume lies in lectures and papers that have been given in recent years. In Part One, the material for the first two chapters is drawn from lectures given originally at Gresham College, London, and published in earlier forms in my *Salt of the Earth* (Continuum, 2001). Chapter three is drawn from more recent material that has been explored with dioceses and clergy in conferences and consultations. In Part Two, an earlier version of the fourth chapter appeared in the *Blackwell Companion to Modern Theology* (ed. G. Jones, 2005), of chapter five in *Reinhold Niebuhr and Contemporary Politics* (R. Harries and S. Platten (eds), OUP, 2010), and of chapter six again in *Salt of the Earth* (2001).

In Part Three, chapter seven has been slightly reworked from an essay that appeared in *Intercultural Theology: Approaches and Themes*, and edited by Mark Cartledge and David Cheetham (SCM, 2011), with chapters eight and nine drawing on some material that has been used in earlier speeches and lectures, and with the purpose of providing some slight intentional overlap and linkage to the two preceding volumes. (I have dared to presume that not everyone who reads this volume will have necessarily read the other two.) The first part of the Conclusion partially draws on an essay that originally appeared in *Religion, Time and Change* (M. Percy (ed.), Sheffield Academic Press, 2000). The second part of the Conclusion draws on a story published in *Modern Believing* (vol. 52: 3, July 2011, pp. 33–40).

Lastly, I once again thank my family for their forbearance during the writing of this book. Their love and support is, always, beyond measure.

Martyn Percy, Epiphany 2012

Introduction

For more than two centuries, secularisation theorists have been asserting that religion must inevitably decline in the modern world; prophesying its final end, as the clarity of modernity gradually dispels the fog of superstition and religiosity. Yet despite much talk, and many theses, much of the world today remains as religious as it ever was. Indeed, it is arguably more so. To lack knowledge of faith, or to be religiously illiterate today, is at best unwise, and at worst dangerous.

This book, however – the third in a trilogy that addresses church, faith and society[1] – is not specifically about the shortcomings of secularisation theses. Nor is it about some of the more dysfunctional morphologies of religion that have emerged in response to modernity. It is, rather, an attempt to sketch out something of spirituality of ecclesiology, and specifically to suggest that something like what could be termed an 'ecclesial canopy' still provides some measure of meaning and value in modern societies. It is primarily a work of practical-pastoral theology – but one rooted in ecclesiological considerations and cultural studies. In hinting at an ecclesial canopy, I am of course making a thinly-veiled reference to Peter Berger's idea of a sacred canopy,[2] and suggesting that our social constructions of reality still contain elements and values that might be inferred from ecclesiological investigations. The volume therefore challenges the belief that the modern world is increasingly bound to a secular trajectory, showing that while aspects of modernity do indeed have some secularizing effects, reactions are also provoked that could be said to consolidate religion and ultimately strengthen faith.[3]

There are several ideas implicit in the concept of an enduring ecclesial canopy. The first is that the church still provides an overarching narrative of meaning and truth in modern life. This may not be, at times, adequate and comprehensive. And at the risk of extending the canopy metaphor, one might argue that the roof has one or two holes, is in need of repair, and can no longer stretch socially and culturally to cover all of life. The second is that the canopy is itself a form of 'stretched social skin' that provides shape and identity for the wider social body, as well as a register of values and moods in society.[4] A third suggestion is that the canopy

---

[1]   See Percy (2005 and 2010). This volume picks up where the other left off, with reflections on spiritual space and the capaciousness of God.

[2]   See Peter Berger (1966 or 1967).

[3]   On this, see Peter Berger (1999).

[4]   For a fuller discussion, see Dan Hardy (2002).

provides social and cultural space – generously, and without calibrating the cost to itself – for society to explore and practice the values it needs to discover and recover for social flourishing. This explains the subtitle of this book – faith, hope and charity – suggesting that there continues to be a link between the values and character of the church, rooted in the transcendent, which have a bearing on the modelling of society. Put another way, how Christians diversify and disagree, and how faith mutates under a range of pressures, may be teaching society more about how to cope with an increasing miscellany of beliefs and competing convictions, than dwelling on the more pedestrian aspects of what Christians cannot agree upon (e.g., sexuality, gender, faith order, etc.). A fourth suggestion is that for all the secularising tendencies of the modern world, the shape and coverage of the church continues to provide an enduring space and shelter under which ideas and values can be explored in a spirit of generosity and openness. A final suggestion is that the churches, in their ministry, are often unaware of the social environments in which they are immersed, and the opportunities they create. For example, both the possibilities and problems of consumerism present particular issues for the churches. The influence of the church in such situations is of course manifest; but often also actualised and experienced in deep, latent, implicit ways that are seldom articulated. This is a pity, because as Reed suggests, the ecclesial construction of reality is a powerful, value-led and socially enriching form of encompassing that often does more than it knows:

> If bees could talk, and we came across them busy in a flower garden and enquired what they were doing, their reply might be: 'Gathering nectar to make honey'. But if we asked the gardener, he would most certainly answer: 'They are cross-pollinating my flowers'. In carrying out their manifest function to make food, the bees were performing a latent function of fertilising flowers. The mutual dependence of bees and flowers is an analogue of churches and society (Reed 1978, p. 145).

Peter Berger's early work on the social construction of reality informs the perceptions outlined above. Indeed, I wish to argue that there is also a public 'theological construction of reality' that is fused within the socio-sacred canopy under which we dwell. The canopy is, of course, only a metaphor – but one that serves us well in thinking about the nature of the universe – the social and sacred canopy that continues to shape our thinking, values, beliefs, behaviours and practices. As Berger says, 'social order is a human product, or more precisely, an ongoing human production' (1967, p. 52). Thus,

> ... a social world [is] a comprehensive and given reality confronting the individual in a manner analogous to the reality of the natural world ... In early phases of socialisation the child is quite incapable of distinguishing between the objectivity of natural phenomena and the objectivity of the social formations .... The objective reality of institutions is not diminished if the individual does not understand their purpose or their mode of operation .... He must 'go out' and learn about them, just as he must learn about nature.... (1967, pp. 59–61).

And it follows from this that what we think we know is, in fact, shaped by innate commitments to higher frames of knowledge that we rarely interrogate. Thus,

> ... theoretical knowledge is only a small and by no means the most important part of what passed for knowledge in a society ... the primary knowledge about the institutional order is knowledge ... is the sum total of 'what everybody knows' about a social world, an assemblage of maxims, morals, proverbial nuggets of wisdom, values and beliefs, myths, and so forth (1967, p. 65).

And from this, it therefore follows, in terms of knowledge and its legitimacy – a canopy, so to speak – is often just beyond our immediate, everyday, critical grasp, such that:

> The function of legitimation is to make objectively available and subjectively plausible the 'first-order' objectivations that have been institutionalised.... Proverbs, moral maxims and wise sayings are common on this level ... [as well as] explicit theories ... symbolic processes ... a general theory of the cosmos and a general theory of man .... The symbolic universe also orders history. It locates all collective events in a cohesive unity that includes past, present and future (pp. 92–104).

Like most other sociologists of religion writing in the 1960s, Berger predicted the eventual and all-encompassing secularization of the world. Yet by end of the twentieth century, Berger's work very clearly recognises that religion (new faiths, as well as older, traditional forms of religion) was not only still prevalent, but in many cases was more vibrantly and intensely practised than in periods in the past, and perhaps particularly in the USA. It would have been a surprise to many sociologists of religion in the 1960s to discover that the first decade of the new millennium was characterised as much by religion in the public sphere, as by any other factors. Berger did, however, qualify these concessions. He does recognise that religion is a powerful social force in later modernity. But he also points to the fact that pluralism and the globalised world fundamentally change how the individual experiences faith (i.e., consumerism, choice, new patterns of believing and belonging, etc.), with the taken-assumed nature of religion often being replaced by an individual's search for a personal religious preference. In this respect, the more recent *Desecularization of the World* (1999) explores how Western academia and Western Europe itself are in fact exceptions to the triumphant desecularisation hypothesis: these cultures have continued to develop into highly secularised ones despite the resurgence of religion in the rest of the world.

Yet it is this notion of 'encompassing' I want to press in this volume. If society is still somehow held and shaped by frameworks of knowledge, assumptions about values, behaviours, beliefs and practices, to what extent is the framework (or canopy) a social, secular or sacred construction? Moreover, is there any sense in which it can legitimately claimed that there is some persistence of an ecclesial canopy – a body of knowledge, constructions of reality, artefacts, beliefs, practices and values, that still somehow shape and hold society? And is there a pastoral, generous and hospitable way of owning and practising a form of ecclesial encompassing in a plural and diverse society? I believe so. Moreover, I also hold that this idea of canopy of knowledge, rooted in institutional life – hence sacred or ecclesial canopies – is also rooted in the Christian scriptures. And whilst this is not an exercise in biblical exegesis or eisegesis, readers will see the inferences drawn from the Old and New Testaments. The comfort, for example, that can be taken from Isaiah's conceptualisation of God's canopy:

> He will feed his flock like a shepherd: he will gather the lambs with his arm, and carry them in his bosom; he will gently lead those that give suck. Who has measured the waters in the hollow of his hand, and meted out the heavens with his span ...? (Isaiah 40: 1–12).

Finally, the concept of the canopy itself intentionally points in several ways. The word has a complex etymology, originally meaning 'bed curtain', but from which we also derive the modern French word 'canapé'. Dissimilated from the Latin 'conopeum', from the Greek 'konopeion' (meaning 'Egyptian couch with curtains'), the same word can now mean 'sofa' and 'couch' (places to lie on) as well as referring to the canopies of heaven and water that ancient societies believed were above the world. An ecclesial canopy, then, is something that is both supportive and above us; but always that larger space which is simultaneously homely and comforting, as well as a virtually limitless and expansive environment in which God both dwells, yet is also above and beyond:

> Thus says the Lord God, who created the heavens and stretched them out, who
> spread out the earth and its offspring, who gives breath to the people on it, and
> spirit to those who walk in it … (Isaiah 42:5).

Inevitably, perhaps, the thesis follows the proximate contours of Peter Berger's
contributions to such debates. Yet whilst these span a considerable period, and
richly deserve the scholarly and journalistic attention they have received over
the decades, the main focus of this book is in providing a sketch that offers a
spirituality of ecclesiology. The use of the word 'sketch' is quite deliberate here.
As with the two preceding volumes, the trilogy as a whole is not an attempt to offer
a systematic account of the church. Others, such as Roger Haight,[5] have already
provided the church and the academy with this kind of illuminating description
and explanation. A sketch, in contrast, is a work in progress. It is an intentional
approach to its subject: a piece of work that recognises that the living, breathing
church – this social skin of the world – can support a form of commentary that
is neither systematic nor dogmatic in outlook, but is rather provisional and
speculative in nature. Indeed, such an approach merely recognises that

> … even in the time of Jesus, and certainly afterward, the Church was not first an
> idea or a doctrine, but a *practice* of commonality in faith and mission (Daniel
> Hardy, 2000, p. 29).

There is a sense, then, in which this volume seeks to sketch out what these
practices looks like, and set against a contemporary cultural context that both
projects and imagines a secular worldview which has no need for the kind of
shape, depth and richness that faith can bring to everyday life. Here, I am drawing
on – though not necessarily fully concurring with – John Milbank's reflective
essay 'On Complex Space' (1997, pp. 268–92). Here Milbank draws our attention
to the overlapping of interests and competing convictions which can be inimical to
Christianity. Whilst I find the tone (and therefore the ethos) of his argument to be
rather insistent (hectoring, even), I nonetheless agree that Christians should refuse
to be 'resigned to the present age' and should 'endorse the Catholic advocacy of a
complex gothic space' in which 'church and society can flourish' (1997, p. 285).
So, by focusing on faith, hope and charity, I am seeking to set out something of
how the church continues to provide a discrete set of practices and values that, in
turn, have some implications for the articulation of any spirituality of the church.
As Berger expresses it,

---

[5]   See R. Haight (2004, 2005, 2008).

> Every human society is an enterprise of world-building. Religion occupies a distinctive place in this enterprise. Our main purpose here is to make some general statements about the relationship between human religion and human world-building (Peter Berger, 1967, p. 1).

Each chapter is a kind of sketch focused on contemporary ecclesiology, rooted in practical and pastoral theology. With a focus throughout the book on the mutations of Christianity in contemporary culture – a theme indeed, of the three volumes – and the ways in which cultural and faith interact with Christian beliefs and practices (ecclesiology), this third and final volume also links the reflections to the principal virtues that concludes Paul's meditation on love in his first letter to the Corinthians, chapter thirteen: faith, hope and charity. The observations and reflections – preliminary, explorative and in some places teasing – are intended to offer some intriguing new ways of looking at the religious issues confronting humanity and society, and the emerging mutations produced by the interactions between Christianity and contemporary culture.

The first part of this book explores Christian faith in the modern world, examining some of the spatial, competitive, consumerist (including commodification) and organisational issues that have an impact on the development of today's socio-cultural space. The second part of the book examines three socio-political situations – social Christianity and liberation; sinfulness and society; and public truth, pluralism and human rights – to look at the kinds of hopes, mutations and transformations that are emerging in culture and contemporary Christian practice. The third part examines charity and ecclesial polity, and, as with the two previous volumes in the trilogy, takes Anglicanism as a kind of default case-study, exploring a range of issues in contemporary ecclesial praxis. With the focus again on mutations and synergies, these final three chapters hint at some future pointers for practical and pastoral theology – as an arena for deeper empathetic critical self-awareness, dialogue, hospitality and hope in ecclesial life. The conclusion is in two parts, and returns to the issue of choice and consumerism for churches explored in Part One (and, indeed, is a major thread that runs through all three volumes). The first part of the Conclusion offers what I have termed a forward-looking critical retrospect, which, amongst other issues, explores the Millennium Dome as a canopy space. In returning to some of the themes explored in the Introduction, this essay examines the contested nature of sacred space and time in the context of a culture that is increasingly shaped by secularisation, pluralism and consumerism. The second essay in the Conclusion, a Coda, is a satirical story. This is an unusual way to end, but one that returns us to the organisational and consumerist concerns that have characterised this volume, and the trilogy.

Sketches on World-Building: Christianity and Contemporary Culture

In a recent essay from Linda Woodhead (2010), she argues that there are at least four models of religion – as belief, as identity-shaping and boundary-forming, as value-commitment, and as power. She also adds a fifth – as 'super-social relations', providing meaning, coherence, direction, unity, easement and a sense of control over events. Rather as Geertz suggested, as a system of symbols that acts to establish powerful, pervasive and long-lasting moods and motivations in people by forming conceptions of a general order of existence and giving these conceptions an aura of factuality that makes them uniquely realistic.

It would have taken a brave cultural commentator to predict that the opening years of the twenty-first century would be characterised by a new awareness of religious resurgence. That the new millennium would continue to provide space for religion, that provided meaning, gave order and substance to lives and wider society, and still have an air of factuality and realism that continues to confound proponents of secularism and humanism. To the casual observer in late modernity, many forms of organised religion looked to be on the wane – suffering from the corrosive vapours of secularism, modernity and consumerism. But the pessimistic prophecies propagated from the pulpits of secular soothsayers have not come to pass. Religion is as strong as ever, and showing every sign of a tenacious resilience for adaptation.

For the most part, the more aware periodicals, journals and commentators have not been afraid to sketch the emerging picture, even if the authors have not always cared for their subject. One thinks of Gilles Kepel's *Revenge of God* (1994), charting the resurgence of Islam, Christianity and Judaism in the modern world. Or again of the revisionist sociology of Peter Berger, who has recognised the capacity of religion to mutate within modernity, rather than merely melt away.

In a similar vein, a religious and cultural commentary such as *God is Back* (2009) – written by two senior editors from the *Economist* – gets to grips with the puzzle of the enduring potency of religious belief and behaviour in contemporary culture. The authors are keenly aware that the 'God is dead' rumour – running from around the time of Nietzsche – is palpably untrue. Indeed, the non-Advent of his demise has generated a kind of cognitive dissonance amongst committed secularists, which in some respects explains the evangelistic zeal of the remaining prophets of secularism such as Richard Dawkins and Christopher Hitchens. But there are now few takers for the crusading rallies of atheism. Moreover, as Micklethwait and Woolbridge point out, religion is now even more visible and demonstrable in many of the spheres it was presumed to be absent from. In public life, civil unrest, wars, ethical debates and social upheaval, religion plays an increasingly significant role – even if it is one that not all faith members of those communities would wish to own.

The authors offer a considerable and perceptive outlook on the role of the USA in religious resurgence. The combination of social, political and market freedom has led to a booming culture of religious competition in North America. Fused with the Enlightenment, globalisation and outright pragmatism, religion has become a successful export. And where the subtle brand of American imperialism has been resisted – especially in the Middle East – religious reactions have flourished. The embers of religion, when not glowing, are aflame.

Micklethwait and Woolbridge seldom take sides in their rich analytical description of the global state of religious affairs. They acknowledge that most of America's so-called 'social capital' has a religious source, and that those civic associations without a religious base are less likely to flourish than those that do. (This is broadly true of Europe too, but we tend to be more reticent in owning and affirming this.) Faith, in other words, is doing a great deal of good for a great number of people over a great span of society. But more often than not, the influence is undetected and mellifluous.

The authors also have a good eye for the apparent contradictions and puzzles of American Christianity. Perhaps too much time is devoted to fallen faith leaders and noted evangelists who have fallen foul of the vices they spent so much time preaching against (e.g., Swaggart, Bakker etc.). And the attention given to some of the more bizarre fusions of faith, leisure and consumerism is a little laboured in places, giving the sense that religion is still something to be treated as specious.

For example, the Golgotha Fun Park in Cave City, Kentucky, we are told, has a nine-hole crazy golf course that begins with creation and ends with the rapture. It is a work of intelligent journalism, which offers a rich tapestry of description and analysis, and makes judicious use of academic insight to support a rather strong thesis. It is not so much that God is back. He never went away. So the emerging puzzle of the third millennium is, therefore, the persistence and vibrancy of religion, and not its absence. Even in the developed nations of the world, it has been strange to observe how much qualification traditional modes of the secularisation thesis now require.

Some years ago, I was involved with a British university in the auditing of an American bible college. Our hosts were always most gracious and kind, but one did not have to spend too long in the conversations over dinner to discover how differently we saw the world. Polite chat would quickly move to a range of issues that clearly perplexed our colleagues from the mid-west. 'Is it true that Britain is now full of mosques, and the churches are all shut?'; 'why do you pay your clergy all the same, no matter how they perform?'; and 'do you really have state-funded church schools?', were queries that typically surfaced. Trying to explain any of the reasons why, one quickly learnt, required much more than a short lesson on the history of religious establishment. There are deeper pulses at work. Our hosts could not understand why Tony Blair 'didn't do God', but still chose bishops. Just as Britons, mostly, cannot understand why Sarah Palin 'doing God' (as much as possible) might influence a single voter at the ballot box.

America and Europe are indeed an ocean apart, and the differences between the two continents are most sharply observed when comparing and contrasting religious identity and patterns of affiliation. The dominant mode of religious belonging in Europe assumes that religion is a kind of utility: always there, and somehow provided by the state or derived from nascent social capital. A kind of spiritual National Health Service (NHS), if you will: extensive, vicarious, and all-purpose. Believing without belonging is quite normative, in the same way that one is comforted by the knowledge that local dentists and doctors exist, but do not need to be troubled unless one requires their services.

In the USA, however, religious affiliation tends to be a conscious choice that is more culturally and socially indicative. Belonging to a church is both voluntary and deliberate, just as one would expect from a society whose very DNA requires consumers – including religious ones – to exercise their freedom, make choices, and then support their chosen affiliation with a degree of dedication and passion. This is a kind of market model of religion, where intensive, personal and collective faith flourishes in competition with other expressions of religiosity.

In *Religious America, Secular Europe? A Theme and Variations* (2008), for example, the authors wrestle with a problem that has become something of a cliché; that Europe is secular and America religious. In seven rich and illuminating chapters, Berger, Davie and Fokas contrast four variant themes that might help to explain the differences and similarities: those histories, intellectual traditions, institutional factors and social distinctives that lead to religion being experienced and expressed in strikingly dissimilar ways on either side of the pond. The authors are well placed to offer their astute and timely observations, and the book is as inspiring as it is informative and thought provoking. For it enables the reader to get to grips with the whys and wherefores of spiritual differentiation: two continents, forever divided by a seemingly similar religious language and culture.

Berger, for example, offers a pithy reflection on having breakfast at a hotel in Austin, Texas, with two businessmen sat near him, eating and reading their newspapers. One looks up and says 'the situation is really hotting up in the Middle East', before pausing and adding 'just as the bible said it would'. His companion simply grunts in agreement, and carries on reading his newspaper. On the other hand, whilst staying in a London hotel, he cannot find a concierge who can direct him to an Anglican service. Berger comments that it is not odd that the staff did not go to church, since 'that is now commonplace in English society'. What is odder is that the hotel staff seemed not to be able to comprehend the request. It is refreshing to find such a cogent argument that debunks so many of the cherished arguments of secularisation theory. The hypothesis that Europe is normal and secular because of modernity and the Enlightenment is no longer plausible. Because the vibrancy of religiosity in America – and other developed and developing nations – suggests that it is Europe's secularity that is specious, and requires an explanation. In their enticing mix of personal musings and sociological reflections Berger, Davie and Fokas offer a rich and thought-provoking account of why two continents, an ocean apart, which have produced such markedly different kinds of religiosity in contemporary society.

The Spiritual, Spatial Turn

The intention, then, in this third volume of the trilogy focused on ecclesiology, is to begin articulating a spirituality of the church, but one that is rooted in the challenges and contingencies of contemporary culture. The foundation for this enterprise is rooted in the conviction that attentive, rich and orthodox spirituality works with boundaries, not barriers. This is not, moreover, a liberal turn. It is, rather, the recognition that God's wisdom and love is what the tradition and fundaments can only witness to; but the two are not to be conflated. There is always more. The infinite expansiveness of God, which is his wisdom, sees to it that we live, move and have our being with a view to being more fully possessed by the truth; to believe that you possess it is therefore always less. Here, I am once again drawing on the life and legacy of Daniel Wayne Hardy's work, who himself owed a significant debt to the life and work of Samuel Taylor Coleridge, the Anglican poet and theologian. For Hardy, Coleridge represented a deep engagement with God and most aspects of God's creation – imaginatively, intellectually, practically, spiritually, emotionally and through creation. Hardy believed that Coleridge responded to the 'attraction of the divine' in all things – something that was fused into his poetry and theology: orthodox liberalism, romanticism, wisdom and a rich imagination.

In this kind of ecclesial spirituality the borders of faith, though prudently policed, are left open; because it is recognised that God is both outside and inside those borders. This then assumes that the only acceptable frame of reference is an open frame, which allows the viewer to look and participate both in and beyond the immediate, and so catch a glimpse of the ultimate. Open frames of reference trust that God is present: not absent, or about to be eclipsed, but rather, revealed. Simone Weil expresses this same dynamic better than most theologians:

> For it seemed to me certain, and I still think so today, that one can never wrestle
> enough with God if one does so out of pure regard for the truth. Christ likes us
> to prefer truth to him because, before being Christ, he is truth. If one turns aside
> from him to go toward truth, one will not go far before falling into his arms
> (S. Weil, 1973, p. 72).

Such an approach is rooted in trust: not in culture or ideology, but in God, who is in all and beyond all. And, for that reason, there can be no argument about turning away from an imperialistic approach to different faiths or beliefs. Characterised by a generosity founded on God, an ecclesiology rooted in faith, hope and charity can bear witness to the comprehensive love of God. Such a theology (and faith) can afford at once to be both confident yet circumspect; definable yet open; certain, yet tinged with faithful questioning. In other words, and to follow oft-quoted words from *The Cloud of Unknowing*: 'By love God may be gotten and holden, but by thought and understanding, never'. This turn towards spirituality reminds us that the forms of ecclesiology, such as have been argued for in this trilogy, and in this volume, are no less an expression of the gospel than other more dogmatic forms of Christianity. We find this generosity, moreover, not just in theology and spirituality, but also in poetry. Think, for example, of Samuel Taylor Coleridge's salutation in *The Rime of the Ancient Mariner*, and penned in 1797–98:

> Farewell, farewell! But this I tell
> Too thee, thou Wedding Guest!
> He prayeth well, who loveth well
> Both man and bird and beast.
> He prayeth best, who loveth best
> All things both great and small;
> For the dear God who who loveth us,
> He madeth and loveth all.

Although this is poetry, it is also a rich form of pastoral theology. Coleridge simply says that the best prayers are from those who love best. It is a capacious and redeeming vision for the world, rooted in God's love and generosity. The world is God's. God loves it. All our social and ecclesial constructions of reality, therefore, should reflect this; and our practices be fully aligned with our beliefs.

For this reason, our attention in this volume ranges over contemporary culture, practical and pastoral theology, and the ways in which religion and spirituality are mutating in modern societies. 'Attention' is the right word to use here, because some aspects of religious belief and practice can be puzzling when they are first observed – and then only begin to make sense when we look into them more deeply. Yet all too often, the spatial and spiritual remain richly and intrinsically connected in our world, and perhaps in such obvious ways as to be too easily missed by the casual and familiar ways in which they are regarded. We are drawn, too, not merely to attention as an abstract, neutral or intellectual exercise that centres on observance and critical reflection. The attention that Christian faith requires of its followers is a loving attention – one in which compassion, grace, mercy, peace and wisdom inform and shape the attention we give. Attention is a skill, to be sure. But it is also a virtue, value and loving practice.

Consider, for example, our dealings with death. Churches, of course, are in the business of death. There are 600,000 deaths per year in the United Kingdom. Over 70 per cent of the population will have some sort of Christian funeral, many of which will be taken by a Church of England minister. The Church of England derives 6 per cent of its annual income from weddings and funerals. And yet very few churches have the courage or the wisdom to invest in new graveyards these days. As in many areas of life, the church lags behind, and it is doing so particularly in the business of death.

Modern society has done some funny things to death. As Tony Walter points out in *The Revival of Death* (1994), few people now experience a death in their home. Death occurs in hospitals, hospices, residential or nursing homes. Death has become something for specialists, and has ceased to be 'ordinary'. Even the relatively modern terms 'undertaker' and 'funeral director' tell a story. We don't know how to make arrangements for the dead; the power is ceded to another. In many towns and cities, death has been pushed to the periphery, with new civic crematoria springing up on the edges of communities, away from where people live. Out of sight means out of mind. There are fewer graves to visit; we are forgetting the value of remembrance. We no longer live with the reality of death. The marginalisation of religion, faith and spirituality – including 'vernacular' and folk religious customs – has followed the spatial constraints placed upon death.

In the last fifty years, churches and clergy have arguably lost their way in death. Britain has one of the highest cremation rates in Europe. As more and more people choose to be cremated, clergy find themselves conducting services in less familiar civic settings, with the time allotted to them controlled not by the church, but by the demands of undertakers and the constraints that crematoria are under. Moreover, many cremations have become 'celebrations' of the deceased's life, and not an engagement with death. Many 'services' are now less religious in tone, and contain forms of sentimentality, spirituality and memorialisation, fused with offerings from popular culture. The business of death has become a competitive one – open to market forces; but also one that is more marginal in a society that tends not to accord death significant social, emotional or physical space.

Arguably, not much can be done about this drift, but churches may perhaps need to fight harder to make death more central to society. How we commemorate the dead, and where we place them, tells an important story about the living. If you give death physical space, you also create a climate in which there can be emotional space. Death and bereavement are natural, not dysfunctional, and churches need to consider again how they can offer better spaces for the dead, if only for the sake of the bereaved. But this is easier said than done, and it is at this point one realises how far churches may have 'drifted' with contemporary cultural tastes. For example, at a church not far from me, a burial ground for cremated remains was recently consecrated. Approaching the Garden of Rest from the church, there is little to mark out the area as sacred. There is no wall or gate, and no railings or religious symbols (such as a cross) that suggest that this garden is different from any other. In the centre of the garden there is small piece of grey slate that proclaims: Jesus said 'I am the resurrection and the life' – but the lettering cannot be seen from any distance.

Inside the church, a notice pinned to the wall explains that no plot for ashes can be marked by a permanent or temporary memorial. Neither can flowers be left in the garden, or on the spot where a loved one is laid. Instead, the bereaved are directed to a Book of Remembrance, which records the name of the deceased and their date of death. The book is kept in a locked glass cabinet, which is in turn kept inside a locked church. The church noticeboard does not say when the church is open – only who to telephone to obtain a key.

What is wrong with this? So many things, that it is hard to know where to begin. It lacks the loving attentiveness of which we spoke earlier. The protocol does seem to match with the sum of human pain and confusion in bereavement, which requires compassion, not (mere) empathy. The desire to leave some offering at a grave – normally flowers – seems to me to be an innate and humane instinct, and possibly even a right. The prohibition on memorials is odd, especially when no inscriptions are allowed. Memorials are a creative opportunity to speak of the after-life, of a love stronger than death, and of the ties that bind us and unite us. To ban such things is to silence the reality of hope in death, and the rumour of resurrection. The Book of Remembrance simply fails to understand what it is like to be bereaved. Were my wife to die, I would surely want to keep *that* anniversary. But what about seeing her name on her birthday, or on our wedding anniversary?

Gardens of Rest are multiplying in British churches at a considerable rate. Most are neat, tidy, and designed to be easy to maintain. The tenants are of the assured long-term variety, so little is given to them in return for the little they offer. Many such gardens are bland and anodyne. Even the best of them are rather bijou and bourgeois. And their proliferation reflects an unspoken English habit that is inclined to sweep death up and put it away: we rarely see it, and we seldom talk about it.

Our continental neighbours, in contrast, are usually more expressive. A trip abroad reveals gloriously untidy and disordered graveyards. There are photographs pinned to wooden crosses and headstones, messages left and candles alight, the poignancy of an unmarked plot next to the grotesque flamboyance of a marbled mausoleum. There is a cacophony of stone and wood, sometimes tasteless (to English eyes) – and yes, often tacky. And there are visitors, the living moving amongst the dead, in silent symphonies of tribute. British tastes can get squeamish here. There is a fear of the unregimented (stones must be this wide, this high and of this stone, and no more – by order). At churches, some congregations regard the burial ground as 'theirs', and legislate against what they regard as the potential poor taste of their parishioners. (Horror of horrors, someone might leave plastic flowers at a grave.) Meanwhile, Diocesan Chancellors and Consistory Courts decide on whether a slab can say 'Dad' or should say 'beloved father of ...', and what motifs are suitable for a child's grave.

In creating good physical space for the dead, the church can also create the right emotional space for the bereaved. The ground we stand on, with the dead, in other words, provides its own kind of spiritual or ecclesial canopy. It makes good pastoral sense, and it might even be good business too. But it is mostly an invaluable service in a society that has forgotten how to remember the deceased. Investing in beautiful gardens of rest might start to stem the flow of religious burials being lost to civic places. In turn, this might give some of the power back to the bereaved, who can often feel de-skilled in death, and starved of voice and choice in funerals, and their aftermath. Many also feel pressed into 'safe' middle-class aesthetics when it comes to tombs or plaques – if they are allowed them at all. The signs at the moment are that churches prefer low-maintenance gardens. They probably need to be more imaginative and relaxed, and less prescriptive.

The dead and their bereaved, meanwhile, vote with their feet. It is a common sight to see flowers tied to lamp-posts in roads at the site of a fatal accident. In the woods near to where I used to live, it is a common sight to see flowers tied to trees, near the places where ashes have been secretly scattered. Some benches have also been bequeathed, often with heartfelt inscriptions. The use of 'natural woodland' burial sites is on the increase. At the local children's cemetery, teddy bears and gifts sit snuggling up to simple gravestones, signs of cherished memories and unfulfilled dreams.

Yet if churches collude with reducing the physical space for the dead in suburban and urban contexts; and are, at the same time, also only tending to speak about dead in 'neutral' and marginal spaces (crematoria), it is little wonder that the public recognition of Easter is in decline. If there is no good place to lay the dead, there is no site for resurrection. Churches without decent gardens of rest or graveyards are missing a dimension of life and liturgy. Death is not tidy, and neither is bereavement. It may be time, then, for churches to think harder about the relationships between the living and the dead, and the spatial and the spiritual. It is the living, though, who will be grateful. They are the ones who will come back to visit, pay their respects, and perhaps say 'thank you'.

Why might death and burial matter in the contexts with which we are concerned in this volume? One reason particularly comes to mind. At a generic level, Thomas Tweed (2006) identifies the core purposes and value of faith as being a matter whereby 'religions are confluences of organic-cultural flows that intensify joy and confront suffering by drawing on human and supra-human (i.e., divine) forces to make homes and cross boundaries' (2006, p. 8).

Tweed therefore sees faith, and religious environments as extensive and intensive – places and practices that afford the opportunity for the beneficent recalibration of human experiences – especially centred on joy and suffering – that draw people in (home), but also enable them to transcend their limitations (internal and external forces), and also move on in their lives, and negotiate thresholds. As David Martin reminds us,

> Not only are they [i.e. churches] markers and anchors, but also the only repositories of all-embracing meanings pointing beyond the immediate to the ultimate. They are the only institutions that deal in tears and concern themselves with the breaking points of human existence. They provide frames of reference and narratives and signs to live by and offer persistent points of reference (Martin 1994, p. 189).[6]

In the same vein, Martin's *The Breaking of the Image* (1980) argues that the relationship between sociology and theology is the world turned upside down: (the theological) in its interaction with the world is the right way up with all its boundaries, partitions, difference, and power (the sociological). As Martin puts it, the fusions of religion and society are all around us, 'in the condensed images of liturgy and scripture, or else in the sound of music and singing' (1980, p. 48). So, in *The Ecclesial Canopy* we seek to discover some of the more hidden purposes of religion in society, and the intra-formational issues that emerge from its persistence and presence as an agent that provides space and time for social shaping, meaning and holding. In so doing, I shall be arguing for the cultivation of a new kind of 'ecclesial intelligence' – one which pays attention to the latent and manifest influence of faith in today's world. The book is, in several places,

---

[6] David Martin, from an unpublished paper, and quoted in Grace Davie (1994).

a rather counter-intuitive approach to ministry, church and society, with insights and hypotheses that look beneath the surface of (apparent) meaning. For this reason, we shall be exploring areas like religion in public life, and the importance of reasoned situational ethics in the public square. As well as the subtleties of ecclesial composition – the cultural practices that shape church life.

We conclude this Introduction, therefore, with a telling analogy from a theologian, and to whom we referred earlier, but who would not normally want to be identified with the kind of theological outlooks articulated here, and in the preceding volumes. Nonetheless, the analogy is a good 'fit' for the capacious spirituality of ecclesiology that we shall be exploring in these pages: a complex, slightly contrary, encompassing canopy – yet *naturally* incomplete, and always pointing beyond itself to something other and higher. The analogy likens faith and practice to a very familiar 'complex space', or perhaps to a kind of canopy – a great Gothic cathedral:

> One walks through such a building conscious of continually unfolding vistas. It is a whole, yet it cannot be seen as a whole. Nor, though it is handed down to us by the past, is it ever completely finished. New spaces expressing new needs, new altars representing a multiplicity of concerns and commitments, new decorative details celebrating new ideas and discoveries, can go on being added. It is also constantly decaying and constantly being rebuilt. It can represent both diversity, and the imperfection of incompleteness, without compromising its unity or confusing its purpose. A cathedral points beyond itself. It is not definable like a city, but open to all. Its verticality is a reminder that it is not just about human beings and human relationships. It provides a complex space which can bring home to us where, as transitory, contradictory, sinful and yet ultimately hopeful and receptive human beings, we really stand before God (J. Milbank, 1997, p. 284).

It is in such spaces that the vision for the ecclesial canopy is born. It is the awning for that big space that speaks of the incarnation, transcendence, and mystery of God; yet also crafted from the stones, wood and endeavours that speak of humanity.

PART I
Faith and Futures

Chapter 1

Fission: Faith in the Market Place

No-one can doubt the powerful fission that takes place when Christianity, consumerism and late-capitalism are in coalescence. The alloy that develops is strong, beguiling and melding. There are obvious examples: the health, wealth and prosperity movement is a powerful fusion of North American positive thinking, quasi-mystical pragmatism (e.g., 'just imagine the dream to make your reality') and the spirit of capitalism present in the Protestant work ethic. The church growth movement – pioneered by Donald McGavran, but also developed by Peter Wagner, John Wimber and others – has developed techniques for the enhancement of numerical growth. And although such techniques can be traced to scripture, the actual tracing is generally inductive and retrospective. The church growth movement begins with pragmatism: what works is good, with legitimation and consecration following only later. Yet there are also subtle, and arguably more insidious, ways in which market-led thinking can shape ecclesial polity and the horizons of spiritual imagination. Because numerical growth – of almost any kind – has become something of an idol within many ecclesial cultures, it has become almost impossible for churches to resist the temptations of literature, training programmes and motivational resources that are designed to increase the power, mass and performance of the body – even the body of Christ.

Yet such trends are not without their critiques. The missiologist Lesslie Newbigin sensed that the church growth movement, for example, was a movement more rooted in late capitalism, competition and consumerism than any kind of original Christianity:

> Modern capitalism has created a world totally different from anything known before. Previous ages have assumed that resources are limited and that economics – housekeeping – is about how to distribute them fairly. Since Adam Smith, we have learned to assume that exponential growth is the basic law of economics and that no limits can be set to it. The result is that increased production has become an end in itself; products are designed to become rapidly obsolete so as to make room for more production; a minority is ceaselessly urged to multiply its wants in order to keep the process going while the majority lacks the basic necessities for existence; and the whole ecosystem upon which human life depends is threatened with destruction. Growth is for the sake of growth and

is not determined by any overarching social purpose. And that, of course, is an exact account of the phenomenon which, when it occurs in the human body, is called cancer. In the long perspective of history, it would be difficult to deny that the exuberant capitalism of the past 250 years will be diagnosed in the future as a desperately dangerous case of cancer in the body of human society – if indeed this cancer has not been terminal and there are actually survivors around to make the diagnosis (Lesslie Newbigin, 1986, p. 82).

One does not need to search far and wide for the kind of Christian literature and training programmes that are of concern to Newbigin. The respected church growth consultant mixes biblical literalism with pertinent anecdotes, and blends them with an undiluted mix of popular motivational books drawn from business, commerce and the world of self-help, to produce the kind of powerful fission that scholars such as Newbigin wished to critically question. In his recent *The Worship Mall* (2011), Bryan Spinks explores, sociologically, the different kinds of worship experience available to believers today. Using the analogy of the shopping mall, he argues that contemporary believers and churches have been able to assemble bespoke and personal identities to express their beliefs in ways that (arguably) are more relevant to society. Increasingly, believers shop for the religious experiences, identities and institutions that correlate to their needs and desires. The competition is, increasingly, with the leisure industry. Religion is now a 'consumable' experience, with denominational or higher forms of allegiance sublimated to that of religious-consumer power.

Moreover, the present, practices of the church tend to collude, albeit innocently, with capitalism, consumerism and organisational thinking. The inexorable rise of 'mission action plans' (MAPs) has a seemingly unstoppable momentum, and an apparently urgent agenda that demands prioritisation. Yet there should be some pause for thought here. Growth can easily be confused with multiplication. The church is not a body that is supposed to be ever-more productive, like a factory or industry that simply improves its output year on year. It is an organic body of wisdom, in which pruning, seasons, life and death course through its very veins. It is about renewal and resurrection – so also about letting go, and death. It is about love and loss, and the hope of things to come. Yet by investing too much in MAPs, the church risks trading multiplication for growth, extensity for intensity, popularity for depth, and acquisition for wisdom. You cannot ignore the call Christ gives to lose your life – even martyrdom. The church is not called to success, but to faithfulness. We cannot swap the via dolorosa for the yellow brick road. Indeed, when such swaps do occur, sustaining and maintaining is quickly devalued, and innovation overvalued. The problems with capitalism and consumerism lie in the degree to which each inculcates the other. Mutual absorption is inevitable, and in some respects, desirable. Yet it is important to remember that there are no bad foods – only bad diets. The heart of the matter is the amount of capitalism and consumerism the church ingests.

None of this should in any way surprise us. The fusion of consumerism, late-capitalist ideology, the sanctification of choice, and all embedded in religion, is alive and well in the church. Often masquerading as mission (when what is actually meant is 'how to be successful and grow ...'). For example, Peter Brierley's work (2010) draws on texts such as *The Success Principles: How to Get From Where You Are to Where You Want To Be* (Jack Canfield), *Winning: The Answers* (Jack and Suzy Welch) and *The Eighth Habit: From Effectiveness to Greatness* (Stephen Covey), to develop a beguiling thesis. Do you want your church or organisation to grow? Assuming you do, Peter Brierley argues that ministers need to ask the right questions – and offers five that are key, and singled out as fundamental for promoting church growth, centred on the articulation and implementation of a clear vision and strategy.

Readers of this book will quickly be divided into two camps. Some will appreciate a thesis that is punchy and directive, and find the style and substance of the book galvanising and challenging. Others will find the thesis problematic from the outset, unable to identify with the assortment of characterisations, prognoses and diagnoses that are proffered. The opening anecdote in the Introduction is instructive. A 'recently retired domineering' member of a congregation, we are told, frustrates a female minister's strategy for growth. But she is 'not strong and assertive enough with such individuals', resulting in the retiree '(winning) the day'. Depending on your point of view, you can side with the author, and ask why the minister lacked sufficient clarity and robustness, resulting in a process that (allegedly) 'took all the church's energies for the next three years'? Or, you might be left dwelling on the underlying ageist and sexist assumptions of the anecdote, with the presumed levels of concentrated power willed into the minister's hands – and against any obstructive laity who might get in the way of a minister's vision and strategy (Brierley, 2010, p. 3).

More puzzling – though alas, hardly unusual for this genre of book – is the continued appeal to late-capitalist thinking that infects this kind of approach to mission and ministry. The book is peppered with references to 'successful' secular companies and organisations, implying that the church can enjoy similar lustre, popularity and prosperity through simple emulation. Ministers, if they acted more like CEOs or company Presidents – leading, strategising, hiring and firing – would be able to direct and shape the church more effectively. Indeed, the book is mired in a curious fusion of unexplored assumptions. North American positive thinking – with books and anecdotes citing principles for success, growth and strength – are amply represented, and left un-challenged. These assertions combine with a kind of literalist biblical pragmatism that suggests scripture provides the church with the necessary blueprint for perpetual achievement.

Yet there are many pertinent critiques of this kind of approach to life and work, and indeed religion. A recent essay from Barbara Ehrenreich (2009) contains a trenchant, searching and analytical judgement of the health, wealth and prosperity movement, and clearly demonstrates how the programmes, techniques and literature of the movement are rooted in the 'dark(er) roots of American optimism', positive thinking and motivational' businesses. Does God want you rich? The health, wealth and prosperity movement doesn't seem to doubt it; but Ehrenreich is not so sure. Just as Eric Fromm questioned the fission of Christianity, confidence and American capitalism some fifty years earlier:

> Religion allies itself with auto-suggestion and psychotherapy to help man in his business activities. In the twenties one had not yet called upon God for the purposes of 'improving one's personality'. The best-seller in the year 1938, Dale Carnegie's How to Win Friends and Influence People, remained on a strictly secular level. What was the function of Carnegie's book at the time is the function of our greatest best-seller today, The Power of Positive Thinking, by the Reverend Norman Vincent Peale. In his religious book it is not even questioned whether our dominant concern with success is in itself in accordance with monotheistic religion. On the contrary, this supreme aim is never doubted, but belief in God and prayer is recommended as a means to increase one's ability to be successful. Just as modern psychiatrists recommend happiness to the employee, in order to be more appealing to the customers, some ministers recommend love of God to be more successful. 'Make God your partner' means to make God a partner in business, rather than to become one with Him in love, justice and truth. Just as brotherly love has been replaced with impersonal fairness, God has been reduced to a remote General Director of the Universe, Inc.; you know that he is there, he runs the show (although it would probably run without him too), you never see him, but you acknowledge his leadership while you are 'doing your part' (Eric Fromm, 1956, p. 98).

So, if the church is (merely) an organisation with spiritual values and some core tasks, aims and objectives, then Brierley's thesis is arguably apposite for our age. Directive vision and strategy will be just what is needed. But if the church is something more than this – perhaps the body of Christ – then the thesis is of rather more limited value. Why did Jesus, to advance the Kingdom of God, avoid emulating the power and growth of the Roman Empire? What do the temptations in the wilderness teach us? Does scripture condone the consecration of pragmatism in order to achieve immediate expediential growth, or ask us to be more discerning?

What is today's church in danger of idolising, and why? When is it right to be faithful, and in so doing, forsake success? Is growth always good? Exactly what sort of questions does God ask of us? As Karl Barth mused,

> The true growth which is the secret of the up-building of the community is not extensive but intensive; its vertical growth in height and depth .... It is not the case that its intensive increase necessarily involves an extensive. We cannot, therefore, strive for vertical renewal merely to produce greater horizontal extension and a wider audience .... If it [the Church and its mission] is used only as a means of extensive renewal, the internal will at once lose its meaning and power. It can be fulfilled only for its own sake, and then – unplanned and unarranged – it will bear its own fruits (Karl Barth, 1958, p. 648).

Berger: Faith and Markets

A contribution from Peter Berger to this debate should not surprise us. In *A Rumour of Angels: Modern Society and the Rediscovery of the Supernatural* (1970), the prevailing assumption that 'the supernatural has departed from the modern world' was challenged by Berger – just as it had been in his earlier work from the 1960s. Dramatic formulations, such as 'God is dead', or that we have now entered a 'post-Christian era', or that the decline of religion may be undramatically assumed as a global and probably irreversible trend, are also challenged directly by Berger. The religious response to the simultaneously crude and subtle pressure of the apparentness and secularisation, argues Berger, are the polarities of relativism and fundamentalism. He writes that

> Contemporary culture (and by no means only in America) appears to be in the grip of two seemingly contradictory forces. One pushes the culture toward relativism, the view that there are no absolutes whatever, that moral or philosophical truth is inaccessible if not illusory. The other pushes toward a militant and uncompromising affirmation of this or that (alleged) absolute truth. There are idiomatic formulas for both relativism and what is commonly called fundamentalism: 'Let us agree to disagree' or against 'You just don't get it'.... For reasons that may not be immediately obvious, relativism and fundamentalism as cultural forces are closely interlinked. This is not only because one can morph and, more often than may be appreciated, does morph into the other: in every relativist there is a fundamentalist about to be born, and in every fundamentalist there is a relativist waiting to be liberated. Most basically, it is because both relativism and fundamentalism are products of the same process

of modernization; indeed, both are intrinsically modern phenomena of going to extremes (Peter Berger, 2010, p. 3).

But what might Berger mean by 'products of the same process'? Here, I suspect, Peter Berger is implicitly returning us to one of his more enduring interpretative analogies for religion, first coined in 1963[1]: namely, a 'market model' for ecclesiology in relation to secularised society. The rough contours of the argument are as follows. In a secular society where State and Church are largely separate, churches can no longer rely on the body politic to enforce their claims of loyalty. Consequently, new religions (or none) are tolerated by the State, which leads to a pluralistic situation. In turn, this creates a religious 'free market', where all religions are pushed into a competitive situation:

> What previously could be authoritatively imposed, now has to be marketed. It must be sold to a clientele that is no longer constrained to 'buy'. A pluralistic situation is, above all, a market situation. In it, the religious institutions become market agencies and the religious traditions become consumer commodities (Peter Berger, 1993, p. 138).

The analogy is intriguing, especially when set against the background of another enduring phrase of Berger's, and his more general theory of 'the social construction of reality' (Berger, 1967). For Berger, this means the totality of 'everything that passes for knowledge in society', especially the common-sensical, that constitutes the reality of everyday life for the ordinary member of society. The work has substantial implications for the study of religion. I shall be attempting to show that whilst it is useful to regard religion as being in a market-orientated situation, the boot may also be on the other foot.[2] Market-orientated situations can be deemed to sit squarely within the context of the religious situation.

Faith, Markets and Pluralism – Berger's Persistent Religion

In a religious monopoly, according to Berger, the content of religion is determined in line with the dominant and established theology or religious leadership. In a pluralistic situation, religion becomes more susceptible to mundane influences and consumer preferences. The principle of changeability is introduced and the content of religions become subject to what we might deem 'fashion'. Correspondingly, it

---

[1]   See Peter Berger (1963, pp. 75–90).
[2]   See Peter Berger (1977, 1979, 1981).

becomes increasingly difficult to defend and maintain religious traditions that are supposed to be based on 'absolute' truth.[3] Thus, traditional religions can suddenly find themselves accused of being 'narrow' or even 'sectarian', whilst new or more adaptable religious groups are valued for their ability to inculcate and reflect contemporary trends and movements. Even so, consumer pressure cannot, *per se*, be said to be the sole determinant in religious content. What is being suggested, however, is that religions are subject to change, even if they choose to position themselves in the religious market by virtue of being opposed to it.

This might be true of our own situation: it is certainly a valid social analogy that 'reads' religion, even if it does not interpret and critique it. Yet Berger's original intention in using the market analogy in 1963 was to provide an account of ecumenism. Churches were still regarded as being in a competitive battle, but the gradual secularisation of society meant a cutback in the size and scope of the religious market. Consequently, denominational particularities were de-emphasised, and the religious product 'standardised' in the interests of providing a simpler market format for potential consumers. Thus, unity is stressed above difference, connectedness over division, and uniformity of purpose against schism. In short, ecumenism is cast as a marketing strategy – a response to the process of secularisation (1963, pp. 85ff).[4] Yet Berger is careful to maintain that the denominations will continue to exist through a process of 'marginal differentiation'. This guarantees that rivalry does not get out of hand between competing denominations, yet, at the same time, keeps the game alive for all the participants. Berger is also careful to avoid addressing the role of theologians in the process of legitimisation here (Berger, 1967, p. 10); a skilful piece of marketing itself.

Berger's treatment of institutions and identities is rooted in his discussion of knowledge or world-views. In the broadest sense, knowledge makes human beings and society; we are orientated by 'pre-theoretical' concepts, or 'common knowledge'. Knowledge itself here is 'shared meanings', which are in turn funded by ideology as a form of social legitimisation. 'Ideology' does not mean a broad sweep of beliefs, or a narrow political agenda, but, rather, a set of ideas that legitimises vested interests and is linked to a larger, symbolic universe. The secularisation thesis and the idea of the marketability of religion rest on these

---

[3]   Except, of course, when they enjoy a brief phase of popularity. The youth attendance at the Pope's recent Mass (September 2010) in Birmingham, England, is a good example. The numbers turning up – in their hundreds of thousands – signify anything from curiosity to respect, but they do not necessarily translate into an increase in vocations or Mass attendance.

[4]   See also Robert Lee (1960), and Johannes van der Ven (1996, pp. 450–67).

presuppositions. Western society and culture are deemed to be undergoing a process whereby the dominating symbols are losing their power and profile (Berger, 1967, p. 129).

Furthermore, because (religious) plausibility is linked to legitimisation, and because the enlightenment, modernity and rationalism are, to an extent, products of Protestantism, Christianity has become 'its own gravedigger' (Berger, 1967, p. 11). Yet Berger is quick to acknowledge that secularisation does not mean religious belief disappears altogether. Secularisation occurs at different levels. It might weaken the religious 'plausibility structures' amongst individuals, but it does not follow that this agenda becomes established in society as an accomplished fact.[5] Moreover, modernity can still create conditions that favour religious resurgence; strong religious impulses still exist.[6] Revivals are episodic in character, spontaneous and unpredictable reactions to secularisation. Ecumenism is a more organised response to the loss of power vested in common symbols, and Berger may be right to dub the ecumenical movement as a market-led response. Yet times have changed since the advent of this original thesis. In Britain at least, ecumenism has been transformed from a process that was crawling towards standardisation to one where difference is celebrated. The British Council of Churches no longer exists: regional devolution has replaced that body with organisations like ACTS (Action of Churches Together in Scotland) or CTE (Churches Together in England). Working together in spite of differences has replaced the agenda of working towards 'oneness'. The creation of a single modernist super-church – a metanarrative – has not occurred. Presumably this is partly because certain particular truth-claims in churches and denominations could not be standardised or negotiated away in the interests of public unity. But it must also be because of the postmodern celebration of difference that treats the metanarrative with incredulity. Berger could still argue here that the denominations are only responding to the market flow: standardisation has given way to specialisation. Moreover, brand loyalty has all but gone, with consumers committed to a range of services and products rather than just one.[7] Yet the problem that remains for Berger is the relationship between the willingness of churches to be adaptable, and the truth claims that many believe they are founded

---

[5]   See Wuthnow, Hunter, Bergesen and Kurzwell (eds) (1984), p. 64.

[6]   The creation of 'shrines' – candles, flowers, notes – to remember and pray for victims of tragedies is but one example. From Hillsborough to Diana, Princess of Wales, 'folk' religion wells up in times of national grief, and is given voice, focus and direction by the established churches.

[7]   A.S. Ehrenberg in *Ogilvy on Advertising*: 'consumers do not buy one brand of soap or coffee or detergent. They have a repertory of four or five brands, and move from one to another' (Ogilvy 1985, p. 172).

on. To an extent, all churches have dimensions to them that are theologically non-negotiable, and are with them irrespective of any prevailing fashions.

Johannes van der Ven (1993) levels two further criticisms at the 'market model'. In summary, he suggests that 'market' is an inadequate term for describing the basic face-to-face interaction in various sectors of the church. In turn, he points out that 'markets' are not pure entities beyond society, but a partial by-product of social relations (1993, pp. 454–5). There is still praise for the 'market model', as an account of the relationship between association, people and movements. But van der Ven fears that it relativises the church, and ascribes too much power to individual choice. Even in trade and industry, competition is not the be-all and end-all – there is no perfect realm of competition. Thus, van der Ven concludes that, whilst the church is influenced by marketability, the mechanisms of supply and demand and the like, it does not follow that it merges into a dominant mode of marketability. It bears the features of a community, a movement and a distinct body, that at times is attractive precisely because it is unmarketable and seemingly unappealing. It is not just a 'product', but also a 'service' with a distinct identity that does not necessarily have an interest in buying or selling itself, or being concerned with its market position.[8] Berger's arguments and the critique of Johannes van der Ven are seemingly mismatched. Berger, as a sociologist with theological interests, assesses contemporary ecclesiology from a height. His analogies provide a 'map' of the cultural situation in which churches find themselves. In his work he talks of 'symbols', 'levels' and 'units': this is a form of social cartography – a detailed description of the 'big picture'. For Berger, religion is a 'social' construction of reality that borrowed sacred ideas to enforce existing plausibility structures. When the religious ideas lose their power, the social construction of reality shifts from being founded on the sacred to that of the secular. This is a sociological approach to religion, in which any form of revelation is necessarily cast in the role of ideological projection, albeit for the prevailing common good. On the other hand, Johannes van der Ven writes from a strong confessional background (Roman Catholic), and although his ecclesiology is occasionally overwhelmed by sociology, its beginning and end lies in theology. Thus, for van der Ven, the lie of the land looks a little different:

> In principle the *Church* encompasses all members of society ... it claims to be universal ... it contributes to personal and social integration. The *Denomination* can be seen as the Church's opposite ... it functions as a societal institution

---

[8]   The obvious example of this is the religious community – perhaps a monastery or convent – that does not primarily seek to attract members. The orientation of the community is prayer, work and contemplation.

amongst other societal institutions. The *Sect* restricts itself to its own circle of chosen or elected members ... throws up relatively high barriers of reception. The *Cult* – meaning religious devotion – is a manifestation of religion in which individual spirituality plays a central part ... [where] the most important thing is the 'personal path' that an individual must look for ... (1996, p. 23).

For van der Ven, there are five models of the church in relation to secularisation and market forces that are based around the organisation of personal relationships, community and society: how the micro relates to the macro. Thus, there are *Amodern* denominations, always resisting modernity, rationalisation and evolving. Faith is 'deposited' in the past, but regularly inspected in the present. Second, there are *Modern* denominations that accept modernity and rationalism, where development is positive. Adaptation to cultural institutions and trends is seen as agreeable; there is an emphasis on openness. Third, *Critical-modern* denominations emphasise personal religious freedom, but also a deliberate non-identification with society. Fourth, there are *Amodern basic communities*, where Believers are deemed to be elected; there is a stress on being 'chosen', or on 'obedience' to God's laws. Small is beautiful, because society sullies holiness. Finally, there are *Critical-modern basic communities* which actively participate in society, re-shaping the world in line with perceived Gospel/Kingdom values.

Only the *Amodern* model of the church attempts to put the church back in the centre of society; a synthesis between a wistful Christendom and totalitarianism. The other four models imply that this cannot now be done, and question whether it ever really was. The churches have always been *associated* with society with varying degrees of strength – but is it right to speak of gradual erosion of power and influence? Surely the situation is one of flux? The church is part of society; in it and of it, even though it may hope to be distinctive. Catholic social teaching permits the church to be viewed as an association, provided it is understood that the *essence* of the church is more than this. 'Association' is an angle and identifier for the church, in the same way that 'market' can be a helpful analogy, indicating the way we see it, but not the way it really is. The church is more than an association. It is also a people's context – a formation; a social movement, but transcendent reality; a community of believers; an organisation and an enterprise; and finally, a mystical body. In short, 'the social transcendent', 'the communion of saints', 'the body of Christ for the world', and so on.

In terms of ecclesiology, markets and strategies, Stark and Bainbridge offer another way forward. They use sociological exchange theory to construct their models. They balance the *tension* a group desires or tolerates with the *rewards* (sometimes called *compensators*, if rewards cannot be actualised) its members seek. Tension signifies the relationship with the world and the internal structure of the group. Rewards are material, physical and spiritual benefits of belonging.[9] Low tension groups are more church-like, and culturally-normative High tension groups are more sect/cult-like, valuing cultural deviance. The degree of 'exchange' or the 'success' of the group is determined, to an extent, by the amount of power the group appears to have, or can call upon, and can exercise. The more powerful a group is, the greater the rewards on offer. For example, a cult may offer a ministry principally concerned with individual salvation. In a 'high-tension' relationship with the world, it assumes sectarian and communitarian properties. However, a neighbouring cult with similar beliefs, but also offering healing and deliverance (i.e., more power) may well be more attractive to consumers in the religious marketplace.

Antithesis: The Market as Religion – or the Ecclesial Canopy

We know that churches do market themselves, and are to an extent, bonded together in a form of a regulated competitive framework. But suppose for a moment we see the market as an extension of religion? Suppose the chief features of advertising and marketing start to lend themselves to a religious interpretation, in which we could meaningfully speak of a theological construction of reality providing us with our sociality? In short, if religion is commercially-minded, why can't commerce be deemed to be religiously minded? Some general examples might help illustrate how Berger's thesis can, in fact, be usefully turned for the purposes of our argument.

Whether it is washing powders, beer or a new spread for bread, television advertising frequently offers motifs that are more at home in religious usage. Typically, the uninitiated consumer is portrayed as ignorant or unconvinced of the new product on offer. The advertisement shows how they are converted – often in a moment of taste, touch or experience – from blandness, nothingness or scepticism – to being a believer. Advertisements that preach brand loyalty appeal to the motif of conversion because of its religious resonance. The new consumer is shown as enlightened, and joins an elite of brand-believers who have discovered the truth. Products, in their competitive strategies, deploy a theological construction of reality, in which enlightenment, conversion, believing and belonging matter. To be

---

[9]   For further discussion, see R. Stark and S. Bainbridge (1987). Stark and Bainbridge offer a theory of religion that explicates its behaviour, beliefs and phenomena through a process of exchange. As a series of theories, social exchange (or rational choice) sees all social processes in terms of give and take, rewards and offerings, compensation and subjugation.

in any market requires a degree of faith and hope, and an appeal to the possibility of perfection.

These themes are obvious in many commercials. Yet the borrowing of religious ideas is even more apparent in the telecommunications industry, where from advertisers of mobile phones, for example, the message is that whilst they give the consumer freedom to roam, the deeper purpose of the product is to bring people together, so that they can always stay in touch. In other words, freedom, properly exercised, can enable deeper relational bonds. Mobile phones are a divine instrument for combating the evils of modernity: overcrowding, traffic jams and insufficient time. Developing this several stages further, British Telecom's classic advertisements preached that 'it is good to talk', and ran all manner of advertisements which offered tips on how to improve relationships. If only people talked more (on the phone), lovers' tiffs could be healed, distant fathers could relate to their children, siblings could get along better, and everybody feel more valued and included in society. Making the effort to talk to your neighbour is a way of showing regard for them, limiting loneliness and misunderstanding. The telephone takes on a quasi-religious dimension.

The comparisons do not end here. Insurance advertisements offer peace of mind and security. Corporate companies sell an image that is flecked with ecclesial themes: the assurance of presence, the benefits of belonging and the size of the body are meant to tell a story of social salvation, but they cannot do that without resorting to religious ideology. Of course, it is not the case that religion once had the monopoly of these concepts and has now lost it. My purpose in highlighting these common motifs is to remind us that 'market' and 'religion' cannot be easily divided, any more than the secular and sacred can be divorced from each other. The social and ecclesial constructions of reality are fused as one; the sacred and secular canopies, an alloy. One of the problems with secularisation theories, in my view, is that many continue to miss the myriad of ways in which life is constantly sacralised. By the same token, 'secularising' the church through cultural syncretism or Church-State alliances is an established part of Christian identity, long before the Enlightenment, Reformation or Renaissance. Furthermore, even if there is something called a 'secular society' now, it still has its 'gods', shrines and idols, even if they were never connected to divinity.

Berger, naturally enough, is alive to this. In his essay, 'Secular Theology and the Rejection of the Supernatural' (1977, pp. 39–56), he recognises that much theological language has been translated into and reduced to (psycho)therapy and emancipatory political movements. Not only that, just as 'supernaturalistic forms of religion' were once imposed on people, so now is the new 'assertive and arrogant' secularism, which Berger interestingly classes as a type of 'fundamentalism'. Berger concludes this essay by suggesting, humorously, that 'secular theologians' such as Schubert Ogden, Langdon Gilkey and David Tracy, although laudable for addressing their work to the apologetic task of reaching those beyond the community of faith, nonetheless represent 'musicology for the deaf'.

There are signs here – the essay was written in 1977 – that the categories of secular, sacred, divine and human are now more fluid in Berger's thinking. A more devastating critique of competition emerges in 1981, in an essay in the *Harvard Business Review*. Here, Berger questions the concept of legitimacy in commerce, and identifies 'class' as a principal but hidden determinant in economic affairs. Because of this, he urges the business community to go beyond economics and politics, and address 'meaning and value', recognising that inter- and co-dependency need fostering. In other words, the market is to be at least partly subject to society if society is to continue as a humane enterprise; if the market dominates, humanity suffers through its subsequent alienation. Markets tend to be rampant and ravenous rather than ethical and self-regulating. They need to be chastened, controlled and put to good use, rather than be the principal determinant in business life. The essay resonates with the conclusion of an article published in 1979 on 'Religion and the American Future'. Here, Berger pleads for the revitalisation of the American political community, and urgently:

> ... the hope of success is not the final motive for our efforts on the stage of history. Rather, it is obedience to the moral imperatives of our situation. I believe that the revitalisation of the American political community is such an imperative .... an awesome number of human values ride today on the survival of the American experiment. The revitalisation of the religious community is an even deeper imperative, for it points beyond America and indeed beyond history ....[10]

The trajectory of Berger's writings reveals a suspicion about the autonomy and power of markets. They also suggest that religion should no longer be commodified as units within secular-led 'market forces'. Instead, churches should stand with humanity, and share in the common task of infusing society with meaning and values, that will in turn check alienation and relativisation. We have therefore come almost full circle. Secularisation, when pressed, ensures that religion and churches survive and succeed (or something like this), since true human value cannot be derived from the market alone, which may turn out to be a 'god'.

In the meantime, society uses religious motifs in the marketplace as a means of arousing a higher individual and communal consciousness, that seeks of the possibility of change and the benefits of fraternity, equality and liberty. It is a secular gospel, but it is still a Gospel of sorts. True, one can speak of a social construction

---

[10]   Berger, quoted in an interview for *The Third Century*, 1979, p. 77.

of reality in religion that is legitimised by ideological projection. Yet at the same time, there can be no full exorcism of the theological construction of reality that imbues much of our sociality. In truth, the modernist meta-narrative remains a child of liberal Protestantism, which is itself descended from Christendom. Secularisation, as Berger acknowledges, is a child of Christian development: part of the family in a long, if allegedly declining, dynastic line. Yet it does not end there. So-called secularization may not be the problem, argues Berger. Rather, it could be the pluralism emerging from capitalism that has produced choices, and ultimately spawned relativism and fundamentalism:

> Pluralism relativises. It does so both institutionally and in the consciousness of individuals. This relativisation is obviously enhanced when the state does not try to impose uniformity of beliefs and values by means of coercion. However, as the fate of modern totalitarian regimes illustrates, even when the state makes this attempt, it is very difficult to block out every form of cognitive contamination. There is now a veritable market of world-views and moralities. Every functioning society requires a certain degree of normative consensus, lest it fall apart (Berger, 2010, p. 5).

The church in the marketplace remains a powerful and enduring image for sociologists and theologians. As a general analogy, it offers some insight into models of the church in relation to one another, and in relation to secularisation. By definition, it also offers a mirror to society; how religious motifs are used for secular purposes, as well as exploring the limits of secular and materialist ascendancy in relation to moral and religious principles that might offer deeper points of reference in the construction of sociality. The wide dissemination of religious symbols in society – including marketing and advertising – suggests that the embers of Christian belief still glow in an apparently secular society. Moreover, this may point to the strength of religion and its capacity for self-gift, even in a secular society that often fails to see it. Equally, this form of implicit religion may also be said to point to the weakness of secularization theses, and its failure to find moral frames of reference that provide cohesion, balance and direction, without going through religious motifs. The ecclesial canopy – that which continues to encompass communities, as a kind of 'social skin', ordering the world and holding it together – may well be more intact than many suppose. Indeed, this is precisely what Berger means us to suppose; faith still forms some kind of firmament. The sacred canopy is intact.

Conclusion

As with the two preceding volumes in this trilogy, there is a marked optimism about the place of faith in the modern world, and the shape and depth of religion's identity. That said, there is no shirking from the challenges that Christianity faces in contemporary culture. The normal response to change, for religion, is to organise and resist, or occasionally organise and adapt. There is nothing necessarily wrong with this, of course. However, it is important to remember that organisation and religion do not necessarily have an easy relationship. Sometimes patience and discernment is needed before organisation, resistance and adaptation are implemented. Patience, indeed, is a key virtue in the formation of the church and its ministry. We forget this at our peril. And this has a special bearing for churches and other religious institutions, which are often offered – tantalisingly – the salvific benefits of the leaner, more functional and capitalist private sector, which we (allegedly) know works well and efficiently. Yet we should perhaps pause at this point:

> I come from the private sector myself but I do get tired of a certain private-sector arrogance. When people say, 'Oh get some private-sector people into the schools, that'll sort them out'. Actually I doubt if there are many jobs in finance as hard as teaching a class of fourteen-year-old boys in a tough school. Because business is in some way quite simple, it has clearly defined aims. The aim is to make money. So you have a measure against which to judge all the subsidiary actions which add up to the overall result. Managing a hospital is rather more complex. Because it's very hard to know what your objective is. There's no money-metric to help make the choice between better cancer care or having a better A & E (i.e., emergency ward). It's a judgement call. And running a hospital is an endless series of judgement calls where the criteria and objectives are very far from clear. So don't tell me that's easier than making money (David Hare, 2009, p. 39).

Many of our great establishments and institutions are under siege at present. Afflicted by spending cuts and an assortment of rationalisations and reviews, not to mention the corrosive rhetoric of late modern capitalism, service, caring, scholarship and learning for their own sake can seem a distant memory. Public institutions are easy prey for the philosophies that drive organisations and privatisation. So where does the mission and ministry of the churches belong in a world besieged by aims, objectives, and outcomes; in an environment that assumes that competition and marketing are natural, and probably intrinsically good?

Clearly, it lies somewhere in keeping space for the sacred and pastoral to be both possible and open, as well as alive and engaged. In offering faith both to and for society, churches have a unique role in calling individuals, communities and society to the horizons that lie beyond the scope of immediate priorities. Pointing beyond the temporal and pragmatic to the world of the spiritual, the domain of values, and to the social transcendent. Indeed, authentic ministry sits in the gap between created and redeemed sociality. It holds the world before God. Like the church, it is the social-sacramental skin for the community. It is not an enclave for the redeemed, but rather a resource for all those seeking meaning and truth in a world that longs for hope. Moreover, the recovery of this vision is vital in a consumerist world, even for those with faith. As Charles Taylor reminds us, faith is now practised in societies which are profoundly altered: specifically we have moved from a context 'in which it was virtually impossible not to believe in God, to one in which faith, even for the staunchest believer, is one human possibility among others' (Taylor, 2007, p. 3).

The phenomenologist Thomas Tweed, as we noted earlier, captures something of what might be required from faith communities today, when he writes that religions, at their best,

> ... are confluences of organic-cultural flows that intensify joy and confront suffering by drawing on human and supra-human (i.e., divine) forces to make homes and cross boundaries (Tweed, 2006, p. 12).

This is a beguiling definition of religion. At its best – and one presumes a passionate real faith in a real God as a basis – good religion performs four important tasks that churches and their ministers will know much about. First, it intensifies joy. It takes the ordinary and makes it extraordinary. It knows how to celebrate lives, love and transitions. It blesses what is good, and raises hope, thanks and expectation in prayer and praise. It lifts an institution and individuals to a new plane of existence – one of blessing and thankfulness for what is and can be. And it not only moves, but also intensifies. Just as a birth becomes even more in a baptism, so in any ministry does a ceremony become more with prayer and celebration. Second, suffering is confronted. Working with pain, bereavement, counselling and consolation will be familiar to all ministers – providing the safe space and expertise that holds and slowly resolves the suffering that individuals and institutions carry inside them. Third, the making of homes is a profoundly analogical and literal reference to the function of faith. Making safe spaces of nourishment, well-being, maturity, diversity and individuation; our 'faith homes' are places both of open hospitality and security. Fourth, faith helps us to cross boundaries – to move forward and over the challenges of life to new places. It can be crossing deserts to find promised lands; or passing from darkness to light. Religion never keeps us in one place; even with our homes, it moves us.

Naturally, the manner in which we engage with their institutions is just as important as the actual programmes and events that might be offered. Sometimes, it is the way of being and the character of individual ministry that carries more weight than and resonance than those things that seem concrete and planned. This is not surprising, since faith communities often make contributions to social capital that are not easily calculated or calibrated. Because they foster and focus distinctive values that provide leaven in complex contexts, faith communities often find themselves promoting forms of goodness that secular and utilitarian organisations might miss. In this respect, Bruce Reeds's analogy of bees making honey, and the incidental pollination of flowers, and as we noted in our Introduction, explains how religion functions by drawing on an analogy from nature: 'the mutual dependence of bees and flowers is an analogue of churches and society' (Reed, 1978, p. 139).

Here, Reed offers us a vivid picture of mission and ministry that faith communities might recognise. Through the simple ministry of 'deep hanging out', or perhaps that of attentiveness, hospitality, care and celebration, churches and ministers frequently do more good for those they serve than they can ever often know. They may simply offer regular lunches, or open house for tea and coffee at any time, or being willingly bound up in time-consuming visiting to those who have too much time.

Only some of these activities are borne of manifest intentions, of course. Yet the potency of the gesture and practice lies more in their latency, and is significant. These practices say something about the possibilities for different kinds of spaces in institutions, communities and wider society – social, pastoral, intellectual, spiritual, to name but a few. They open up a different side of the humanity. Churches, in being there with programmes and events, as well as in being purposefully hospitable, actually enable the institutions, communities and society they serve to begin transcending themselves. Put simply, any ministry that says 'there is more to life than what you are currently absorbed by', 'look deeper', 'think with your heart', 'let your mind wander and wonder' and 'we are all beginners in prayer' is providing an ecclesial canopy under which all can reside, replete with faith and doubt, questions and answers. Indeed, the nature of this canopy does not require explicit recognition, much less thankful acknowledgement. Its mere presence is enough – a kind of translucent social skin for the world that allows us to see out and beyond, yet lets in the light.[11]

---

[11]   The Darby Translation renders Isaiah 40: 22 as 'It is he that sitteth upon the circle of the earth, and the inhabitants thereof are as grasshoppers; that stretcheth out the heavens as a gauze curtain, and spreadeth them out as a tent to dwell in …'.

Chapter 2

Shopping for God: Consumer Religion

In a world of globalised markets, consumerism and technology, it is no surprise that religious culture is increasingly conflated with the materialities of life. The rise of the consumer – Tesco Ergo Sum – 'I shop, therefore I am',[1] is a form of eleutheromania, in which the very exercise of choice is a sign of freedom, enabling the establishment of individual or group identity. It may be accurate to state that 'you are what you eat', or then again that, to paraphrase Alfred Gell, 'homes are the distributed personhood of their makers'. People can be defined, or at least interpreted, by their materiality: what they consume or produce, save or waste, says something about who they are. Our homes are concrete configurations of meaning; as they are defined, so they set about defining the definer.[2]

If this is true, though, how might spiritual choices be indicative of consumption and production within contemporary culture? The purpose of this chapter is not to consider the material objects of religion, and what these may or may not say about the lives of their adherents. There are plenty of fine studies that have interpreted the accidental artefacts of religious culture – tableware featuring famous revivalists such as Wesley, ornaments commemorating a shrine or event, through to the more commonplace bumper stickers, posters and fridge magnets, conveying romanticised sentiments about the closeness of God, so beloved of contemporary Evangelicalism.[3] Rather, in this chapter, we are concerned with what apparently cannot be seen so easily: spirituality. It is my contention that an understanding of the exercise of spiritual choice in religious consumers has the capacity to illuminate the study of contemporary ecclesiology and culture.

Seeing consumerism as an issue for religion is a comparatively recent phenomenon. Alan Aldridge, a sociologist of religion, interprets a variety of religious happenstances through consumerist themes. For example, he sees the debate in the Church of England over the relation between The Book of Common

---

[1] This parody of postmodernism in a single phrase, borrowing from Descartes' 'cogito ergo sum' ('I think therefore I am') is often cited by Evangelical authors who commentate on contemporary culture. The original source of the quote is, however, not known.

[2] For further discussion see D. Birdwell-Pheasant and D. Lawrence-Zuniga (eds) (1999) and M. Kwint, C. Breward and J. Aynsley (1999).

[3] For a fuller discussion, see D. Morgan (1999).

Prayer (1662, BCP) and The Alternative Service Book (1980, ASB) as containing consumerist and anti-consumerist elements. The consumerist element is that the ASB is what it says it is – 'alternative'. Only by being an alternative could it gain the necessary support in Parliament, Synod and with the public. Supporters of the BCP could therefore develop a number of lines of argument that were anti-consumerist: (1) the ASB lacks the poetic and aesthetic language of the BCP; (2) continuing to support the BCP defends high culture and 'legitimate taste'; (3) the cultural resonance of the BCP, rather like the King James version (Authorised) of the Bible, appeals to an organic community – it is 'common' prayer or language (Aldridge, 2000, pp. 192–4).

It would not surprise Aldridge, therefore, that the successor to the ASB (its licence expired in 2000) is simply called Common Worship, and that instead of one single volume, there are several, covering many eventualities. There are no less than eight eucharistic prayers to choose from (the BCP had just one), and the appointed readings for those services run in three-year cycles, rather than the BCP's own annual cycle. There is choice as never before. Common Worship can be purchased on cd-rom, downloaded from the internet, and adapted to suit every need and every occasion. It even includes the main liturgical texts from the BCP, so traditionalists can no longer complain; the new alternative now incorporates the traditional, and, in so doing, will surely eventually replace it.

The relationship between religion and consumerism is ambivalent. Like the media or advertising, it is normally regarded as a culture that is to be resisted by the churches. Bocock, somewhat crudely, defines consumerism as 'the active ideology that the meaning of life is to be found in buying things and pre-packaged experiences' (R. Bocock, 1974, p. 50). One of Berger's early assertions about American religion was that it did not respect the 'pedigree in Christianity', but rather offered 'the religion of your choice' – differentiated brands, but essentially the same commodity (Berger, 1966, p. 117). Yet as we saw in the previous chapter, there are elements in consumerism that support the sacred realm rather than undermining it. Then again, the unmistakable vitality and vigour of religion in certain contexts – perhaps especially America – suggests that the religious marketplace is hotly contested.

These diametrically opposed views of consumerism are two sides of the same coin. On the one hand, consumerism can be all about the sating of appetites, which then drives markets, desires and social life. On the other hand, consumerism provides a format for social intercourse, and produces a degree of individual and social satisfaction. As Aldridge points out, religious consumers also share a double identity. Are they active searchers in the spiritual marketplace, exercising their autonomy? Or, are they prey to every passing religious fad, at the mercy of cults, sects and new religious movements and the latest spiritual fashion? Or can the consumer be both? The contours of the cultural milieu are far from clear (Aldridge, 2000, pp. 187–90, 207–8).

Yet, for Aldridge, the customer is already emerging as king, with religious practices and beliefs becoming increasingly pliable to 'fit' the lives of the hoped-for adherents.[4] Citing Beckford, Aldridge notes how religion is now not so much a social institution as a 'cultural resource' (Aldridge, 2000, p. 212).[5] The firmness and anchorage of religion is lost in the waves and currents of modernity; the sea of faith has become the ocean of doubt, and faiths are struggling to keep afloat. That said, Aldridge has enough historical knowledge of church-going habits to know that consumerism may not be inimical to religion. True, consumerism is now very much part of the sacred realm, insofar as there is now a consciousness of choice. (At conferences, I regularly meet post-Evangelicals, ex-Catholics or former Anglicans who have all 'found something else', be it alternative liturgies, meditation, or even part of another religion, yet all the while remaining as part of their original faith.) Thus, Aldridge claims that the contemporary consumer culture does not only enable people to make their own faith – people frequently demand the right to choose. Adherents to religions often do not see their faith-related practices as mandatory or obligatory, but rather as vocation, voluntarism or simply a matter of selection (Aldridge, 2000, p. 213).

Aldridge's insights owe much to the anthropologist of contemporary culture and mass consumption, Daniel Miller.[6] Much of Miller's work concentrates on the apparently mundane matters of modernity such as shopping; yet he 'reads' such activity in a way that opens up the possibilities of seeing consumerism and religion as being inextricably linked. For Miller, shopping is not a form of 'hedonistic materialism that we enjoy abusing', but 'a vicarious journey through sacrifice' (Miller, 1998, p. 5). How can this be? Miller uses the concept of 'the treat' to explore how the shopper rewards him or herself, and the groups or individuals they are buying for. Anthropology is frequently concerned with how boundaries and borders are developed (e.g., soil in the garden, but 'dirt' on the carpet), and how activities are differentiated. The 'treat', therefore, is what allows the rest of this consumer activity to defined as 'shopping'. Miller develops this further by exploring theories of sacrifice, arguing that shopping itself may be viewed as sacrifice in three stages. In stage one, the vision and rhetoric of excess is explored:

---

[4]   Aldridge doesn't offer examples, but recent traits in English Roman Catholicism bear out his thesis. Many parishes now offer Sunday's Mass on Saturdays and Fridays, in order to accommodate the needs of families, and their working or leisure activities. An eclectic approach to the teachings of the church in respect to contraception is taken as read.

[5]   Cf. J. Beckford (1989), pp. 170–72.

[6]   See D. Miller (1987, 1997 and 1998).

'both the discourse of shopping and that of sacrifice represent a fantasy of extreme expenditure and consumption as dissipation'. The second stage is a more explicitly religious interpretation, focusing on ritual:

> ... the core of this ritual is a splitting of the objects of sacrifice between that which is given to the deity and that which is retained for human consumption. An equivalent central ritual to shopping expeditions is found to be that which transforms a vision of spending into a vision of saving ... (D. Miller, 1998, p. 7).

This leads Miller to conclude that the third stage is directed towards expressing the real benefits of the ritual through relationships and love. This is the dissemination of the sacrifice, which, for Miller, arises out of modernity being 'under the pressure of secularisation [where] the romantic ideal of love comes to substitute for religious devotion'. Miller's argument is certainly novel, and to some readers may seem far-fetched. Yet underneath the narration, his presuppositions appear to be sound. Commodities are used to constitute the complexity of social relations. Religion and shopping share a common practice, whereby the practice of sacrifice is intended to create desiring subjects. A shopper does not merely 'buy' goods. They buy in the hope of shaping the lives of the recipients, maintaining the community, and creating new patterns of meaning that can be shared. As we shall see shortly, when exploring the Alpha course as a paradigm of 'consumer-led' religion, his insights go some way to explaining the success of this type of evangelism.

The rhetoric of consumption and sacrifice opens up important new vistas in the debate about religion in contemporary culture. For David Lyon, 'religious consumers' are now a fact of modern life, although he acknowledges that 'the privatising of religion antedates the consumer society' (Lyon, 2000, p. 81). This, he claims, is in part due to the gradual disappearance of institutional religion from social life, which in turn has led to a situation where competing convictions (to borrow a phrase from Robin Gill) now vie for religious consumers. The 'market' then, can actually 'lead' religions, or at least shape what they offer to the public, assuming that they are interested in acquiring more adherents.[7] Lyon reflects on how the 'frequently caricatured Puritan ideals of asceticism, self-denial and fixed boundaries ... are clearly out of kilter with [today's] culture' (Lyon, 2000, p. 82). Yet I suspect he is only partly right. The irony of the 'market' is that it also spawns radical alternatives. For example, holidays and the holiday industry largely trade on offering a carefree, relaxing time in sunnier climes. Yet the rise of the rugged trek or holiday in difficult terrain as a viable form of 'relaxation' cannot be ignored.

---

[7]   Cf. J. Esposito and M. Watson, *Religion and Global Order*, R. McCutcheon (1997).

The consumer-led 'soft' religions of late modernity will lead to an alternative or counter-cultural movement.

More convincingly, Lyon aligns himself with the insights of Daniel Bell and Michael Featherstone, and argues that consumerism is:

> ... no longer about utilities that address fixed needs, but about constructing an expressive lifestyle in which 'individuals are encouraged to adopt a non-utilitarian attitude towards commodities and carefully choose, arrange, adapt and display goods – whether furnishings, house, car, clothing, the body or leisure pursuits' to make a complete statement ... (Lyon, 2000, p. 83).[8]

For some, this necessarily leads to the creation of 'religious enclaves', or of religious traditions simply offering their spiritual 'provisions' to a hungry market that will, characteristically, shop around. In other words, the danger may be that 'religion', in terms of its ability (and etymology), will no longer provide the basis for social glue; it will not, literally, 'bind together'. Rather, it will find itself as just one more commodity within a market, which itself a form of binding. This realisation may not be surprising, and, indeed, some regard it as a blessing. R. Laurence Moore's Selling God observes that American religion, and especially Protestantism, has an inbuilt commercial bias:

> religion, with the various ways it has entered the cultural marketplace, has been more inventive than its detractors imagined ... as a commodity, it [has] satisfied many buyers (Moore, 1994, p. 10).

For Moore, American Christianity, which is devoid of the legal privileges enjoyed by state and national churches in Europe, has led to American denominations and congregations investing heavily in cultural relvance, reflecting popular taste and proclivities where possible. This 'supply' fits the 'demand' of American life, and increasingly, much of life through the 'first world'. Because the customer is king, religion no longer imposes, but invites. Thus, Reginald Bibby, commenting on his native Canada, notes the phenomenon of á la carte religion, of religion as a consumer item, and of how religious consumers are highly selective in what they consume (1993, p. 169 and 1987, p. 35). In other words, the husk of religion is increasingly discarded in favour of the kernel of spirituality.

For many religious adherents, this may seem like a parlous state of affairs. Yet in Britain, religion retains a strong pulse through what scholars variously term as 'common' or 'folk' religion. In North America, it is simply the case that

---

[8]   See also M. Featherstone (1991), p. 114.

the equivalent phenomenon has a particular commercial edge to it, which is itself culturally normative. Moreover, the cultural domination of American life, globally, therefore now impacts many other cultures and their own enculturation of religion or spirituality. It cannot be surprising that many peoples in Europe, Asia or the Pacific now find their innate spiritualities evolving at rapid rate. Or, as Davie notes, religious memory is constantly 'mutating', but possibly faster now than at any time before. Believers, she notes, 'select at will from the package of religious goods on offer ... and mould these into a variety of packages that suit a variety of lifestyles and subcultures' (Davie, 2000, p. 199).

Consumerism – and perhaps especially its American forms – appears to have been a key driver in this mutation. Vincent Miller, in his prescient *Consuming Religion* (2004), argues that the most profound problem is not so much the consumption of goods, but rather the ways in consumerism trains us to treat everything, including religion, as an object or goal. Moreover, new synergies are formed through consumerism, and most especially between commodities and values. Belonging, success, and fulfilment become attached to objects of consumption – including classes and courses that can be purchased – so that the consumer can sate their desires. 'Wholeness' – that place where values and needs (or rather desires) are integrated for the consumer becomes an attainable goal, or even a right (p. 121). In religion, spirituality becomes the default category for locating and purchasing such wholeness. Yet, as Miller points out, when consumers become trained to lift cultural or religious objects, motifs or ideas from their original contexts, they are less likely to be influenced by the deeper purposes and longer-term trajectory of the tradition to which they belong. Thus, 'nice icons' become decorative art, or possibly with some personal inner meaning for the purchaser, but not objects of devotion that are located within the context of the catholicity of collective worship. Evangelistic courses for individuals give them the challenge, stimulus, transformation and affirmation they desired; but not necessarily the demands of deep discipleship.

It is to such a consumer 'package' that we now turn; an example of a commodified, globalised, contextualised presentation of the Christian faith, that is marketed, copyrighted and consumed throughout the world: Alpha. What follows is a form of cultural and critical-theological reflection, which explores both the strengths and the weaknesses of a religion that is both sold and bought within the postmodern spiritual marketplace.

Consumer Choice? Assessing Alpha

Alpha courses appear to be a phenomenal success. Their own publicity suggests that hundreds of thousands of people have taken part in a course in this country, the Commonwealth and beyond. Alpha News is full of good reports and self-publicity, smattered with quotes from appreciative academics, bishops, and others.[9] The Alpha Course itself has now become a business operation, with its own staff, teaching materials, sweatshirts, videos and books. Of its type, it is one of the slickest commodifications of the gospel. There are books, videos, t-shirts and bumper stickers. The books and videos are available in dozens of languages.[10] Moreover, there are signs that the success of the course has broken through into mainstream culture, with a major national advertising campaign during the Millennium celebrations, and David Frost, erstwhile TV presenter, hosting a range of programmes that featured Alpha.[11] Alpha, inevitably, has also prompted some significant critiques.[12]

Alpha has a number of features that commend it to the postmodern consumer-led spiritual marketplace. First, it is a course, not a 'hit and run' exercise in evangelism. Alpha is local and relational. It is not an event, or abstracted away from normal life. The context of meals and fellowship is normalising. Alpha, not necessarily embarrassed by the particular local church; it claims to build on it. Thus, the course offers local ministers or laity a number of evenings, a weekend away and a final supper, which they organise, which clearly can facilitate the building up of community relationships.[13]

Second, because it is designed to be locally based, and from the church, it avoids the pitfalls of some itinerant evangelists who might not relate easily to local contexts and churches. Typically, a course is run through a series of twelve meetings, with people often being personally invited. Each meeting often begins

---

[9]   Cf. *Alpha News*, London, Holy Trinity, Brompton, London – a quarterly newspaper that appears as an 'insert' in mainstream denominational newspapers. The academics who support Alpha tend to be lecturers at theological colleges of an evangelical persuasion.

[10]   The majority of these are written and presented by the Revd Nicky Gumbel, a staff member at Holy Trinity, Brompton, London.

[11]   Celebrity presenters are highly prized by Evangelical initiatives, since they underline the cultural relevance of their message. Alpha has also attracted celebrity converts such as Jonathan Aitken, a former Minister under the Conservative government, but jailed for perjury.

[12]   See Steve Hunt (2004) and James Heard (2008).

[13]   For an account of one person's involvement with the Alpha course, see J. Ronson, 'Catch Me if You Can', *The Guardian Weekend Magazine*, 21 October 2000, pp. 10–23.

with a meal, followed by a presentation (a mixture of video and lecture), followed by discussion. The atmosphere is intentionally relaxed.

Third, there is a wealth of supportive literature to aid enquirers. It is well-marketed, and written and presented in a 'light', chatty and apologetic style, formed from an evangelical-charismatic basis. A version of David Watson's popular *Jesus Then and Now* (1980) – a 'primer' that introduced the basics of Christian faith – but with much more emphasis on the individual, the therapeutic; and a rather personable Holy Spirit. Unlike Watson, however, internationally known preacher though he was, Alpha claims to have converted 'millions' to Christianity.

People who attend an Alpha Course seem to enjoy the fellowship and find their faith refreshed.[14] Amongst most, if not all charismatic-evangelical churches, the Alpha Course has now become almost obligatory; a logo that makes a statement about being in the vanguard of fashionable evangelistic techniques. Yet there are some who have serious reservations about the style, content, approach and results of Alpha. How, though, can something apparently so successful be flawed? Three theological reasons immediately come to mind.

First, there is very little attempt to present the Church as the body of Christ which is the initial repository for the Gospel. The assumption Alpha appears to make – common to a good deal of evangelical apologetics – is that people become Christians first, then think about joining a church. The disociation is highly problematic. Whilst individual evangelists and various agencies target the millions beyond church structures, the majority of conversions often fail to be properly inculcated into the church. This is, in part, because these same people are embarrassed by the church, and offer a Gospel that barely mentions it, if at all. Evangelicals tend to have little theology of place, or an appreciation of directional plurality (i.e., a place of collegiality where differing opinions are held together by the tensions, bonds and love of communion), regarding the church as a collection of people who are in agreement with one another. A focus on the church and sacraments would deepen the course, and ensure the material was more firmly rooted as an arm from within the church, rather than an external agent being used as a go-between. Some Roman Catholic and liberal Anglican churches have 'tailored' the course in this way, although the authors forbid this.[15]

---

[14]   Some fairly straightforward critiques are now beginning to appear, most notably S. Hunt (2001). See also J. Freeman (2000), 'Christian Evangelism and Nurture in Contemporary Britain', BD dissertation (University of Birmingham: unpublished) and M. Ireland (2001), 'A Study of the Effectiveness of Process Evangelism Courses in the Diocese of Lichfield with Special Reference to Alpha', MA dissertation (University of Sheffield, Cliff College: unpublished).

[15]   The course and the trademark are protected by copyright law in Britain.

Second, the genius of Christianity lies in its contestability. In the relentless appeal to 'basics', the course obviates the implicit and explicit paradoxes in the Gospel, as well as its breadth. It offers Christianity as a simple, un-contextual, boundless project that is 'learned' through a course offering certain types of knowledge and experience. Any group that offers a course on 'Basic Christianity' needs to address who chose the basics, and why certain 'basics' were selected and not others. In Alpha, the basics turn out to be an appeal to a largely inerrant Bible, attenuation of a homely and powerful Holy Spirit, and expression of an Evangelical atonement theory. They are not, interestingly, the Trinity, baptism, communion or community, which might be more appropriate for other groups. Moreover, the authors apparently do not like the course being adapted or enculturated. This suggests that a 'package' of truth is being sold. Yet Christianity is arguably not something we 'possess'; like God, it possesses us, but is beyond us too.

Third, the focus on the Holy Spirit is one of over-emphasis. The Spirit on offer obviously arises from a personable, therapeutic, home-counties context that is concerned with the individual.[16] The dynamics of the Spirit's work in creation, justice, peace, reconciliation and the wider church receive scant attention. This is because the authors of the course reflect their origins: an elite, upper-middle class outlook (Eton, Cambridge, Brompton), which, quite naturally, has also enculturated the Gospel. In introducing the Gospel from here, there is inevitably no real social mandate, no prophetic witness and no serious appreciation of theology or ecclesiological breadth and depth.

Alpha trades on the fact that the gospel is free for all, and correspondingly offers a highly successful 'trial pack' (a 'nice' version of Christianity), yet one that does not actually relate to what is ultimately on offer, namely the complexity of salvation from within the church. It does recognise that 'lasting conversions' are made through local church connections and friendships, with less coming from hyped-up rallies or events that are outside the church. But the weaknesses lie in its theological foundations. It sets its own 'questions', and then offers the 'answers' to them: a classic technique in apologetics – caricaturing 'objections' to faith, then demolishing them. There is little space for people to actually reflect on and vent their own serious social, personal, moral or theological concerns. The appeal to 'basics' seems to assume that all Christians are more or less the same underneath, and that their ecclesial expressions are merely cosmetic. They are not: for many they are matters of theological and aesthetic substance.

As a course, it is therefore somewhat prescriptive, a package rather than a pilgrimage. Participants are locked into a hermetically-sealed hermeneutical

---

[16] Part of the whole course includes a mandatory weekend away for participants, which introduces them to 'encounters' with the Holy Spirit.

circle that keeps more issues out than it actually addresses. It is a confident but narrow expression of Christianity. As we shall see in a moment, it represents a trend that some scholars now define as 'McDonaldisation' – global yet local; a franchise on every street corner, which offers a very limited and tightly controlled range of products.[17] The secret of the success is that the menu is reliable, and the diet unvaried. In the case of Alpha, the mixture of the didactic with the relational and the existential 'encounter' is a perfect postmodern recipe. The teaching is not intrusive. The stress on the personal experience of the Spirit over the Spirit in the whole church, in all its plurality and depth, is highly individualistic. It attempts to transform course members into converts, and then again into church members. Converts become consumers, buying into the 'Alpha world'.[18] Ironically, the skeleton of the course does provide a good template that parishes could adapt and deepen according to need and context. (A number of parishes I know have adapted the middle-class presuppositions of the course for their own situations where 'supper parties' are not easy formats in which to discuss life and faith. It is odd then, that the authors of the course programme are against this. Presumably, this is because there is a real bias in the material that is not to be ignored, and is to be protected from dilution. So here we have a technique with fundaments, Patent Pending. A kind of 'brandalism' visited upon Christianity, where a commonly expressed faith has been redefined and appropriated by a subordinate brand.)

Most observers agree that Alpha ultimately does to churches what any revival does. Mostly, it excites and galvanises existing believers, and encourages them to ponder (briefly) the world outside the church. Then to engage with it more openly than they might otherwise have done, albeit temporarily. However, although this form of apologetics is to be preferred to some itinerant evangelism or mass rallies, insofar as it is locally based, it has still done little to address the theological vacuity of its parent missiological models. It is still more monologue than dialogue. People are still mostly 'sold' a gospel that is independent of the church –and then the course organisers wonder why the attendees don't translate into members.[19] It also offers

---

[17]   On this, see P. Ward (1999). Ward bases his approach on G. Ritzer's *The McDonaldization of Society* (1993) and *The McDonaldization Thesis* (1998). See also J. Drane (1999).

[18]   Some parishes report that they have not been able to inculcate Alpha converts into the mainstream church. The converts have remained within their original Alpha nurture groups, where they continue to meet and discuss.

[19]   Steve Hunt, a sociologist of religion, notes how in Wokingham, a prosperous suburban town in the South of England, 22,000 Alpha invitations were issued to the population. However, only five new members of the church resulted from this extensive exercise.

a version of the Gospel that is weak on sin, suffering, atonement, sacraments and sacrifice. True, people have to start somewhere with the claims of the Gospel: milk precedes meat,[20] and you learn to walk before you run. But does the presentation have to be so sugar-coated, simplistic and narrow?[21] People's previous experience of the church is deemed to be peripheral, and the selected 'basics' presented as central. For example, one cannot imagine receiving any reasonable answer to a question like this: 'What did God do for me when I was baptised as child?' Such issues are omitted from the agenda. They are just too complex to form the basis for a discussion about divine action and the graciousness of God.

The danger of a therapeutically tuned version of the Gospel that is intentionally socially relevant is that it will itself become a fashion-victim. The course comes from the same church – Holy Trinity, Brompton – that introduced John Wimber's 'Signs and Wonders' (miracles are the best form of evangelism: 1984–86), the 'Kansas City Six' (1988–90: a group of strange American 'prophets', now widely discredited) and the 'Toronto Blessing' (RIP, 1994–96). In their own way, all these phenomena were rather ordinary within the context of revivalism and enthusiastic religion, yet they were marketed and sold well, particularly by Holy Trinity, Brompton. They had a shelf-life of between 18 and 24 months and, in spite of some of the same bishops and personalities who promote Alpha giving each of these movements their full imprimatur, they fizzled out. So what they actually point to, ironically, is the lack of a deeply formed ecclesial identity and enduring spirituality in these faith-expressions. Without something new to sing about, punters in the pew eventually become bored. 'Success' is therefore about being at the forefront of spiritual fashion, riding along on the crest of the latest wave or craze.

Modernity's Spiritual Marketplace?

Mention was made earlier of the relationship between Alpha and what sociologists and cultural theorists term 'McDonaldisation'. Ritzer describes the 'M word' as

> the process by which the principles of the fast-food restaurant are coming
> to dominate more and more sectors of American society as well as the rest
> of the world ... the emergence of what [Weber] called Formal Rationality,
> that is, a collection of rules, regulations and procedures, and the growth of

---

[20] 1 Corinthians 3:2.

[21] For a further reflection on dietary metaphors as a way of reading contemporary religion, see M. Percy (2001).

the bureaucratic systems necessary to ensure the smooth operation of such practices … (G. Ritzer, 1993, pp. 28–9).

Pete Ward sees five similarities between Alpha and McDonald's. First, and as we have already seen, Alpha is a 'simplification' of religion. Second, it represents an 'iron cage', creating systems that bind and stifle; it is initially 'novel', but ultimately suppressing. Third, it is a form of imperialism, spreading a uniform spirituality across the globe. Fourth, it is an 'illusion' – what Baudrillard calls 'simulacrum', a copy of a copy of which there is no original. Fifth, it is 'convenience' mission, in which the relationship between production and consumption is transparent.

Whilst Alpha, as a product, should clearly not be identified with hamburgers and French fries, Ward's point is that the productive processes are similar. How then, would Miller's thesis on shopping as sacrifice fit within this analysis? Three points need making. First, for Miller, the concept of 'the treat' is closely related to the virtue of 'thrift'. Alpha is a deliberate 'economising' of the gospel, in which only the 'basics' are offered. However, the religious shopper or consumer may also acquire benefits that relate to this thrift: food and friendship as part of the course, or extra merchandise that will enable them to appreciate what they are being offered. As Daniel Miller says,

> splitting of the objects of sacrifice between that which is given to the deity and that which is retained for human consumption. An equivalent central ritual to shopping expeditions is found to be that which transforms a vision of spending into a vision of saving (Miller, 1998, p. 7).

Second, the religious consumer must sacrifice his or her time to achieve consumption, and more besides. It is in the very act of giving themselves that the course participants learn to receive. In turn, the consumer of Alpha can also turn into the provider for others, providing further opportunity for sacrifice. This is made possible because 'salvation' has become an 'object' in Alpha, which characterises and defines subsequent relationships, in terms of who has 'bought' it, 'sold' it, or is still waiting to be reached by the commodity:

> As in the anthropological concept of The Gift (Mauss, 1966), the object constitutes the relationship, transcending the separate identity of both parties. Commodities have replaced the gift because under modernity a relationship is no longer understood as existing between people as signs of social categories. Rather the ideal is that as characters in a good novel we explore ourselves and develop each other in terms of the potential of the relationship … (Miller, 1998, pp. 7–8).

Third, the 'dissemination' of the sacrifice, which for Miller, as we noted earlier, arises out of modernity being 'under the pressure of secularisation [where] the romantic ideal of love comes to substitute for religious devotion' (Miller, 1998, p. 151) turns out to be one of the main benefits for Alpha course participants. In this regard, there is something ironic about Alpha. It is, in one sense, 'conservative' in its theology and overall outlook. And yet it is also profoundly liberal, being predicated on encounter – both spiritually inner and existential – as well as relationality.

Thus, the religious consumer does not merely 'buy' the goods on offer. They purchase in the hope of shaping the lives of the recipients, (including their own), maintaining the community, and creating new patterns of meaning that can be shared. In other words, it is the very act of enduring Alpha and persisting with the course that the consumer is rewarded; what is spent will most likely correlate with what is saved. For believer and unbeliever alike, it is a case of reap what you sow. There is a further irony for Alpha, alluded to earlier, insofar as it is both a form global imperialism and de-contextualised, whilst also being perceived as local and neighbourly. This is, of course, the achievement of Coca-Cola or KFC; though global, it is known locally, and the franchisee plays a significant part in establishing this axiom. Here it may be important to understand globalisation as a process of compression rather than oppression. This takes us beyond the notion of capitalism or organised commerce as being necessarily imperialistic (suggested by Ward), and suggests that globalisation is better viewed as 'the compression of the world' in which increasing socio-cultural density is linked to rapidly expanding consciousness.[22] There are pluses and minuses to be noted here, which relate to our earlier remarks.

On the plus side, this means religion, as a commodity, may now be viewed as or manufactured to be handy, compact, portable and adaptable. Like any other 'global' product, its minimalism guarantees that it can be placed almost anywhere, and used by almost anyone. On the other hand, the very fact of compression is problematic. It can feel oppressive, lacking the space in which to grow and develop. Moreover, the very size of the compressed product might also make it vulnerable to competition. For Alpha, the danger of a course that claims to be global and introductory is that it can tend towards trivialising the totality and breadth of Christianity. To pursue the McDonald's metaphor for the last time, there are no bad diets, only bad foods. The compression of the menu and the marketing of 'basics' in the interests of maximising the volume of consumers is a substantial achievement. However, maintaining the customer base requires both innovation from the producer and loyalty from the customer. At the moment, nobody knows

---

[22] On this, see R. Robertson (2000).

if Alpha will have the longevity to continue to be the staple fare for religious consumers in the years to come. Brandalism of this kind, or any other, and in consumerist terms, tends to have a short lifespan.

It is perhaps not surprising that scholars are divided on the likely implications of globalisation for the churches, Christian culture and other faiths. For the phenomenon, whatever it may be, has a variety of effects that seem to run in contradictory directions. On the one hand, it is possible to conceive of an organisation or product that comes to dominate a market, and thereby gain global recognition. On the other, that which is 'local' may offer a form of cultural resistance. However, in both cases, compression is a key. The local is compressed by the global; the global achieves its glorious reification by being compressed in the first place. From an Evangelical perspective, commentators such as Max Stackhouse see this phenomenon as a challenge to the ministry of churches, fearing that faith will itself be subject to forces of reductionism. Where liberalism arguably failed (or at least could be resisted), globalisation threatens to conquer. The shrinking of the world will necessarily shrink faiths within it, and the only 'winners' in the competition will be consumer-shaped religions that 'work'. And the arbiter of the winner can only be the market itself, which now assumes a passive but nonetheless dominant role. At least one other problem that may arise out of this dynamic is that concepts such as 'charity', be it local, national or international, become a matter of 'balancing interests', rather than an un-negotiated gift.[23] Stackhouse calls for prophetic resistance and a critical public theology.[24]

That said, the reality of the spiritual marketplace is undeniable. David Lyon describes the situation in America and Europe as one in which 'a vague, inchoate, but seemingly serious religious quest is in evidence', and notes how, following Wuthnow, religious appetites have shifted from 'dwelling' to 'seeking' (Lyon, 2000, p. 88).[25] The modern spiritual consumer is shopper, not a loyal stay-at-home settler. Lyon cites Wade Clark Roof in support:

> Many within the baby-boomers generation who dropped out of churches and synagogues years ago are now shopping around for a congregation. They move freely in and out, across religious boundaries [combining] elements from various traditions to create their own personal tailor-made meaning systems (W.C. Roof, 1993, p. 5).

---

[23] See R. Williams, *Lost Icons: Reflections on Cultural Bereavement*, Edinburgh, T&T Clark, 2000.

[24] See M. Stackhouse (1988); Cf., 'If Globalisation is True, What Shall We Do?', in *St Mark's Review*, no. 180, 2000, pp. 25–32.

[25] See also R. Wuthnow (1988).

Roof's insights look to be a good 'fit' for our modern and postmodern eras, and they certainly confirm what many in faith communities fear. Roof's narration takes account of the rise of 'self-help' culture, the glorying of the self as the centre of consumerism, the triumph of spirituality over religion, of 'reflexive' faith, of communities of memory losing out to in individualism, and more besides (W.C. Roof, 1999, p. 8).

Conclusion

These observations notwithstanding, it is important to get things in perspective, and ask what is really so different about the present time? Is it really true that people have never really had religious choice before, but that now they are subject to what David Ford terms 'the multiple over-whelmings of modernity'? Certainly, a casual glance at the advertisements in contemporary church newspapers seems to reveal a curious obsession with new, faddish and consumerist forms of faith:

> '... the church is transitioning from a pioneer phase into a more established maturing phase as our strategic objectives become more focused and our distinct organisational character emerges more fully. We need an outstanding organisational shaper to implement our CityShaper vision. Reporting to the Vicar, you will ....'[26]

> 'The sense of purpose comes out of Tim's conviction that things are changing these days. Having spent his recent years helping lead Worship Central, travelling the world to resource and equip churches and their worship leaders, Tim has a great view on the current state and coming waves within the worship movement. 'I feel like we're on the cusp of a fresh move of worship', he explains. 'In some ways it feels like we have got a bit stale; maybe we're in danger of settling on a formula in congregational worship ....'[27]

To be sure, there can be no doubt that faith in the developed world is followed, in large measure, by 'autonomous religious consumers'. As Warner notes, 'brand loyalty is in decline and increasingly transient'; the religion of choice has replaced

---

[26] Advertisement for a 'Director of Operations' at St Paul's Hammersmith: *Church Times*, 18 December 2009, p. 28.

[27] Advertisement for 'Love Shines Through' (worship album), *The Door*, March 2011, p. 4. For a fuller discussion of the ambivalence of modern worship music as in contemporary evangelicalism as both spiritual and consumerist, see Anna Nekola (2011).

the religion of birth. The individual consumer is king.[28] Yet following our earlier discussions, we would be wise to be cautious about alarmist cultural critiques driven by confessional antipathies or sympathies. Historically, it is not safe to assume that previous generations did not experiment with alternative religious and spiritual beliefs, even at those points when Christendom was at its highest float. Keith Thomas recalls that

> what is clear is that the hold of organised religion upon the people was never so complete as to leave no room for rival systems of belief (K. Thomas, 1971, p. 178).

Any examination of the veneration of saints in medieval times, or of post-enlightenment esoteric religion, or indeed of almost any period in history, can demonstrate a spiritual efflorescence that is beyond the immediate control of the church. People have always adapted religious tradition, privatising it, enculturating it and reshaping it around their needs, desires and contexts. It may be the case that the only things that are unique about our times are these: individualism is on the increase; in turn, that is closely related to the capacities of production, which are shaping consumption; globalisation has led to a consciousness of choice, which people feel it is their right to exercise; spirituality is evolving into a credo which is more materially concerned;[29] and religions are increasingly enduring a tension, between becoming more democratised and more centralised, as globalisation and consumerism demand.[30]

However, the biggest paradigm shift in late modernity is the way in which mass consumption and production is 'squeezing' religion into new shapes – a kind of brandalism, and to which we referred earlier. Alpha is but one example of a beginners guide to Christianity for people who are already too busy, which offers a 'light touch' in terms of the demands of the gospel, in exchange for a commodified knowledge, a network of new relationships and a range of different experiences. The product is a good fit for consumers, offering a subtle blend of affirmation and challenge. But information, contacts and encounters are not the same as wisdom,

---

[28]   See R. Warner (2011). See also G. Davie (2007).

[29]   See S. Collins, 'Spirituality and Youth' (2000). In saying 'materially concerned', I am alluding to the transference of spirituality into either hedonistic interests or environmental concerns. However, the spiritualities that emerge do not necessarily become politicised, or develop into variants of liberation theology, although this may happen. Where it does not occur, the tendency is to sacralise the object of desire, be it the forests, the earth, crystals and the like.

[30]   For a fuller discussion on the subject of religion and consumerism, see Eric Fromm (1941) – and especially the third chapter on freedom in the age of the Reformation.

deep forms of socio-spiritual bonding and transcendence. Yet there are two final factors to mention that will determine how Alpha remains as a sustainable feature within the ecclesial landscape.

The first factor is this nagging sense of simulacrum when one attends an Alpha course. Clearly, and on one level, no-one can fault a course that is popular for outsiders, galvanising for insiders, and to all intents and purposes, welcoming. The slick advertising campaigns that offer to answer the deepest questions in life are also compelling. Yet, it is the genuineness and depth of welcome, hospitality and faith that is most at issue. The hospitality on offer is pleasing on the surface, but harder work underneath. Of course, many might desire tight programmes that must be followed, and overseen by charismatic leaders. At issue, therefore, is pedagogy (what kind of education is this?) and hospitality (is it genuine, or a means to an end?). Both are connected, of course. But I am struck by how one might want to interrogate the relationship between education, learning, and pedagogy; hospitality and welcome; and ecclesiology – the latter, I think, because many are drawn to genuine forms of religious community. Yet joining Alpha is not quite like that. Too much cannot be said; many things cannot be asked; the welcome and hospitality is, in other words, subordinate to the 'processing' that the enquirer must undergo:

> We want students to listen to us because we want to share our truth with them; but students have their truth to share too, and perhaps the greatest respect we can extend to them is to take their truth seriously. Hospitality in teaching is a harbinger of hope because the more we attend to the insights, experiences, fears, joys, and humour of our students, the more we not only see their goodness precisely in their otherness, but also realise how they can bless and enrich our lives (Paul Wadell, 2002, p. 132).

This suggests, therefore, that Alpha is more of a simulacrum than genuine pedagogical and relational hospitality. And here its on-going development may find questioning and opposition from the very grounds that currently provide it with such success. If the developed world begins to turn against capitalism and its values, Alpha may find that its assumptions about individual and collective growth are challenged.[31]

The second factor is the development of technology that will have the greatest effect on spirituality in the years to come. Sylvia Collins argues that

---

[31] On this, see Benjamin Barber's *Consumed: How Markets Corrupt Children, Infantalize Adults and Swallow Citizens Whole*, New York, Norton and Co., 2007, and his *Jihad vs McWorld*, New York, Norton and Co., 1995.

cybernetics and virtual technologies will have a significant impact on spirituality. These technologies offer young people an experience, if not the reality, of intimacy. Paradoxically, they seem to offer postmodern youth both increased uncertainty and ultimate control. However, this spirituality does not come at the expense of consumerism. There is very little to suggest that young people will be spiritually sensitive ... rather, the spirituality of intimacy of the millennial generation will be deeply bound up with the consumerism that has increasingly concerned youth throughout the postwar period (Collins, 2000, p. 235).

If Collins is right, then we would expect to see the churches developing a complex portfolio of events, networks and systems that allows believers a high degree of reflexivity within a comparatively well-defined compressed context. All the signs are that this is already happening. For many churches, the point of judging their success by Sunday attendance figures has long been passed. Instead, they can be assessed on the totality of their output: various groups for various ages; special events; new networks to explore new ideas; traditionalism affirmed and radicalism embraced; the new mixed with the old; reflexive teaching on issues of concern, but little sign of a systematic theology. Most, if not all of this, can be found at the average parish church. Consumer-led religion has already arrived. This may not be a bad thing, of course. But the signs of the times need reading and discerning with great care: caveat emptor.

Chapter 3
Formation and Embodiment:
Sketches on Sacred Space

O tell of his might,
O sing of his grace,
Whose robe is the light,
Whose canopy space.[1]

We have considered the ambiguities of Christianity's presence in the marketplace – the ways in which faith mutates and reacts to late capitalism – in chapter one. Chapter two then offered an explorative sketch on the ambivalence of consumerism, commodification and Christianity in contemporary culture. So, in this third chapter, we turn to a different kind of contrariety, namely the ways in which competition for and over sacred space affects the performance and polity of faith. The competition can be between secular, consumerist and sacred claims to human habitat and values. It can also range over religious difference, including fiercely contested ideologies. Here, we explore how faith is both formed and continues to form in relation to competition for space; and in the conclusion to the chapter, suggest that this formation is an on-going project for transcendent values embodied in the church.

In *The Illusionist* (French: *L'Illusionniste*), an animated film directed by Sylvain Chomet in 2010, and based on an unproduced script dating from 1956 by the French mime, director and actor, Jacques Tati, we encounter a modern parable of religion and public life. Of sorts. The main character in the animated version of the Tati story is an illusionist (magician), who plays the theatres and music-halls of France and London. But much to his puzzlement, he is rapidly watching his career give way to rock and roll, and to the emerging popular culture that would come to dominate the 1960s. In the film, this new mood of modernity is represented by the advent of modern technology, and specifically electricity – guitars, lighting and amplification – none of which the illusionist requires for his trade.

We see the illusionist head off to new virginal pastures, unsullied by the advances of modernity and technology, and the animated story follows him to a

---

[1]   *O Worship The King*, by Robert Grant (1779–1838).

community that bears more than a passing resemblance to the Island of Iona. Here, he books into a guest house – the Abbey Church clearly visible in the background – and that evening entertains the Gaelic community with his repertoire. The villagers are awestruck. We sense that the illusionist has finally found a place that will truly appreciate his talents – disappearing rabbits in hats, bouquets of flowers pulled from coat sleeves, and coins found behind children's ears – an environment where he is no longer competing with modernity.

The evening is a great success. But as the illusionist soon discovers, the whole community has not come together to marvel at his magic. They are there in the bar to celebrate the ceremonial turning of a single light bulb. Electricity has arrived on the island. And before the evening is over, the pub landlord has pulled out a brand-new jukebox from the cellar. Everyone dances – not to sound of the Gaelic fiddle, but to the new sounds from the jukebox, and under the perpetual lighting that is now strung across the bar. There is, it seems, no place left on earth where the illusionist can hold people in awe with his magic. Technology and modernity are in the ascendancy.

The illusionist leaves Iona. But he is followed by a young girl who is smitten with his art, and they go to Edinburgh together. Here the illusionist tries to ply his trade again, but all we see are a few old people and a tiny number of children. His magic no longer holds people in any kind of thrall. He is forced to get a job in a garage to make ends meet, whilst the young girl tends to their lodgings. There is a brief revival, of sorts. The illusionist is hired to do magic in a shop window for passing customers, but it is schematised around the products the store is promoting. The work soon goes awry, and our last glimpse of magic at work in the public sphere is a turbaned magician (a Turk – perhaps representing Islam?), who sticks at the job well, but with ever-depleting audiences. The story ends with the magician leaving the girl, who has found love with a boy of her own age. The message of the film is that illusions do not work: only love is real, and we must seek it and find it.

I should say at the outset that Tati's intention in writing the story was almost certainly autobiographical. Conjecture from theorists suggests that he wrote the story for the daughter he had become estranged from (Helga Marie-Jeanne Schiel). So the story is not a romance, but rather a complex narrative about a father and daughter, and one that both apologises for and partly justifies the absent father.

And yet I think Tati, and especially the interpretation given by Chomet, is also capable of being read parabolically. Tati set his original script in Czechoslovakia. Chomet's choice of Scotland, and Iona indeed, in the 1950s, is therefore intriguing. Moreover, the resonances with the story of religion in late European modernity can hardly go unnoticed. The illusionist is a plying a kind of priestcraft, and as modernity and technology advance, he is driven in to more rural, marginal and basic communities where his work still captures the imagination and inspires awe. When even this fails, he is reduced to aligning his magic to a more subservient end, namely commercialism. But by now, religion (in the form of magic) is truly marginalised. Only the very old and the very young are watching; the rest are indifferent.

The film's ending sums up the apparent fate of religion in public life and space. There is no mystery and awe in a word shaped by modernity and technology. There is only love and each other – and this is the rather hopeful and hopeless note the film leaves the viewer with. The illusionist retires, in an echo of T.S. Eliot's poetry – motoring and modernity have taken over. Religion can no longer enchant and hold the public spaces as it once did.

I am well aware that this is a contentious and rather forced reading of Chomet's animated film. Yet it serves to highlight how easily space is taken for granted, and what the empty or filled places of modern life might be saying about religious purposes and Christian identity. With reference to three brief sketches, I intend to highlight how we can see and imagine space differently – and in a theologically literate way – that resonates with the insights and imagination we commonly find in the writings of Richard Giles.[2] This is not, however, a direct engagement with his books and lectures on the uses of space for worship and enchantment. This task is undertaken by others, and by those who know far more bout architecture and liturgy. Rather, this essay is an analogical expansion of Richard's work, and is therefore an invitation to the reader to begin to read spaces and places in ways that are theologically literate and culturally prescient.[3]

Sketches on Space, Place, Ministry and Meaning

To that end, we turn to three brief sketches. And we begin by noting that the very nature of contemporary parochial ministry in England can place a demanding onus on institutions preparing individuals for the ministry of the church. This might include, for example, instilling some sort of recognition that the (somewhat dubious) distinction between mission and maintenance is often a false dichotomy in the majority of parochial contexts, where the historic religious resonance of the church building will have a widespread (if sometimes unclear) spiritual

---

[2]   See Richard Giles (1999) and (2005).

[3]   (I also owe a debt to Stephen Pickard's reflections in his 'Church of the In-between God' (2009). Here, Pickard teases apart the dialectic of space and place more formally, to reflect on how the places of Australian Anglican identity are shaped by the spaces they inhabit. In this essay, I use the space-place dialect more broadly. For more detailed reflections on St. Paul's Cathedral and at Cuddesdon, see Joseph Sterrett and Peter Thomas (eds) (2011), *Sacred Text-Sacred Space: Architectural, Spiritual and Literary Convergences in England and Wales*, Leiden: Brill. See also John Inge (2003) and J. Milbank, 'On Complex Space', in *The Word Made Strange* (1997).

significance. Thus, good maintenance of a building ('sermons in stone') is likely to be, *de facto*, good mission in any parochial context. The building may involve and affirm the neighbourhood in myriad ways (beyond the merely functional operation of providing a place for meeting), thereby nourishing social and spiritual capital. The relationship between a church and its people in many parishes is essentially perichoretic – the 'mutual indwelling' of various cultural and religious currents that blend and inter-penetrate, producing new spiritual meanings, whilst also maintaining distinctive sodalities.

The spiritual relationship between individuals, communities and their buildings is a complex one that merits some elucidation in terms of implicit theology. Even a simple shared space, such as a student or community common room, can suggest a complex nexus of theological formation and ecclesial participation. For example, I am often struck by how students, spouses and children inhabit the common room at our college in Cuddesdon.

There are three entrances or exits to the room, a small bar, and a variety of different types and heights of seating – fixed benches, comfy (and rather worn) sofas and easy chairs, and some upright chairs positioned informally around tables. The room is arranged in such a way that it is easy to move in and out, yet also linger and chat. Smaller and larger conversations are possible, and the room as a whole manages to feel both snug and open – helped by a fireplace that is one of just several focal points. The room, in other words, is a kind of parable of Anglicanism: it embraces commonality and diversity. It is neither circular nor square; but rather a kind of parallelogram that invites movement and circulation. It is also a place of both settling and journeying; literally a *via media*, expressed in architectural form. The layout of this one room is also matched by the overall architectural layout of the buildings – open in texture, facing outwards to horizons both near and far, and yet sufficiently composed to convey a sense of being apart from its environment as well as within it.

Whether or not the architect (G.E. Street) designed the buildings to somehow be a lived parable of (idealised) broad Anglican identity cannot be known. But what can be said is that the way in which the rooms and spaces are occupied is a matter of deep interest to those who are concerned with the articulation of implicit theology. Here, how space is inhabited and understood has a deep impact on formation and identity, and on composition and vocation. If further proof were needed of this, one need only observe how other, similar, spaces are used in other institutions, yet in very different ways.

At a neighbouring theological college, the common room had only one entrance. The chairs – all of one kind – are laid out to both sides of a rectangular room, with a path dividing the chairs; an aisle within a nave comes to mind. Students therefore tend to cluster (if standing) in the aisle, or sit in small groups with their backs turned to other groups if they occupy the seats. It is the very antithesis of the first room described. Standing in the centre means that pathways are blocked; but being seated is also, potentially, an exclusive decision. The layout of the room, in other words, is uncomfortable for ambivalent lingering, and forces people into choices. The composition of the room (matching theological ethos), is somewhat divisive in character.

These remarks are perhaps especially suggestive for parochial ministry, but also for formation and theological education more generally, whether in residential or non-residential contexts. Quality may need to be valued more than quantity; pace, solidarity and connectedness more than haste, energy and apparent achievement. It may be important to encourage ordinands to see that the worth of affirming the resonance of the past may have a higher spiritual value than the apparent obviousness of the need for relevance and progress.

Indeed, one can sometimes suggest that Cuddesdon – and here this is shared with many other theological colleges – is a parable that dwells on unity and diversity. The buildings of Cuddesdon are mostly hewed from the honey-coloured stone that is common for many Oxbridge colleges. There is a pastoral warmth in the hue and density of the stone, which the sunlight catches and illuminates at certain times of the day. The actual stones are, on closer inspection, arranged in an ordered way, but not a uniform way. Every stonewall testifies to the mantra that unity is not the same as uniformity: diversity of size, shape and sequence is easily found. And there are the wings. Cuddesdon, as a College, looks like a single building. But looked at more carefully, one can see subtle differences in the stonework of Gore, Liddon, Rashdall and Major – and where these have been joined. And such differences are now more apparent in the Edward King Chapel, and Harriet Monsell House, both of which are more contemporary in design, and newer additions. Yet the buildings as a whole express a delicate ecology of unity and diversity – the many different eras that have shaped its life and witness. It is one, yet many; diverse, yet singular. It is, in short, a parable in stone that speaks of Anglicanism: plurality and unity.

Moreover, I hold that this kind of deep relational engagement with spaces and places may have a greater missiological impact than overt evangelistic schema and initiatives. And clearly, the ministerial 'blend' of being and doing (i.e., the clergyperson as both contemplative and activist) may need to be adjusted in any transition from urban or suburban contexts to rural ministry. Context may have a direct bearing on theological output. In other words, theology can be a rather 'slow' discipline; it takes time to accrue wisdom for the journey. Part of the process of formation is to comprehend the vision for theological reflection, which is attending patiently and deliberately to all kinds of material, including the spaces and their possibilities, and buildings and their potential meanings. This means helping ordinands to 'loiter with intention' in spaces and places, noting how issues and encounters surface in different environments. Indeed, good training might help clergy to purposefully dwell and dawdle in their loci, so that deliberations can inhabit the spaces they need, and so that clarity and wisdom might more easily come to fruition. Theology is not a discipline for hurrying.

Yet it is a discipline that should lead to action. I recently found myself on the other side of the world from Cuddesdon, and in Macau, as a guest of the Anglican Province of Hong Kong. Macau was, for centuries, the gateway for Christianity to enter China. Matteo Ricci, Francis Xavier and Florence Li Tim Oi (the first ordained woman in the Anglican Church) all have associations with the Island. The feature that will strike any visitor to Macau, however, is its Portuguese heritage.

Settled by traders and missionaries from Portugal in the sixteenth century, Macau quickly became a place of distinctive fusion – cultures, faiths and trade combining to shape architecture and identity. Macau became a Portuguese colony in the nineteenth century, and in 1999 was handed back to China – although it remains, like Hong Kong, a 'special' territory of the motherland, still with its own currency, police and laws.

A walk in Macau's densely populated city and suburbs is a surprising experience. Many streets lead into public squares – the kind one would typically find in Portugal and Spain. Originally, these squares had several functions. First, it was a liminal meeting place immediately outside a church, and could also be used for trade, meetings and relaxation. Often the *Communidade* (administrative building) was also to be found flanking the square, and then prominent families would build their residences to provide further flanking, with the school (usually run by the clergy) completing the enclosure of the space.

In common with Mediterranean and Latin Catholic Europe, these squares evolved into places where boule could be played, villagers or townsfolk could gather, and children could play. And in Macau, these spaces have indeed been faithfully re-created. However, where Macau is different from Portugal is in the density of population. The houses and flats on Macau are tiny, and overcrowding in family dwellings a significant problem across the territory. At the same time, the main source of income in Macau is gambling, with almost forty licensed casinos. These are substantial in size, and gambling takes place on an almost industrial scale. (A walk in one of the larger casinos was not unlike the experience of stumbling into a vast battery-chicken farm – except filled with humans at tables and machines, in their many thousands, seemingly unaware of the date, time and climate outside.).

The Anglican church that day was introducing me to a new kind of space in Macau. The Taipa Youth and Family Integrated Service provides space for development in a city that has little room to develop the (moral?) character of its inhabitants. The main work of the centre focuses on youth and family work, offering what must seem, to many Westerners, a rather innocuous set of services.

There is a television lounge that families can book to watch a DVD. And a small library, karaoke room, dance studio and arts and crafts rooms. There are also rooms set aside for education, catering, counselling and simply meeting.

This project is government supported but church-run, and it recognises that in a place where there is little private space, and what public space there is often commercialised; simple space for youth and families that is adequate for developing social skills and moral character is at a premium. The community halls and church rooms that many Western Christians might take for granted are simply not there in the same way, so the Shen Kung Hui Macau Social Services Coordination Office provides a valuable service to the community by simply offering adequate space that enables families to meet and relax in such a way that many homes cannot offer or afford. This is a deep ministry of social engineering, generating moral capital through the provision of a place and space that is affordable, commodious, non-commercial and unthreatening.

Of course, other ministries are on offer too – with specialist advice for young people, school counselling, addictions (gambling and alcohol) and family mediation all catered for. Yet the striking thing about the place is the space in the place – for Taipa is one of the most crowded new cities in the Far East, and here the church offers a simple (Benedictine-style) ministry of hospitality that is mostly a form of 'anonymous Christianity'. Yet it is a remarkable ministry, born out of a vision of how open spaces and places can transform the lives of those who have little space, and little sense of the identity of the place to which they now belong. In some sense, then, the Taipa Youth and Family Integrated Service provides the same kind of environment that the Portuguese no doubt intended with their original public squares in the older parts of Macau. A space and a place to be together – gently watched over by the church, surrounded by good neighbours, and with food, drink and education all near to hand. All the things needed for life, in an open, yet bounded, space.

For our final sketch, we turn to St Paul's Cathedral in London. Situated on Ludgate Hill, which is the highest point in the old City of London, the present building was constructed by Christopher Wren in the late seventeenth century, after the Great Fire of London of 1666. It is generally thought to be the fifth cathedral on that site, the first being built by St Mellitus in AD 604. The cathedral is one of the city's most distinctive and recognisable sights, standing at 365 feet (or 111m) high. From 1710 until 1962, it was the tallest building in London, and its central dome remains one of the highest in the world.

Wren was given the task of rebuilding the cathedral in 1668, along with dozens of other city churches destroyed by the fire that began in Pudding Lane. There were several design stages for the new cathedral, with at least four design schemes rejected on either practical, ecclesiological or theological grounds. By the time

Wren came to complete the ultimately successful fifth design, he had resolved not to publish his drawings in advance, as consultation was proving to be divisive and time-consuming. The final design incorporated concepts drawn from the Renaissance, fused with a more Gothic style, and drawing some inspiration from St Peter's Basilica in Rome. The first stone of the cathedral was laid in 1677, and the cathedral came into use twenty years later. It was finally completed in 1708 ('topping out'), some forty-two years after a spark from Farryner's bakery had caused the Great Fire of London. At the time of completion, some remarked that it was 'un-English', whilst for others there was an air of 'Popery' – the sense of the space and the dome being unlike anything seen before. Yet this extraordinary space may have another origin, rooted in Wren's childhood, and the religious and political settlements that emerged in the late seventeenth century.

Ask any schoolchild what the most traumatic and violent period of English or British history was, and the chances are that they will say the First or Second World War, or possibly the Black Death, or perhaps even the Great Plague. Yet without doubt, it is the English Civil War – which, of course, extended to Ireland, Scotland and Wales, and lasted from 1642 until 1651 – and with sporadic violence and repression continuing until the restoration of 1662. Family members turned on each other. There was betrayal, death and suffering on an unprecedented scale. The war was waged not only over the right form of governance for the country (monarchy or democracy), but on the theological vision that builds societies, and shapes human behaviour.

The statistics for the Civil War, insofar as they can be deemed to be reliable, are startling. The English suffered a population loss of almost 4 per cent as a direct result of violence (these figures do not include those who perished through disease or neglect), which is a greater percentage per head of population than the First and Second World Wars combined. The losses in Scotland and Wales eventually stood at 6 per cent, and in Ireland, where Cromwell conducted a vicious and visceral campaign, may have been as high as 40 per cent, a figure that is more than twice that of the losses suffered in the great famines of the nineteenth century. Or, put another way, more than double the losses the Soviet Union incurred in the Second World War. Whilst the Irish statistics are disputable, there is no question that the scale of loss and atrocity was considerable, and Cromwell's name and legacy remain permanent features etched into the Irish psyche.

As a young adult, Christopher Wren was caught up in all of this. He was a teenager when Charles I was executed. His father was Dean of Windsor, and deprived of his living and housing under the Cromwellian reforms. His uncle was Bishop of Ely, and spent a good deal of the Civil War in the Tower of London. He survived – but as an emaciated and broken man. The deep psychological trauma of the Civil War has had a lasting impact on the British psyche. It was in fact three wars that took place over a nine-year period. And it was, let us not forget, a religious war. It led to new ideas in religion (e.g., Levellers), breakthroughs in medicine (Harvey and blood circulation – far too much opportunity for fieldwork), weaponry, and techniques in war (some of the first PoW camps).

The outcome of the war, however, is perhaps what is most interesting in relation to Wren's project at St Paul's, and the emerging settlement under the reign of Charles II. In a decade of some of the most brutal and bloody conflict seen on British and Irish soil, the English learned some important lessons about religion – lessons that had begun in the Reformation and Counter-reformation of the previous century. What were these lessons?

The first had been rehearsed in the Reformation, namely that you cannot change people's beliefs by beating them or persecuting them, or through war and violence. This would lead to a new accent in English Anglican identity. It led, for example, to the emergence of 'dinner party rules' for religion – we can worship together, but we seldom talk about it afterwards This was a new extension of the Elizabethan settlement – you cannot make a window into men's souls. The second lesson was a harder one, and Anglicans still live with this agenda. We, as a nation, found out the hard way that we prefer peace to truth. The war was essentially over imposing truth as a precondition for peace. We realised that you cannot do that. Peace is the priority, because truth is contestable and contingent. Third, and because of this lesson, the eventual settlement of English identity is one where an uneasy peace is usually valued over and against settled and theistic solutions. Because the latter, as the English learned, led to division, hatred and violence. It is better to live in love and charity with our neighbours, and disagree with them, than to try and impose our truth on them through indoctrination or violence. The lesson of the war was simple: it can only be done at a cost – and that cost is too high.

So the post-1662 Settlement is, essentially, a liberal one. But not liberal in the sense of campaigning or winning victories against conservatives or fundamentalists. Liberal, rather, in the sense of being open, tolerant and capacious. Politically, such liberalism will express itself in a coalition rather than a government of one single party. It will consist of allowing different viewpoints to flourish, including ones it does not agree with. In this sense, English or European Christian liberalism is rather different to the kind of 'party' or campaigning liberalism one might find in the USA. This side of the pond, liberalism tends to seek peace, not victory. In contrast, liberalism in the USA is more of a party matter; it has a tendency to want to win, seek vindication, and not to compromise.

So how does all this have any kind of impact on a space like St Paul's? Whilst there is clearly a history to the design – a fusion of gothic and renaissance styles – the striking thing about St Paul's is the sheer size of the space, and the relatively muted décor. Wren's reified psychological and spiritual response to the trauma of the

English Civil War – one in which stained glass windows were blasted by muskets, people died for their faith, and churchgoers argued intently about surplices, altars and lecterns – is to produce a capacious space in which all can co-exist but find little to focus their disagreements on. In some sense, the cathedral expresses the new English need for sufficient space, yet enclosure – something achieved by Wren in height, length and breadth of the project. It is an inclusive space, with an oddly early enlightenment feel to it. It is no accident that the *Book of Common Prayer* project (1662), which was now in its third edition (after 1549 and 1552) and an attempt to be universal and inclusive, should also find expression in stones and spaces.

So, in St Paul's we have a huge dome, with not too much in it to cause unease or controversy. A big space, not lacking in décor; but equally nothing that oppresses the eye or offends the sensibilties of more Puritan-minded worshippers. A place to be, but devoid of controversy and overly-ritualistic or divisive-symbolic foci. Indeed, perhaps the dome should be seen as a singular weaning breast? Or perhaps we can see the space as an expression of Newton's early thinking on space, and the Enlightenment's interest in the possibility of new life in new spaces. Here is a new space for light, truth and peace. Australia, after all, was 'terra nullis' (empty space) for some while before it became populated and colonised.

So Wren's architecture, following the English Civil War, is clean, uncontroversial, tidy and neat. You look up and see light. It is the proverbial Big Tent. It is charity and capaciousness in stone. It is not filled with objects that mediate many messages; but a space that invites new possibilities for thinking and being. It is, in short, a space of Religious Enlightenment. Then it all begins to makes sense. Especially when you discover that for a few brief years, whilst a student at Westminster School, Wren sat next to a child called John Locke, one of the fathers of the Enlightenment, and therefore of open and inclusive liberalism. It is a space that, as the theologian Dan Hardy would have said, is like so many churches: it is layered, and interwoven with many meanings, which all point to the infinite expansiveness of God, which is his wisdom.

Keeping the Space: Formation for Society

We began this chapter with some observations about Chomet's interpretation of Tati's tale. Granted, this was a tendentious reading of *The Illusionist*, yet it served a purpose, namely to suggest that one of the challenges faced by faith groups today is the marginalisation of religion in public life – the pressure placed on belief (and the space the practice takes) to move into the shadows and corners of modern life. This is partly due to the gradual weakening of the capacity of faith to offer enchantment. Yet our three sketches – Cuddesdon, Macau and St Paul's London

– are, in their different ways, all rooted in a vision of faith that is public, alive and central. For Cuddesdon, the space exists precisely because the clergy of the nineteenth and twentieth centuries needed new forms of training, education and formation that would enable them to contribute to the increasingly compressed and oppressive spaces of industrialisation and urbanisation. It was also a response to their own perceived sense of marginalisation in these new secular spheres. The church centre in Macau is, in a different way, a counter-cultural space in another kind of secular sphere. Not only symbolically, but also as a place where the advances of capitalism and urbanisation can be resisted. St Paul's, as we have seen, represents a form of space that articulates a new form of peace after the trauma of violent social and religious division; settlement and orthodox liberalism that aspires to be inclusive rather than divisive. In each case, the church has sought to pitch a tent in the age in which it is set. Each kind is a Big Tent; one that serves God, society and the needs of the church (and in that order).

Our age has a high view of freedom and variety, and low view of habit and discipline.[4] It is also an age where regular, frequent committed church-going – and indeed belonging to any other kind of voluntary institution – is struggling against the weight of secularisation, consumerism and individualism. Religion in the developed world is adapting – mainly by placing a greater emphasis on spirituality rather than institutional religion. Regular week-by-week church attendance (dispositional and disciplined) has had to concede significant territory to more episodic forms of faith, such as pilgrimages, celebrations and shrine-based worship. These are more intensive and personal; but less time-consuming too – suggesting, perhaps, that religion has been quietly pushed into the corners of modern life.

We have been here before, of course. The no less traumatic revolution or civil war that took place in France at the end of the eighteenth century, and saw a variety of experiments with monarchy, republicanism and democracy before the current settlement, also finds expression in religious and civic places. The Pantheon of Paris is partly a church, and partly a secular space for national heroes. Unlike Westminster Abbey, it has been unable to find a unity of purpose (note, not uniformity). The Pantheon bristles with tensions: religious paintings competing with clean, empty spaces that memorialise philosophers and writers who would more readily be recruited to the secularist cause. Yet in the middle of the Pantheon sits a vast dome – the same kind of space that Wren had conceived of – in which co-existence is both taught and caught. Wren's clock tower at St Paul's is replaced in the Pantheon by Foucault's pendulum. The message is clear. Take time and space.

In offering faith both to and for society, churches have a particular role in calling individuals, communities and society to the horizons that lie beyond the scope of

---

4   On this, see Eric Fromm (1956).

immediate priorities. Pointing beyond the temporal and pragmatic to the world of the spiritual; to the domain of values and to the social-transcendent. Indeed, authentic ministry sits in the gap between created and redeemed sociality. It holds the world before God. Like the church, it is the social-sacramental skin for communities. It is not an enclave for the redeemed, but rather a resource for all those seeking meaning and truth in a world longing for hope and change. Clearly, the mission of the church lies somewhere in keeping space for the sacred and pastoral to be both possible and open, as well as alive and engaged with wider society.

For faith groups today, the normal response to imposed change is to organise and resist; or organise and adapt. There is nothing necessarily wrong with this. However, it is important to remember that organisation and religion do not necessarily have an easy relationship. Sometimes patience and discernment is needed before rationalisation and adaptation are implemented. Patience, indeed, is a key virtue in the formation of the church and its ministry. We forget this at our peril. And this has a special bearing for churches and other religious institutions, which are often offered – tantalisingly – the salvific benefits of lessons from the leaner, more functional and capitalist private sector, which, as we saw earlier, are known to work well and efficiently (allegedly). The church, however, is a body mystical and organic, as well as politic, institutional. It is Christ's: not just 'something' to be rationalised and organised.

Here, the ethos of our institutions might just be as important as the actual services, education and hospitality that might be offered to any parish or community. Sometimes, it is the way of being and the character of individual ministry that carries more weight than and resonance than those things that seem concrete and planned. This is not surprising, since faith communities often make contributions to social capital that are not easily calculated or calibrated. Because they foster and focus distinctive values that provide leaven in complex contexts, faith communities often find themselves promoting forms of goodness that secular and utilitarian organisations might miss.

That is why it is so important to comprehend the nature of the body of Christ in relation to its actual practices. Ministry or the practice of the church cannot simply be reduced to aims, objectives and outcomes. Only some activities in ministry are borne of manifest intentions. Many that are latent, rooted in ethos, are no less significant. Such practices may open up a different side of humanity and society. Indeed, the nature of this kind of social body does not always require explicit recognition, much less tacit acknowledgement. Its mere presence is sometimes enough – a kind of translucent social canopy made up of values and practices that the world can both shelter under yet also see beyond; and lets in the light.

Moreover, being formed in this kind of body is not necessarily straightforwardly equivalent to being prepared for service and leadership in other kinds of apparently comparable institutions and organisations. Attention to the idea of the church as a complex body at this point is pertinent. Bodies contain systems and forms of organisation that require meticulous regulative management. Not all of these will be consciously apparent to the mind. But a body is clearly more than one single form of organisation. It contains naturally functioning parts that need no conscious instructions; it responds, reacts, grows and declines in relation to different circumstances and environments. It is something that can be trained and educated; yet is also in constant state of complex formation, which may involve instinct, growing self-consciousness, wisdom, memory and innate calculation.

Correspondingly, Paul's analogy of the church as the body of Christ allows us to reappraise the richness of the church as an institution (1 Corinthians 12: 12–26.). The human body is, as Mary Douglas reminds us, a 'natural symbol' by which people often order the systemic nature of their corporate life. The human body is often an image of society; how a group views and values its own members will reflect upon notions of corporate and individual life. Therefore, to contemplate the church as a body is to invite reflection on the sensitivity of the church, its receptivity, its boundaries, barriers and definitions, all processes of exchange, as well as its natural death and replenishment. It is 'osmotic' in character: giving and receiving nourishment, identity and love. The body is inescapably part of its environment, as well as separate and distinct. The body – with all its members – is incarnate in space and time.

So, though we are many, yet we are one. Our identity, of course, is complex and contestable; yet obvious. It has to come to terms with the multiplicity of meanings that it inhabits, which vary across the range of discourses in which the body engages – medical, anthropological, sociological, spiritual, and so forth. The body is one, yet capable of multiple interpretative possibilities.

Why, though, do these reflections matter in terms of the space given over to formation in churches and congregations? Arguably because ministry in the church requires taking responsibility for a highly complex organism, where obvious clarity of intention and attention cannot be taken for granted, and are not always apparent. The systems and micro-organisations within the institution/body will maintain their foci in a dedicated (even myopic) manner, almost independent of any willed tactics or strategy that the body may consciously have articulated. Thus, the 'head' may well prioritise a range of tasks or opportunities. But the heart will still beat on, and other micro-systems within the body will still carry on with their primary functions. This does not mean, of course, that the body is divided, or in any sense schizoid. It is simply the recognition that its complexity is part of its organic and mystical given-ness.

So, leading a body like the church is *not* always like leading other kinds of ordinary organisation. Good theological leadership comprehends that much of ecclesial polity is open; and although has a shape, can sometimes remain provisional. It is, like a body, replete with creative dilemmas; checks and balances; the reactive and proactive. That is partly why scripture is so rich here, since it offers not answers to questions, but images in the midst of dilemmas – ways of living and being together that allow for the fourfold cyclical momentum of communication, conflict, consensus and communion. The Holy Spirit is at work in the totality of this cycle – yes, even in conflict.[5]

So in terms of resolving some of the apparent conflicts we face, and in inhabiting dilemmas, the desire and need to sometimes reach settlements that do not immediately achieve closure is actually a deep *formational* habit of wisdom that has helped to form Anglican polity down the ages. Essentially, the calling to be formed for ministry in this body is all about inhabiting the gap between vocation, ideals, praxis and action. Some neutral or universally affirmed settlements are easily reached on a considerable number of issues within the church. But sometimes settlements have to be reached that allow for the possibility of continuing openness, adjustment and innovation. Inevitably, therefore, consensus and communion are slow points to arrive at and, even when achieved, usually involve a degree of provisionality. This is a typical Anglican habit: embodying a necessary humility and holiness in relation to matters of truth and pragmatics, but without losing sight of the fact that difficult decisions need to be made. This is the nature of the body.

Paul's image of the body of Christ, therefore, is not an (or *the*) answer to questions about how to shape the church and congregations of the future. It is, rather, an image that invites us to dwell on the ways in which Christians live together in the here and now. It invites us into a set of relationships in which we can contemplate and own our individual distinctives, as well as our inter-connectedness. It is not a final answer; but rather an invitation to engage in living and discovering together. And, like a body, is subject to daily change, adaptation and fresh challenges; as well as being constant and self-conscious. So, the feet should not be treated like the ear, or the eyes as the hands. Paul's image of the body teaches charity, mutuality, interdependence and cohesion. It teaches us to value the differences we have, to cultivate an awareness of the common vocation we share and challenges we face, as well as those that are particular to various regions and contexts.

Conclusion

Ulrich Beck's teasing thesis, *A God of One's Own* (2010) has some pertinent things to say about our present time. Writing as a sociologist and religious commentator,

---

[5]   See Luis Bermejo SJ (1989).

Beck suggests that just as one has a life of one's own and a room of one's own, western modernity has created an ethic of individual self fulfilment that allows believers to shape and determine the God they believe in. This powerful current is channelled through the individual's life, experience and self-knowledge, permitting religious people to construct their own religious shelters, thereby making decisions about faith rather than deferring them to the power and authority of the institution to which they belong. Indeed, the very act of belonging, and of believing, is defined on terms set by the individual. This opens up two kinds of chasm. The first is between the believers and the rest of the world; and the second is between believers. Beck argues, therefore, that Berger's 'scared canopy' is no longer intact – if by that, we mean a shared over-arching meta-narrative. It does, however, persist in two senses. First, as something which individuals may continue to interpret, albeit on their own terms, and as a hypothesis that attracts wide 'buy-in', but not necessarily with shared agreement on contingent or ultimate meaning. Second, as a kind of 'micro-canopy' – that need only work for the individual or group, and does not necessarily require a wider and shared understanding in order to acquire its validation for the individual or group. Thus, 'this works for me/us' is somehow sufficient, since the individualism is now so complete as to have no need of wider corporate or catholic validation.

Beck does not believe this situation spells the end of religion, but merely its 'entry into the self-contradictory narrative of secular religiosity' (2010, p. 16), which is produced through pluralism, individualism, consumerism and capitalism. Indeed, such factors simultaneously bloat and diminish religion: greater individualism and an increase in committed church-going are highly compatible. The winner is not necessarily religion or faith, however, but ultimately choice, since the individual gains greater reflexivity and personal power through the exercise of choice. But it is a power that places them above the authority they have selected; it is the consumer saying to God, 'you did not choose me, I chose you' (to invert John 15:16).

There is one further and final issue with the sacred canopy that should be mentioned here. Peter Berger and his colleagues, in *The Homeless Mind* (1974) point out how pervasive rationalistic, technical and bureaucratic ways have emptied life of meaning, corroding the scared canopy of meanings in relation to life, death and beliefs about the way we should live. Processes have eclipsed wisdom, resulting in a kind of modern *anomie* – the loss of bearings and the demise of a shared structure of values, truths and stories. Civilisation cannot be built and sustained upon a general plea for respect for all, a commitment to recycling, and an anti-bullying policy – these being the three 'values' promoted by the school my son attends, and posted in the reception area. Here, reasonableness has simply replaced rationality. And it is precisely this kind of anomie that drives individuals to seek their own sacred spaces and canopies, which are stubbornly rooted in the therapeutic, immediate and personal. Yet this individualism is ultimately unable to sustain our neighbourhoods, communities and nations.

In a highly influential essay, Dan Hardy writes that

> The task of theology, then, is to begin from common practice and examine its quality in open trial by the use of natural reason in order to discover the truth of this practice, by a truth-directed reason … (including) practical reason. And the outcome … should be an agreement on the proper organisation of common life which would actually promote the practice of society …. The concern is public … the use of public reason, open trial of the truth and the achievement of truly social existence (D.W. Hardy, 1989, p.33).

In creating the sense of time and space – whether at Cuddesdon, in Macau or in St Paul's – the Christian cadences that are present in the provision of this space actually help to form, create and re-create new possibilities for sociality. This space may be pastoral or performative; or peaceable and prescient. Yet the spaces and places testify not only to a story about their origins, but also one of aspiration. This is the congenial sense of community at Cuddesdon which carries a message about the reality and possibilities of the Anglican Communion. It is the emergence of alternative space in a church-based project in Macau that affirms family and youth, and resists the tide of commercialism and individualism that otherwise might reign in the city. It may be Wren's extraordinary domed cathedral that quickly complemented the spirit of the *Book of Common Prayer* with a sense of common space that was intended to be non-divisive and all-inclusive.

The burden of such places, and the vision for such spaces, is not simply that they serve the church, or even that they are at the disposal of their local communities. It is, rather, that as holy and inhabited places, they actually make for a better society. As Hardy says, the outcome 'should be an agreement on the proper organisation of common life which would actually promote the practice of society'. It is here that we may find the coalition of Christian belief, practice and artifact (i.e., spaces and places) can be at its most dynamic, and truly shape the common practice of our social life. This is partly what it means to pitch God's tent in every age. But such a vision for the world, under God, to be enabled and achieved, requires a real sensitivity to the character and nature of the spaces and places we inhabit, and the people we serve. When we begin to reflect deeply on what we have, we can start to glimpse some of the possibilities for the church and world that God might intend; how his nature might shape the world. But to do so requires some vision, courage and adventure on our part: as well as faith, hope and love.

PART II
Hope and Transformations

Chapter 4

Liberating Captives: Theology and Social Christianity

How are Christians supposed to engage with the world when they are, in truth, expecting a new world that is yet to come? Why bother with the temporal when minds and hearts are meant to be fixed on the eternal? What can theology offer the churches to help Christians of all persuasions maintain their poise and prophetic witness within a public and plural world? These questions pepper the pages of the New Testament as much as they have absorbed Christians for two millennia. On the one hand, Christians are called out of the world, and are to no longer regard themselves as belonging to it. On the other hand, they are to be engaged with the world in all its complexities and ambiguities as fully as possible, being salt, light and least in society, incarnating the life of Christ into the hubris of humanity. The apparent dilemma is expressed by one early Christian writer in this way:

> Christians ... reside in their respective countries, but only as aliens. They take part in everything as citizens and put up with everything as foreigners. Every foreign land is their home, and every home a foreign land .... In a word: what the soul is in the body, that Christians are in the world. The soul is spread through all the members of the body, and the Christians throughout all the cities of the world. The soul dwells in the body, but is not part and parcel of the body; so Christians dwell in the world, but are not part and parcel of the world... (Kleist, 1948, p. 139)

The unknown author of the late second century *Epistle to Diognetus* expresses a paradox that is at the heart of Christian engagement with social ordering, the political sphere and public life. He or she speaks for the first generation of Christians as much for those of the twenty-first, by formulating the sense of divided loyalties that can sometimes threaten the very identity of the church, and the place of Christians within the world.

Yet this tension – with all its possibilities and problems – is at the heart of the Christian gospel. The ministry of Jesus was inherently political in character as much as it was 'other-worldly'. The Gospel of John presents the reader with a

Christ who calls Christians out of the world, but at the same time leaves them in it (cf. Jn. 15: 19, 17: 14, 18: 36, etc). In the same way, the radical words and actions of Jesus appear (at first sight) to point in opposite directions.

For example, consider the miracles of Jesus. Whatever significance may be attached to their historicity, it is the social and political implications that flow from these narratives that are the more compelling. Jesus seems to go out of his way to embrace the 'untouchables' of society – lepers, the poor, the unclean, people of other faiths and those who are marginalised because of their creed or colour (Percy 1998, p. 29). Jesus tends not to heal those who already possess significant social, moral, religious or political status. Instead, much of his healing activity appears to question boundaries and taboos, theologies of taint and forms of social exclusion. Invariably, the healings question the social forces that divide society between the pure and the contagious, between the righteous and the sinner. Jesus, in other words, acts as an alternative boundary keeper, and his healing miracles (like many of his parables) fundamentally question the values that underpin the social ordering of his day, suggesting or demanding a radical reordering.

Yet to only understand Jesus as a radical interferer within the social order of first century Palestine would be to ignore another dimension of his agenda: the kingdom of God which is to come. The radical discipleship demanded by Jesus may be said to dwell less on reform and more on revolution. Employment and families are to be forsaken for the kingdom – the ushering in of the new reign of God. Even the dead can be left unburied (cf. Matt. 8: 22; Lk. 9: 57–62). Moreover, the disciples are not to anticipate reward or rule in this life; all recognition of costly service and devotion is postponed until the *eschaton*, where the wheat will be separated from the chaff, and the righteous rewarded (Matt. 6: 19–21). (In very early Christian tradition, the apparent imminence of the kingdom of God led some to give up work, and others to lead a life of celibacy. But by the time the later documents of the New Testament were being written, Christians were being urged to respect and work with temporal authorities, get on with their ordinary labours, and to apply gospel principles to this life, rather than speculating about the date of the *parousia*.)

These two distinct traditions within early Christian teaching are, of course, closely related. Each act of service (e.g., hospitality, charity, etc.), the extension of costly love (e.g., of turning the other cheek, loving your enemies, etc.) and of vicarious sacrifice points towards the kingdom that is to come. Within Christian tradition, the kingdom is the place where society is reordered; captives are liberated, the lame walk and the blind are restored to sight (Lk. 4: 18–19). It is also the place where the poor inherit the kingdom, the mourners are comforted, the meek and the peacemakers rewarded, and the persecuted redeemed (Matt. 5: 3–11). In other words, Christian social teaching anticipates the rule of God in prayer and action: 'your kingdom come, your will be done, on earth as it is in heaven' (Matt. 6: 9–13).

This tradition and teaching is reflected in the very first Christian communities. Stephen, the first Christian martyr, is a deacon with special responsibility for the daily distribution of alms to widows and orphans (Acts 6: 1–3), reflecting the commitment to charity and service that is advocated in the gospels. In character, the first churches, although diverse in practice and belief, appear nevertheless to have exhibited a radical openness to questions of parity and inclusion. The term for 'church' is the simple Greek word *ekklesia*, meaning the 'assembly of the people' who belong to but are called out of their community. All over the Mediterranean world, assemblies determined the politics, polity and civic ordering of communities and cities. But they were usually only open to citizens, and the power to speak and vote was normally confined to men. The assemblies of the New Testament church – the deliberate adoption of the more internationalist term must have caused confusion to potential converts, as well as making a point – were, in contrast, inclusive if alternative. In these *ekklesia*, women were admitted, as were slaves (cf. Paul's Letter to Philemon), children, foreigners and other visitors. In other words, the character of the New Testament *ekklesia* represented and embodied a different kind of spiritual and social ordering that eschewed discrimination on grounds of race, gender and other criteria.

Closely allied to the notion of *ekklesia* is its apparent antithesis, the *enclasia* – an idea developed by Coleridge (amongst others) to specify that Christians may not (only) be called out of the world, but are also called into it. Coleridge (1839) regarded the idea of *enclasia* as a gospel mandate. Christians were called to be light to the world, the salt of the earth and the leaven in the lump. Correspondingly, churches, rather than being separatist and alternative bodies within their broader communities, were to be deeply embedded within the civic, social and moral ordering of society, contributing to the overall commonwealth. This theological approach led Coleridge to justify the Church and State being closely inter-related for the sake of the common good.

From this brief introduction, it should already be clear that Christianity was, from the outset, an inherently political and social faith. Its expression always challenges the present world order, but is, at the same time, prepared to work within it, regarding nothing as being beyond redemption. It is incarnate, and yet also prophetic. At the same time, Christianity exhibits a typical feature of many world religions – etymologically, the desire to *bind* spirituality to life, and to make a difference to the present in anticipation of God's future. To consider the social and political character of Christianity further, the remainder of the discussion is grouped under three (somewhat arbitrary) headings: social order, political spheres and public life. The categories are not exhaustive, and in a chapter of this size it will only be possible to outline the sketchiest dimensions of Christian thought within each arena. A conclusion will explore why theology and the churches continue to need more tenacity, acuity and wisdom in their engagement with the contemporary world.

Social Order

It is a little-known fact that part of the Edict of Milan (313), which was an agreement between the emperors Licinius and Constantine to recognise the legal personality of churches, to treat all religions equally, and to restore lands and property confiscated under persecution, also made provision for donkeys. According to the agreement, Christians, calling on all others of good will, were to see that beasts of burden were not abused in transporting heavy loads uphill. Such concerns may seem trivial to modern readers, but the Edict provides an early piece of evidence to support the view that the Christian faith had extensive interests in contributing to social order – even in the minutiae of everyday life. Generations of Christians would follow suit on other issues where prevailing standards and constructions of reality had to be undermined and cast aside if justice was to be done. The emancipation of slaves (Samuel Wilberforce), equality for Blacks (Martin Luther King) or the alleviation of poverty (William Booth) are but a few examples.

The Edict of Milan is widely regarded as the point at which the foundation for established Christianity was first laid, although the Edict did not establish Christianity in the formal sense. The emerging Constantinian settlement did, however, provide a paradigm that was to influence much of Europe as it embraced Christianity. This was to link civic governance, religion and the economy in the interests of providing sustainable patterns of social ordering that were of benefit to communities (e.g., such as the prohibition on usury). In England, for example, the relationship between a parish and its church was intrinsic to the identity of a place. Communities that were economically and socially viable were able to sustain a church and the ministry that issued from it, which in turn guaranteed a certain level of moral welfare, social improvement and pastoral provision (including the availability of the sacraments). Or, put another way, the very existence of a parish church within a community confirmed the identity of the place, conferring it with recognisable significance that invited a form of social ordering in which (amongst other things) the needs of the poor and other matters of moral concern could be addressed on behalf of the community (Pounds, 2001).

Similarly, the genesis of many hospitals, schools, hospices and other agencies for welfare (e.g., adoption, fostering, etc.) began their life as an extension of the pastoral provision of the churches, intended for the common good. Throughout

Christian history, there have been many movements and individuals whose faith has spawned something particular that has directly contributed to the re-ordering of society. Christianity has been especially prominent in healthcare, welfare and education, but has taken no less interest in the moral well-being of society, most often manifest in areas related to sexuality and procreation, and in various arenas of censorship.

Readers with a more secular outlook on life might wonder at (and perhaps flinch away from?) a faith that aspires to shape society. How can one credo help order societies where there are many beliefs, and none? Are the interests of society not better protected by faith remaining private, and keeping out of the public arena? The fear of fundamentalism (or of religious oppression through the state) is what drives many secularist critics to distinguish sharply between church and society, and to maintain their separateness. Like the Republic of Gilead in Margaret Atwood's apocalyptic *The Handmaid's Tale*, some secularists fear the advent of a theocratic hegemony, the establishment of religion over and against all competing frames of reference (Atwood, 1985). Equally, the fear of taint and dilution is what motivates a handful of Christian denominations to withdraw from the world in the interests of maintaining their purity and distinctiveness. In both world-views, religion and society don't mix, and should be kept apart where possible.

Yet for the majority of the world's population, religion and society are inseparable; they mix, are mixed, and are not easily extracted one from another, or capable of being told apart. The shaping and ordering of societies invariably has a religious character to it; sometimes seen explicitly, it is more often than not implicit within many aspects of polity. Yet theologically, the ordering of society is a contentious arena. What sources and authorities are to be brought to bear upon pressing social issues? To what extent is a Christian world-view (assuming that this could even be agreed upon) possible in the complexity of the political sphere? What exactly is a Christian government? And what would the city of God look like? (From Augustine to Calvin and through to Milbank, the idea is seldom as attractive as it first appears.) There are many examples of types of Christian social ordering, but space permits only three to be discussed here for our immediate purposes. The theological outlooks to be briefly considered are social justice, social intervention and social advancement.

The modern notion of social justice can be traced to nineteenth century Christian Socialism in Britain and the more dispersed notion of Social Christianity in the USA. (Liberation Theology is discussed as a separate approach later in this chapter.) The birth of Christian Socialism in Britain can be dated precisely: 10 April 1848. F.D, Maurice, John Ludlow and Charles Kingsley, three theologians who were already prominent, met to consider a response to the Chartist demonstration that had petitioned in London for political reform. Motivated by a concern for the conditions of 'working men' as much as they were to relating the gospel to contemporary culture, Maurice, Ludlow and Kingsley produced a series of tracts that were to have a significant impact on the social and ideological landscape of Britain (Atherton, 1994, pp. 1–49).

The presuppositions of the early Christian Socialist movement were comparatively simple, and perhaps to modern minds, obvious. Taking their cue from an emphasis on incarnational theology, they held that as all were in Christ, so was God, in Christ, bound up in the *material* of humanity as much as its spirituality. This meant that the agenda of the kingdom of God was closely related to the concerns of the world, and most especially where suffering and injustice could be located and experienced. Correspondingly, an interest in the extension of suffrage, the relation of capitalism to the labouring poor, and addressing and alleviating the conditions of poverty became primary arenas for debate, and for developing a Christian perspective. And yet an ideological shift would not be enough for the protagonists. To be sure, Christian Socialism fundamentally challenged the prevailing and complacent views about the scope of theology and the place of the church in society. In effect, the dominant other-worldly piety of Evangelicals and Anglo-Catholics, which had been so strong in the early nineteenth century (a mainly spiritual response to massive social and cultural upheaval, including the rise of industrialisation at the expense of agrarian communities), was undermined by the incarnational emphasis Christian Socialists placed on social action and solidarity with the working classes. Initiatives such as the Working Men's College, founded in 1854 to enable adult education, were simply the practical Christian extension of the theological presuppositions that underpinned Christian Socialism.

This emerging tradition of social justice – championed by the early Christian Socialists – evolved steadily throughout the nineteenth and twentieth centuries. Stewart Headlam took the conflation of the secular and the sacred (implicit in Maurice's incarnational theology) and helped to develop the Fabian Society and its championing of collectivism. This outlook, which espoused a kind of organic society and humanity, was directly opposed to the *laissez-faire* capitalism of the same era that had championed individualism, competition and the freedom of the markets (and repeated under Thatcherism in the late twentieth century).

The aspirations for social justice that had begun with theologians such as Maurice were to be further developed and enhanced by the commitment to social intervention and reform that emerged in the first half of the twentieth century. The nurturing context for the possibility of radicalism cannot be over-emphasised. Just as Maurice, Ludlow and Kingsley had responded to and fed off the work of the Chartists, so were the Christian Socialists now able to situate their work in relation to the rise of Communism in Russia and Europe, the poverty wreaked by two world wars, and the stark economic depressions of the 1930s. The new heirs of Christian Socialism in the twentieth century included R.H. Tawney (his 1926 critique of the acquisitive society in *Religion and the Rise of Capitalism* is classic modern theology, blending social theory with ethics and history), Ronald Preston (who espoused middle axioms in dealing with the ambiguities of capitalism and socialism), and William Temple.

Temple's *Christianity and Social Order* (1942) reflects the extent to which the established church had now adopted the agenda of social(ist) radicalism, and was prepared to argue for reform and intervention. Temple's work – written when he was Archbishop of Canterbury, giving it even more of an edge – argues for a church that would not only point out Christian principles (especially where they conflict with existing social order), but also help to re-shape the existing order so that it more closely conformed with Christian principles. Again, this may not sound radical to modern ears, but the impact of Temple's work at the time should not be underestimated, for it situated the church firmly within the arena of political and social debates, giving it a role of social advocacy. *Christianity and Social Order* is therefore less than circumspect in arguing that 'every child should find itself a member of a family housed with decency and dignity, so that it may grow up ... in a happy fellowship unspoilt by under-feeding, overcrowding, by dirty and drab surroundings or by mechanical monotony ...'. The primacy of human dignity emerges as a key, as Temple goes on to press for access to free education, fair income, representation and advocacy in employment, leisure and liberty.

This theological programme was, as Temple acknowledged, mildly Utopian. The aim of his Christian social order is 'the fullest possible development of the individual personality in the widest and deepest possible fellowship'. In turn, this order was founded upon the conviction that the resources of God's earth should be used as God's gifts to the whole of humanity. Not all politicians were impressed with the attempts by English bishops to bring Christian principles to bear upon the political, social and economic order. In 1926 a group of bishops had attempted to bring the government, coal industry and miners together to end the disastrous strike. Stanley Baldwin, then Prime Minister, asked how the bishops would like it if he passed the Athanasian Creed to the Iron and Steel Federation for revision (Atherton, 1994, p. 90). The controversy over *Faith in the City* (1985) in England simply continues the tradition of church-government antipathy on issues of social and economic justice.

Lastly, social advancement may take a variety of forms. Perhaps the first thing to say is that the commitment to justice and intervention is usually a form of advancement in its own right, and it should not be implied otherwise. However, in exploring social advancement, it is useful for our purposes here to single out two distinct schools of thought: the social gospel movement (largely confined to the USA) and that of Christian Conservatism. The social gospel movement in the USA arose in response to the industrialisation and urbanisation of America from the 1860s. Rather like the emergence of Christian Socialism in England, church leaders became concerned at the massive inequalities that were produced by a booming economy, and sought to address the needs of workers. That mode of address required the reformulation of Christian tradition in order to engage with the complexity of the economy. According to Atherton, this involved the rejection of *laissez-faire* Protestantism on the one hand and, on the other, a recognition that the world of work was treated seriously as God's arena of activity, which was underpinned by a liberal theological stress on the solidarity of Jesus within social situations. The movement took a serious step forward with the work of Walter Rauschenbusch (1861–1918 – Rauschenbusch's thought was to significantly influence the theological development of Martin Luther King), whose *Christianizing the Social Order* (1912) offered a radical critique of capitalist society, and advocated a social order organised according to the will of God.

Yet in spite of the promise of the social gospel movement, the agenda began to flounder in the mid-1920s. The liberal theology underpinning the movement began to wane, and its critics argued that the social gospel movement had overestimated the prospect of changing society (bringing about the kingdom on earth), and had underestimated the forces of self-interest and sin that were endemic within all classes and races, which in turn challenged the collaborative ethos that supposed that people would work together for the common good.

What began to emerge in place of the social gospel movement was an altogether more pragmatic approach to the problems posed by the market to theology, churches and society, with scholars such as Reinhold Niebuhr (1892–1971) leading the field. Niebuhr is a pivotal figure in the history of theological engagement with the economy in the USA, since he held a critical perspective on the idea of the social gospel and its possibilities: he called for 'more radical political orientation and more conservative religious convictions' (Atherton, 1994, p. 31) to comprehend the culture of his day. The fusion of the radical with the conservative was to pave the way for the emergence of a neo-Christian Conservatism, which would lay stress on the capacity of markets to increase prosperity, improve life and empower people. Its champions have included Michael Novak in the USA and Brian Griffiths in Britain, who have argued that faith in the market might be said to open up a pathway to social and individual liberation.

Political Spheres

All of the approaches discussed above – and these are only a tiny representative sample – can be understood as critically empathetic theological approaches to the ordering of society. Each tradition is securely based on a theological presupposition (e.g., solidarity, freedom, etc.) that aspires to shape society in relation to market forces, capitalism, industrialisation and the common good. Although politically active, the traditions may be generally characterised as reforming rather than revolutionary. Christian Socialism and Christian Conservatism, even at their most radical, posed no substantial threat to the existing social order of their time. The former may be said to place its main emphasis on sharing wealth as the pathway to creating a fairer and just society, and valuing the commonality of humanity. The latter tradition concentrates on creating wealth as a primary means of generating social and moral improvement. Both traditions share a commitment to social justice, intervention (which would include withdrawal – the practice of non-intervention championed by Thatcherites, for example) and advancement through their particular theological outlook; liberty, dignity and a God-fearing society remain common goals. It is only the methods of achieving these ends that separate the parties.

The approaches to social ordering outlined so far have assumed that Christianity, theology and the churches have a certain place within society, and are respected within their various political contexts. William Temple's theological views gain their prominence partly because of his position as Archbishop of Canterbury within a church that is established, which gives bishops in the Church of England a role in the affairs of the state at all levels (from membership of the House of Lords to territorial representation of all the peoples within their dioceses). In the USA, although there are no ties between church and state, the character and influence of the churches, coupled to the status of theology within the public sphere, constantly creates the potential for Christianity to involve itself in social and political life – which society mostly welcomes.

However, there have been and are situations in which theological discourse and the practice of the churches are seen by the state and (perhaps) by society to be essentially undermining of the status quo, and potentially threatening to the prevailing social order. Here, the shape of theology can be characterised as one of resistance rather than critical-compliance. Consider, for example, a well-known twentieth century example: Dietrich Bonhoeffer. Bonhoeffer was a Lutheran pastor and theologian who witnessed the rise of the Third Reich first hand. He was fundamentally opposed to the philosophy of Nazism, and was one of the leaders of the breakaway Confessing Church that dissented from offering religious support to Hitler's state. He was quickly banned from teaching, and generally harassed by the Nazis. When war broke out, Bonhoeffer was actually on a lecture tour of the USA. Electing to return to Germany he carried on the fight against Nazism from the inside. He was arrested in 1943, and executed at Flossenburg concentration camp, 9 April 1945. His ground-breaking *The Cost of Discipleship* had already been published (1937), in which he had meditated on demands of the Christian life in an oppressive political situation.

Martin Luther King is another example of a theologian who paid specific attention to the relationship between theological concepts of power (e.g., the reign and kingdom of God), and the actual experience of powerlessness that may be common to certain social or political contexts. In common with other figures (such as Desmond Tutu in relation to Apartheid) and movements (such as Liberation Theology), he linked the two together. The love, power and justice of God are not only eschatological concepts; they are also to be worked out in contemporary life, and perhaps most especially through a prophetic social gospel, working alongside political action (including resistance) and appropriate civil action.

King's political life and civil action cannot be understood without reference to his religious convictions, which determined the particular stances that he took, as well as influencing the timbre of his stirring and charismatic polemic. King's theological and political methodologies were often 'pragmatism based upon principle', in which negotiation and engagement with culture – in King's case, an often hostile and violent white supremacist culture – required imaginative and reflexive responses. King was, in other words, not only a significant black theologian: he can also be claimed as a pre-eminent practical theologian, set within the earliest paradigms of Liberation theology. King's theology was part of a political struggle, and to succeed it needed to mobilise believers and non-believers alike to resist the very real alienating social structures and cultures that oppressed them.

This brings us, lastly in this section, to Liberation Theology itself. The term is normally associated with Latin American theologians such as Leonardo Boff, Gustavo Gutierrez, Ruben Alves, Juan Luis Segundo, Jon Sobrino and Jose Miguez Bonino. In truth, however, Liberation Theology is an umbrella term that embraces a range of approaches to contexts and various sub-disciplines or penumbra within the wider theological compass. At the risk of generalising, Liberation Theologians work contextually, explicitly addressing social situations that are deemed to engender oppression. The theological interpretations tend to be 'inductive' in character – working from concrete facts and experiences of oppression, then reflecting and theorising, before finally turning to issues of praxis (normally a militant demand for reordering). At the heart of Liberation Theology is an antipathy towards 'abstract' theology or private piety, and a radical commitment to justice through interdisciplinarity, utilising insights from the social sciences in the construction of theological critiques and solutions. Liberation Theology can cover a number of theological initiatives: Black Theology (e.g., James Cone), Feminist Theology (e.g., Mary Grey), Gay and Lesbian theologies, as well as the responses of South African theologians to Apartheid, or the emergent Minjung Theology in South Korea.

The specific features of Latin American Liberation Theology have arguably provided the key contours for recent theological critiques and forms of ecclesial resistance within a number of political spheres. Liberation Theology sets out to be a practical theological discourse of the poor, determining that this is the primary *place* where theology must be done. Looking to the socio-analytical insights of Marxism, Liberation theology seeks to address the nature and cause of oppression, emphasising solidarity and political action as a pathway to empowerment and salvation. However, with the collapse of Communism (coupled to the inexorable rise of capitalism), the initial thrall of Liberation Theology appears to have waned over the last decade. As more reflexive liberal social democracies emerge in Latin America, the fundamental antinomies that produced Liberation Theology are now less apparent. Capitalism, instead of becoming the (obvious) enemy of the poor, has emerged as a potential partner in liberation and regeneration, and part of the solution in the ending of economic and political oppression.

Whilst solidarity with the suffering continues to be the abiding passion and a fundamental rationale for Liberation Theology, the discipline is nevertheless beginning to gain a new sense of poise: in a globalised economy its praxis now lies somewhere between the participative and the prophetic (Bell, 2001). Once again, we see that something that initially began as a principled revolutionary movement has now evolved into a more pragmatic reformist agenda, in which the original sharpness of theological acuity has become widely accepted and dispersed amongst churches and a variety of theological outlooks. Even so, methodologically, Liberation Theology remains one of the most influential movements within twentieth century theology, and shows every sign of continuing to make a significant contribution to the social and political complexities of the twenty-first century.

Public Life

The distinctive theological contributions outlined in the previous section – characterised by their resistance to the prevailing social consensus and to political oppression – are markedly different from the kinds of theological and ecclesial paradigms to be discussed in this section. Here, we are concerned with how theology and the churches continue to guide and shape society through a critical-support for public life and for the state itself. This position is, arguably, the dominant mediating axiom that synthesises the social ordering and the social resistance discussed in the previous two sections. At the same time, it is arguably the least obvious paradigm, since the 'religion' in question is not encountered so much in the intensity of ecclesial communities (where it may obviously still be found), but is rather dispersed extensively within the overall shaping of society. Theologians such as Andrew Shanks argue that this is a vital dimension of Christianity:

> the innermost essence of Christianity drives it out beyond the Church; it has to
> seek embodiment in nothing less than the body which encompasses the entirety
> of human life, namely the state (Shanks, 1990, p. 114).

Whilst Shanks acknowledges that churches need to retain their identity as distinctive bodies, independent of the state and the public, if they are to be the yeast and salt of the Kingdom of God, they are also there to help fund civilising strands within society. But the churches do not own society, and neither do they entirely generate all the moral strands that might guide and make sociality. As Coleridge suggested almost two centuries ago, the Church of the nation is not quite the same as the Church of Christ, yet it is there to secure and improve the moral cultivation of its people, 'without which the nation could be neither permanent or progressive' (Coleridge 1976, p. 44 – first published 1839). The Church is, therefore, not a world to come, but another world that now is, whose role is to combat political evil, not just institutional defects – but through critical-support, rather than separatism.

We might say that as public space becomes more complex and atomised – in effect, a morass of competing convictions – 'public religion' becomes more difficult to articulate. In other words, *which* public might we be talking about? *What* religion? *Whose* faith? There cannot be one univocal answer to these questions. Robert Bellah noted some time ago how 'pluralised' civil religion had become, being now made up of an eclectic mix of symbols, beliefs and ideals. Granted, these probably performed a similar legitimising function to the one Rousseau had in mind, insofar as they provided a fairly simple creed that supported civil society (e.g., integrity, neighbourly regard, decency, truth, etc.). Yet Bellah also observed how the very foundations of postwar American civil religion were now threatened by vapid individualism (Bellah, 1975). The present parameters of the debate are perhaps best described by another American theologian, Richard John Neuhaus. On the one hand, Neuhaus maintains that an American civil society cannot exclude religion from shaping public life and discourse. On the other hand, he also argues that religious traditions can only inhabit such space on the condition that they respect the rules of open public debate, and do not themselves become tyrannical and autocratic (Neuhaus, 1984, p. 258).

Mindful of the improbability of recovering Christendom, Ian Markham suggests that there are now just three ways in which religion can properly enable a process of what he describes as 'cultural enrichment' within 'secular' society:

> Instead of a unitary culture in which one language, one religion, one history and one set of images dominate, we need a diverse culture in which different languages, many religions, and several narratives and images coexist in stimulating tension .... Cultural enrichment requires three different processes. First, we must develop the separateness of each community. We should empower communities to create the space for their tradition to be affirmed .... The second process within cultural enrichment is that of community engagement, implying dialogue, disagreement, and a mutual exploration of truth .... The third process is that of faith communities discovering their voice within the public square. Public policy requires a moral dimension (Markham, 1999, p. 151).

These are fine sentiments, to be sure. Yet it is not difficult to probe and proscribe the limits of this paradigm; even a brief global survey shows how complex the tensions in public life can be. It is not clear, for instance, that all cultures will agree on what constitutes a 'freedom of expression'. In a liberal climate within the USA or Europe, say, this may appear to be obvious. There are public standards of taste and decency that reflect sensate values. Western cultural assumptions concerning the freedom that the media offers society may, however, be a problem for Islam. (All societies may have interests in controlling or policing the media, due to particular cultural, political or religious reasons.) In other states where there is religious tension between competing convictions, the state may also exercise censorship of religious communication. In Nigeria, for example, this may prohibit the practice of tolling church bells or public calls to prayer broadcast from minarets. The publication of Salman Rushdie's *The Satanic Verses* in 1988 caused a series of international incidents, many of which raised the spectre of the antinomy between freedom and religion, especially in European countries where Islam was a minority faith. Even in apparently progressive pluralist countries such as Singapore, where modernity, consumerism and globalisation is bountiful, media censorship abounds.

These developments arguably represent a stage beyond the civil religion in the sense that Rousseau might have originally meant it. 'Civil' has now become elided with 'public' and, in the process, faiths are now more sharply defined and (perhaps) narrower in their outlook. But what does this mean? In essence, it suggests that the very 'public spaces' that religion once nestled within are now either deemed to be empty of values, or, alternatively, are full of competing convictions that need policing. This may mean, ironically, keeping religion out of the very public spaces that faiths may once have helped to create. Casanova is probably right when he asserts that religion in modern times is differentiated, but not privatised. It continues to have an influence on the public and political landscape, even though it may now only mainly consist of protests – either against secularism, consumerism or liberalism, or just more generally against the excesses of the modern state (Casanova, 1994).

So, ideally, a public faith is not merely an imposed faith, but rather also a servant of society. Here, a single concentrated religious tradition may better represent and serve the interests of the many, than can other forms of quasi-democratic representation in which all have a voice. The role of a national church should therefore be primarily sacrificial and sacramental in character. Incarnate, it must live with its ambiguities, lack of definition, mystery, distinctiveness and power. It actively seeks intra- and inter-dependent social, political and constitutional relations for the sake of social flourishing, to bear witness to the incarnation, and to anticipate the Kingdom that is yet to come.

Tariq Modood has argued that from the perspective of minority religions in Great Britain, 'establishment' remains a sign of hope:

> The real division of opinion is not between a conservative element in the Church of England versus the rest of the country, but between those that think religion has a place in secular public culture, that religious communities are part of the state, and those who think not … the minimal nature of an Anglican Establishment, its proven openness to other denominations and faiths seeking public space, and the fact that its very existence is an ongoing recognition of the public character of religion, are all reasons why it may seem far less intimidating to the minority of faiths than a triumphal secularism (T. Modood 1997, p. 4).

Here Modood shows that a practical argument for establishment remains powerful and reasonable, even for someone who doesn't share 'the faith of the nation'.[1] All of which is another way of saying that the church does have an interest in keeping a positive stake in the articulation of the social consensus, and that any neutrality towards the state is not necessarily desirable. Unlimited freedom of choice can lead to social fragmentation; collective provision and universal service, though sometimes weak, is at least, close to being comprehensive, and

---

[1]   See also A. Hastings (1997), p. 41.

therefore ultimately catholic. However, any partnership between faith and public life sometimes comes at a cost.[2]

Either way, the place of religion in the public life of the developed world has shifted slowly but surely over the last two centuries. It has moved from a position of relative privilege where it habitually and naturally shaped sociality (what Coleridge quaintly called 'the clerisy of the nation' in England), to one where it is one voice amongst a number that may now claim to create, order and sustain public life. Arguably, this apparently new situation of religion is conditioned as much by pluralism, globalisation and modernity as it is by secularisation. To conclude, therefore, we shall briefly explore how theologians and the churches are to face the task of social ordering, political engagement and the shaping of public life in a more obviously pluralised and atomised future.

Conclusion

Politics and the ordering of society is a contested arena of debate and praxis. So, for that matter, is theology. So the idea of a political theology is bound to be contentious and is unlikely to achieve consensus. In this essay we have drawn attention to the inherently political character of early Christianity and that of its founders. In turn, this has led to perspectives on how sociality might be ordered, politics engaged with or resisted, and public life shaped. The sequential history (albeit briefly sketched) has hinted that Christianity and its theologians have, over the last two centuries, progressed from advocating justice, to arguing for a state based on common welfare, to finally arguing for social advancement, either through liberal socialism or conservatism. Yet some theologians continue to deny that Christian theology can have anything to say to politics or society. Edward Norman's *Christianity and World Order* (1997) argues that whilst theological truths may have derivative *consequences* for the political, the actual truths of Christianity are inherently non-political and transcendent in character. Yet from our survey, it should be clear that our early contention, namely that Christianity *is* an inherently political and social faith, is a no less defensible theological stance.

---

[2]   On this, see Oliver O'Donovan (1996). O'Donovan contends that, to pass beyond suspicion and the totalised criticism of politics, and to achieve a positive reconstruction of thought, theology must reach back behind the modern tradition, achieving a fuller, less selective reading of scripture, and learning from an older politico-theological discourse which flourished in the patristic, medieval and reformation periods. Central to that discourse was a series of questions about authority, generated by Jesus' proclamation of the Kingdom of God.

Perhaps the only matter to discuss is what kinds of sociality and what kinds of politics might arise from Christianity in its many and various contexts.

That said, how are theologians and the churches to engage with politics and society at the dawn of the twenty-first century? The range of forces that bear upon the identity of the church, Christian discourse and praxis, and general theological acuity are bewildering enough in late modernity, without getting further drawn into the shaping of society and its political life. Yet theology, if it is to continue to offer a public voice for the churches in the marketplace of modernity, will need to adapt the tone and content of its discourse to fit the pluralised, globalised and atomised world in which it speaks. In part, this project would need to recognise that one person's or communities' liberation may be another's oppression; theology will need to discover its mediating skills, as well as recovering the prophetic.

Part of the difficulty that theologians now face in addressing politics and society is that much of the 'old world order' has vanished, and the shape of the new world order is, well, more liquid than concrete. With the collapse of Communism, and the shrinking powers and influence of many nation states, there are now many fronts on which to engage. Many countries now live in more politically post-ideological phases. Liberal social democracies – delicate reticulate combinations of socialism, capitalism, liberalism and conservatism (and perhaps infused with other political timbres) – abound all over the world, even in the poorest continents. The hard ideological certainties of Communism or Fascism are hard to find let alone fight. Many of the old antinomies that once provided the fertile soil for some of the germane theological movements and ideas we have been discussing are now no longer apparent. Industrial relations are now more complex than the (apparently simple) workers versus the owners paradigm; politics is more multifaceted than simply being the poor against capitalism. In short, the situations of the twenty-first century seem to warrant theological responses that will be more fluid than those of their forebears, perhaps recognising the 'liquid' character of late modernity. Under such conditions, there continues to be a need to recognise the rights and dignity of workers, but this may be extrinsically linked to a notion of market sustainability, adaptation in productivity and economic viability within the global marketplace. In other words, capitalism may be here to stay: but how can theologians shape it ethically, socially and responsibly?

In this new world order, Christian prophetic witness and theological critiques have started to turn away from governments and political ideologies, and concentrate on issues and parameters of common concern. This may include such things as a new consciousness about the environment and the sustainability of the earth. Campaigns for justice and equity may now be directed more at businesses and global capitalism than any one nation. The recent Jubilee 2000 Campaign received widespread Christian support, and achieved substantial results for the poorest of the Earth. Other Christian organisations (e.g., Christian Aid, Oxfam, Tear fund, Traidcraft, etc.) have challenged big business to trade fairly, and in so doing have begun to shape consumer choice, investment policies and the global economy. On a more local level, churches have become active in community regeneration, employment, debt counselling, housing the homeless, adult education, and more besides. The breadth of reflexive and imaginative work alluded to here is impressive, and serves to remind that as much Christianity may be involved in the liberty of captives, it also has its eye on the captives of liberty: those who are left behind by an increasingly mobile, prosperous world, and who are excluded from the global marketplace.

In all of this, it is important to stress that few of the recent theological responses to the new world order now seek revolution. In many spheres of Christian engagement, of charity work and relief for the poor, capitalism has emerged as a partner within the framework of the solution, even if it remains part of the problem. It is the recognition that theology and the churches now function within an age of conversation, participation and negotiation that is the key to envisioning the theological engagements of the future. Here, theologians will need poise, reflexivity and imagination if theology is to contribute to the shaping of public life and the ordering of politics and society. As a discipline, it may yet prove to be even more useful to society in a public and mediating role.

At the same time, the prophetic vocation of theology should not be ignored, and this must be an essential component in any true Christian theological engagement with the re-ordering of society. The liberty of captives remains a primary focus of concern for the Christian gospel and its witness. Those enslaved by debt, the lack of rights, injustice, sickness, poverty and discrimination were close to the centre of God's concern in the ministry of Jesus, and the church continues to define itself by embodying that same love, care, compassion and advocacy for those who suffer in the same way two thousand years later.

Of no less concern, however, are those who are captive to the more subtle forces of late modernity, such as the thrall of the media, entertainment and consumerism. What will Christianity have to say about a saturated visual, sensate culture, in all its plurality and techno-politanism, and yet which leaves humanity increasingly de-sensitised to the sufferings of the Third World? In the new public square (for all its unevenness) theologians and churches will need to continue to develop viable alternatives and critiques of consumerism and media-saturated societies, perhaps even providing some competition for the very things that beguile, seduce and enslave humanity. What are the alternatives to an acquisitive society going to be, and how might theology offer them in the shaping of public life? As Brueggemann suggests, prophetic ministry will need to continually penetrate the numbness of humanity, and enable people to once again face reality (including its pain and death). And beyond that, prophetic theology might then seek to break through the despair of all communities, and imagine, create and embrace new futures (Brueggemann, 1978, p. 109). Social ordering, political theology and the shaping of public life through Christian witness will need to blend together the participative with the prophetic. As we noted at the beginning of this chapter, Christianity will continue seeking the kingdom that is to come, whilst all the time hoping, praying and working for the signs and values of that same kingdom in the here and now.

Chapter 5

Falling Far Short: Taking Sin Seriously

The landscape of contemporary religious belief is often a puzzling vista to contemplate, and one of the more baffling features of modernity is the relatively rapid dissolution of the doctrine of sin. As David Lodge remarks in his novel *How Far Can You Go?* (D. Lodge, 1980), it seems as though hell disappeared in the 1960s, and that nobody noticed.[1] And if there is no hell, then there is nothing – such as sin – that can really take us there. Hell, therefore, becomes an abstract concept; something to gaze on and ponder in literature and art, perhaps puzzle over in primitive religion, but only to ultimately rejoice in our deliverance from such a manipulative and fear-inducing theological construction of reality.

Central to the Christian theology of forgiveness and salvation is an understanding of sin. The church teaches the universality of sin; as St. Paul puts it, 'All have sinned and fallen short of the glory of God.' In different periods of the church's history, and within its many and varied traditions, the focus on human sinfulness is relatively constant. Sometimes human depravity and sinfulness is a major focus of Christian teaching; and at other times the essential goodness of the created order has, whilst not denying human sinfulness, shifted the focus away from indebtedness to one of blessing. Yet whilst one can be reasonably clear about the teachings of the church throughout the ages (variable though they may have been), much less is known about how notions of sin have been constructed and understood in the pews and the wider public sphere. Society has been lenient on some issues that the church has taken a tough line on; and vice versa. What might have been condemned as a vice by some has been condoned by others. Furthermore, the lines between sacred and secular ideologies of sin are far from neat – something readily apparent in Joanne Harris' novel, *Chocolat* (1999), where vices masquerade as virtue, and apparent vices assume the status of saving graces.

To be sure, sin has a complex history. There will be few candidates today, even amongst the most ardent of bible-believing communities, to rise up and condemn mortgages, wearing clothes of mixed weave or the eating of black pudding, all of which are condemned in scripture. But it was not always so. Of course, the church is largely in agreement on what sin is; there are ten commandments, seven deadly

---

[1]   See also Martin E. Marty (1985).

sins and more besides. But it is also fair to say that constructions and foci of sin are contested within ecclesial communities. Some will stress personal sin (including sexuality), whilst others place an emphasis on the collective (e.g., political, social and environmental).

Conceptualisations of sin are deeply embedded within cultures. What is taboo amongst one group of people may be quite commonplace in another. Our identification of what is and what is not a sin can be temporal and relative rather than necessarily absolute. Moreover, there are new debates about 'choice', 'cultural practice' and 'nature' in relation to sexuality, which further cloud the picture. The expression of our sexual behaviour may turn out to be a mixture of nature and nurture, although the location of any genetic drivers in this respect remains contentious.[2] Sin, in the English language, simply means 'transgression of the divine law, and an offence against God, or a violation, especially wilful or deliberate, of some religious or moral principle'. But the *Oxford English Dictionary*[3] also suggests that 'it is a violation of some standard of taste or propriety', implying that sin is as much related to constructions of reality (such as decency and desire) as it is to revealed truth.

As with previous chapters, the discussion cannot be exhaustive, yet it is intended to be indicative, suggesting for the churches a more accommodating attitude to areas of moral disagreement and ethical enquiry. If it is correct to describe one of the effects of globalisation as 'compression',[4] then the moral and social 'norms' within any given culture will find themselves being squeezed and hardened through increasing exposure to other standards of taste, decency and morality. The issue is raised sharply in Tom Stoppard's memorable play, *Jumpers*, in a speech by a fictional professor of philosophy, who is troubled by relativism and a new kind of radical liberalism that is being espoused:

> ... The tribe which kills its sickly infants, the tribe which eats its aged parents, without pausing to wonder whether the conditions of group survival, the notion of filial homage might be one thing among the nomads of the Atlas Mountains, or in a Brazilian rain forest, and quite another in the Home Counties. Certainly a tribe which believes it confers honour on its elders by eating them is going to be viewed askance by another which prefers to buy them a little bungalow somewhere .... What is better? The savage who elects to honour his father by eating him as opposed to disposing of the body in some – to him – ignominious

---

[2]   Two fairly recent socio-biological studies are worthy of note. See L. Rogers (1999) and B. Bagemihl (1999) the latter of whom advances a new theory of ethology.

[3]   *The Oxford English Dictionary: On Historical Sources*, Oxford, OUP, 1978.

[4]   See M. Stackhouse and P. Paris (eds) (2000), pp. 53–68.

way, for example by burying him in a teak box, is making an ethical choice in
that he believes himself to be acting as a good savage ought to act (T. Stoppard,
1974, p. 54).

The musings of Professor Moore are hardly answered by Stoppard's work;
all normative moral boundaries are challenged by a new political rhetoric that re-
narrates standard principles of justice as well as social and religious practice. What
emerges in *Jumpers* is a new secular age, in which religion has been put firmly in
its place. Stoppard shows us that with religion and morality effectively relativised,
one consequence is that you can get away with murder, literally.

Secularisation, as a term, is normally understood to be a descriptive framework
that itemises two distinct but related trajectories: the general decline of religious
belief amongst people, and the process of detachment by society and states from
religious authority and spiritual points of reference. The shift in society is a profound
one – from a time when belief in God was largely unchallenged, and certainly
unproblematic, to one where it is one option amongst many, and often narrated as
one of the more difficult choices that one might embrace. In this chapter, I propose
to lightly sketch the contours of the difficulties churches currently face, within
the context of secularisation, of talking about sin. Implied within that, of course,
comes a complementary struggle: how to talk about salvation and redemption,
but in terms other than those that reflect our zeitgeist, namely greater spiritual
fulfilment and personal development. The grammar and doctrine of sin, however,
remains the focus for this chapter: pondering its absence in public space, some
of the consequences of that absenteeism, and how Reinhold Niebuhr's insights
contained within the two volumes of *The Nature and Destiny of Man* might help
us to reflect on this situation.

Sin in Our Time

But let us begin with our time: the century in which secularisation is said to
cultivate and delimit late-modern and developed societies. However, secular
society, whatever it is or might be, is clearly not that state in which unbelief
has triumphed over belief. It is, rather, that space and time where belief is no
longer hegemonic (save only in a variety of fundamentalist ghettoes and tightly
controlled theocracies), yet remains an entirely reasonable option. Consequently,
the persistence of belief does not require any particular kind of justification or
explanation. Yet at the same time, religious belief (or indeed any kind of belief,
such as communism) in most modern states can no longer assume the place and

privilege of persuasive hegemony. Pluralism is essentially the normative state of modern societies: the right to choose is assumed.

This is indeed ironic. Just as Weber argued in *The Protestant Ethic and the Spirit of Capitalism* (1930), those who set out to reform religion (unwittingly) ended up laying some of the foundations for things we now take for granted in modern societies: the right to believe and practise religious alterity, agnosticism or atheism has become enshrined, such that it is an endemic dimension of our freedom, individual and collective identity. Nothing can be imposed; religion, along with other creeds and ideologies, has become a matter of choice. The frames of reference and ideological paradigms that individuals and groups choose to live by is now a matter of selection rather than non-negotiable imposition; faith is not enforceable. These seeds – of (initial) religious disenchantment, disembedding and disengagement – and all in the name of freedom, alteration or development, were carried in the (if you will) DNA of the Reformation. And this would lead, as Charles Taylor puts it, to a seismic shift in the capacity of religion to form polity:

> Once disenchantment has befallen the world, the sense that God is an indispensable source for our spiritual and moral life migrates. From being the guarantor that good will triumph … in a world of spirits and meaningful forces, he becomes (1) the essential energiser of that ordering power through which we disenchant the world, and turn it to our purposes. As the very origin of our being, spiritual and material, he (2) commands our allegiance and worship, a worship which is now purer through being disintricated from the enchanted world (Charles Taylor, 2007, p. 233).

Of course, the Reformation could not possibly have brought about such a change by itself, and so quickly. It required the accommodationist tendencies of benevolent seventeenth and eighteenth century deism to further the anthropocentric agenda, which steadily began to identify God's primary purposes with human flourishing: divinity and humanity, often through nature, reason and art, were slowly conflated. Gradually, religion receded into the realm of the private and the sentiments; and public space therefore became something in which religious could participate, but which God no longer ordered. With the arrival of the nineteenth and twentieth centuries, replete with industrialisation and other socio-cultural transformations, modern societies had now developed: from being polities that hitherto could not have conceived of their origins and ethos without God as the fundamental point of reference, to being states and nations that were their own guarantors of social flourishing and human freedom.

Granted, this is not the only way of looking back over several centuries of Christianity: there are more positive alternatives to this kind of 'history of subtraction'.

Nonetheless, Charles Taylor, in narrating this history of the secular age, does not capitulate to the kind of reactionary nostalgia that some scholars might be tempted to indulge in. Nor does he look back to an (imagined) age of Christendom and call for its immediate restoration. Rather, he suggests that faith will have to find its way in modernity through a subtle mixture of challenge and reformation; picking its way through pluralism, as it were, but with renewed hope and confidence. So that for true and deep forms of social flourishing to take place, religion (or more particularly, the church) might have to rediscover its nerve:

> The Church was rather meant to be the place in which human beings, in all their difference and disparate itineraries, come together: and in this regard, we are obviously falling far short (Charles Taylor, 2007, p. 272).

Falling far short? This seems a curious and resonant phrase with which Taylor chooses to conclude his magnum opus. He means by this, I suppose, the loss of catholicity from the churches; the omnipresent seduction afforded by creeping denominationalism that allows churches and faiths to individualise, specialise and homogenise in a consumerist culture (and thereby compete); but surely at the expense of pursuing a much richer and larger vision that might be rooted in a deep fission of sociality and transcendence. Such a vision is beyond the temporal aspects of simply being 'established', or, for that matter, of concordats; or, indeed, of alternative models of ecclesial polity that are communitarian, sectarian and disestablished. It is, rather, a hope that the church can be broadly and deeply incorporative within its given social context, providing the necessary shape, ethos and purpose for life that enables true flourishing, and enables the horizons for social flourishing to be elevated beyond our collective interest. Put another way, the church can be the place that orders the world in a way that makes common sense; but without losing the humility that must accompany worship and mystery.

The connections between Christian vision and social flourishing are of course particularly thick in the writings of Reinhold Niebuhr, and most especially apparent in addressing some of the emergent tensions in late modern society. It is commonplace, for example, to regard Niebuhr's stance on economics and socialism as a good example of his theological realism, whilst seeing the advocates of liberal social gospel thinking as rather naive idealists. In fact, the history of the debate at the time, and in the aftermath of the Great Depression, is rather more complex. Niebuhr initially opposed President Roosevelt's New Deal – the term given to a series of economic programs he initiated between 1933 and 1936 – with the goals of giving work (*relief*) to the unemployed, *reform* of business and financial practices, and *recovery* of the economy during the great Depression. Niebuhr regarded the proponents of social gospel as those who were tinkering with a broken system, and the New Deal as an altogether different aberration. Yet he was to change his mind by the 1940s – embracing the spirit of the New Deal – and arguing for realism in state welfare, which placed him securely within mainstream liberal democratic politics.

Niebuhr, perhaps inevitably, developed a Christian critique of the inequality he had witnessed: and it partly gave rise to the new Niebuhrian realism that addressed the countervailing power relations between capital, labour and government. Echoing Augustine, Niebuhr's writings (especially in *The Nature and Destiny of Man*, 1941–43, volumes 1 and 2) began to express that sin is any word or deed or thought against the eternal law. Correspondingly, the injustice of structures – be they social, commercial or of governance – needed to be challenged. The sins of modernity were bound to be more subtle forms of oppression that had found their ways into the polities and praxis of society, as a direct result of gradual processes of secularisation.

Which brings us, neatly enough, to the problem of sin in modern society: if hell did indeed disappear in the 1960s – and no-one noticed – what has happened to sin, trespassing and transgression in late modernity? Even the mention of the word seems faintly problematic. Setting aside Advent or Lent as periods of penitence and holy preparation at the beginning of the twenty-first century (at least in developed countries) seems almost risibly counter-cultural. Few Christians (let alone agnostic members of the public) appreciate churches that dwell on sin and moral shortcomings too much. In our therapeutically-attuned culture, the very concept has been somewhat downgraded. Sin may induce guilt and shame. Such concepts, we are frequently assured, are paralysing and unhealthy.

Indeed, a recent local survey of children's attitudes to sin suggested that the concept is becoming rather outmoded (Richardson, 2009). Even the children from quite religious families struggled to explain what sin was. One child said biting his sister was 'bad'; another, that jumping on the sofa was 'naughty'. And from their schools, including those that are Church of England, the children seemed to have learnt that the great evils of the day are global warming, pollution and bullying. And the answers to these vices? Take more care of the world; and be nice to other people.

Yet a culture that is mainly formed out of desire and achievement may find itself in the grip of a subtle temptation. Namely, to confuse sin with imperfection; with what we lack as people, and on how to achieve greater fulfilment. Falling short, in other words: but not by much. To be sure, it is often helpful to be conscious of sins of omission and negligence. Indeed, there are many popular definitions of sin to be found in Christian paperback books that simply conceive of sin as some kind of shortfall. Yet a society that plays down the idea of serious personal and social sin, and even apparently unfashionable concepts such as original sin, does so at its peril. For in ignoring the dark side of human nature, there is a risk of collapsing into a falsely optimistic and even utopian world-view that then struggles to cope with the reality of evil when it strikes. Rather than accepting sin as commonplace, modern societies often presume to regard the state as exceptional, and even as a private matter.

I suspect that one aspect the problem may lie in language. Sin is a short, simple word – almost too easy and quick to utter. The very accessibility of the word has arguably played a part in the weakening of its power. Our older and arguably denser religious vocabulary preferred the word 'trespass': 'forgive us our trespasses as we forgive those who trespass against us'. The word captures something active; the idea that lines have been crossed; that some of the things we say, do and think are actually offensive, and grieve God. Cranmer's majestic collect for purity in the *Book of Common Prayer* understood that a great deal of sin is concealed inside us. Yet to God, all hearts are open – replete with their miscible emotions and motives. And all our desires are known, too, with no secrets hidden. All of them are seen by the one who is returning. Yet the prayer continues in petition, 'cleanse the thoughts of our hartes by the inspiration of thy Holy Spirit'.

A second aspect of the problem lies with churches themselves, some of whom have unintentionally colluded with the demotion of the concept as a meaningful part of public discourse. The word has been attached to a select range of vices, which though they may be serious and potentially harmful (or corrupting), has lessened the range and scope of the concept more generally. Too much focused attention on sexuality, for example, exacerbates the heightened sense that some kinds of relationships are always 'right' and others always 'wrong'. This then robs the church of the possibility of talking critically and empathetically of the need for confession and absolution in *all* relations of loving intimacy. True enough, some relationships are invariably wrong: those that are abusive, selfish and exploitative, for example. But other forms of relationship that struggle for recognition and affirmation in modernity may be the portent and bearer of many virtues, and not be sinful in the ways that appear to be immediate and obvious. Correspondingly, the very idea of sin might be something that needs to be rescued from fundamentalists and other Christian groups that have appropriated it in order to focus on a relatively narrow range of personal and social vices. Only when society faces and names the fuller range of thoughts and actions that grieve God can culture be truly challenged, and humanity gently ushered into a more restorative notion of flourishing and relationality.

A third aspect of the problem may lie in the subtle yet insidious ways that churches and faith communities have been seduced into colluding with consumerism. As Robert Bellah notes, multiple-choice ('niche spirituality') 'suggests the possibility of over 220 million American religions – one for each of us'. Yet the very possibility of choice (over and against obligation) puts the survival of the community of memory at risk – and to be replaced by 'empathetic sharing' by loosely associated individuals and networks. Under such conditions, faith can quickly become privatised; the property of a sect that sees itself as engaged with but apart from society. Thus, faith becomes 'overspecialised' in the sector, and what Bellah terms 'quasi-therapeutic blandness' quickly sets in, which cannot resist 'the competition [with] more vigorous forms of radical religious individualism, with their dramatic claims of self-realisation, or the resurgent religious conservatism that spells out clear if simple, answers in an increasingly bewildering world' (R. Bellah, 1985, pp. 113ff).

A fourth and final aspect to mention is that in falling far short of the vision of catholicity – both social and ecclesial – churches have not been slow to attract spiritual consumers, hunting for meaning and fulfilment. As Peter Schmiechen perceptively points out, the emphasis on pragmatism (or technique) and consumerism in American Christianity creates a range of problems:

> ... one is that the techniques can be borrowed from general organisational theory and marketing strategies and have no goal other than meeting people's needs as a way of expanding membership. This opens the door to the great debate over what are legitimate and illegitimate needs for religious communities to meet. While Jesus Christ does in fact meet our heartfelt and deepest needs, in America the gospel too often has become a technique for self-improvement and personal happiness ... (Peter Schmiechen, 2005, pp. 364–5, n.5).

Such 'user-friendly' forms of religion abound in America, and increasingly in other developed nations too. Schmiechen has in mind church-growth movements like Willow Creek, and also the writings of Rick Warren.[5] The common thread is the promotion of religion as something that will solve problems and improve the lives of individuals. The highly successful publications of Rick Warren appear to place the emphasis on God's purposes for the individual. However, nagging questions remain. Are churches and individuals being asked to really give their lives over to God's purposes? Or, is it the case that God's alleged purposes are simply a veneer of techniques to enhance the quest for meaning and success?

To be sure, it is easy enough to survey contemporary life in most developed countries, and join in Ezekiel's ancient lament for a nation:

> In those days they shall no longer say: 'The Fathers have eaten sour grapes, and the children's teeth are set on edge'. But every one shall die for his own sin; each man who eats sour grapes, his teeth shall be set on edge .... Behold all souls are mine; the soul of the father as well as the soul of the son is mine: and the soul that sins shall die (Ezekiel 18: 1–4).

---

[5]   See especially his Rick Warren (1995).

To take one example here of what a latter-day Ezekiel might have in mind, consider the consequences of unfettered consumerism in late-modern capitalist societies, which are perhaps all too well known. Children, exposed to relentless advertising for their foods of choice (rather than what might be good for them, less preferable, but arguably more obligatory), eschew vegetables, fruit and balanced diets in favour of snacks and foods that are high in fats, resulting in obesity. Further exposure to commodities may lead to children knowing what they want to have (i.e., acquisitions), but not what they want to be (i.e., vocations, careers, etc.), with the latter simply being the means of obtaining the former.

Here, of course, we may discover that less is more; that by reducing choice we enhance our enjoyment of ourselves and one another. But to appreciate this, unfettered capitalism has to be checked and challenged as not only unwise, but also probably sinful too. The illusion of endless choice turns our gaze away from the other to the self. So, even the innocent 'gap years' (i.e., between school and college) have begun to suffer from apparent commodification, increasingly becoming 'off the peg' consumer items that are now more like touristic rites of passage rather than a means for constructive engagement with the needs of developing countries. No-one is suggesting, of course, that children and young adults are now no longer moral. However, the problem is more subtle than that, for there seems to be no compass.[6] Morality is obscured by consumerism. The master narratives that would inform moral horizons and provide depth and density in content have been quietly left to one side. The consequence of religion becoming a private matter – and with no accompanying common 'grammar of sin' – is that individualism and expressivism flourish at the expense of the social and collective. When it becomes impossible to talk about sin seriously, the scope for discussing goodness is also diminished.

Illumination – Niebuhr's Theological Contribution

How, then, might Reinhold Niebuhr help us to think through this? For Niebuhr, one of the most important insights into the modern doctrine of sin was that the truth is 'hidden from them' (Luke 18: 34), and they (i.e., human beings) constantly 'delight in their own good' (Isaiah 66: 3). Thus,

> Man is insecure and involved in natural contingency; he seeks to overcome his insecurity by a will-to-power which overreaches the limits of human creatureliness. Man is ignorant and involved in the limitations of a finite mind;

---

[6] On this, see Paulhus and Bradstock (2007).

but he pretends that he is not limited. He assumes that he can gradually transcend finite limitations until his mind becomes identical with the universal mind. All of his intellectual pursuits therefore become infected with the sin of pride. Man's pride and will-to-power destroy the harmony of creation (R. Niebuhr, 1941, pp. 190ff).

Correspondingly, sin is both passive and active. It is passive in the sense that it is often a subtle form of subtraction: ignorance of ignorance. The fathers that ate sour grapes could not know what they were doing; nor could they know of the consequences. Niebuhr argues that because we are ignorant of so much (for example, we cannot know the future); we are also often unaware or ignorant of the very limitations that might accompany such ignorance. Sin is also, however, active: the will-to-power. Here, sin is partly conceived of as the effort to obscure individual and collective blindness, but only by overestimating the degree of sight; and, in Niebuhr's thinking, this simply obscures humanity's insecurity – by stretching power beyond its limits.

Pride, then, becomes an important key for Niebuhr in understanding the nature of the human condition and its problematic dimensions. For Niebuhr, the insecurity of the ego, and the grasping after power to make itself more secure, is a fundamental issue, since it leads to the quest for sufficient power to guarantee security. Linked to this is intellectual pride. For Niebuhr, every ruling oligarchy in history has found its ideological pretensions as important a bulwark of authority as its own policing power. So, intellectual pride is a pretension that all human knowledge is actually truer than it really is or can be. Here, Niebuhr has Marxism and other ideological frameworks in mind: the modernist meta-narratives of Communism, Fascism and (to a lesser extent) social democracy that form credulously complete templates through which individuals are supposed to construct lives and their meaning. Niebuhr sees an all-too-present danger with such political and social systems: erroneous moral pride and self-righteousness. Goodness becomes something that is personal, social and temporal; but is now no longer unconditional:

> The whole history of racial, national, religious and other social struggles is a commentary on the objective wickedness and social miseries which result from self-righteousness (R. Niebuhr, 1941, p. 212).

But in case one begins to detect some kind of competition (or even war) for the supremacy of types of knowledge in modernity, or the restoration of (mythic) Christendom over and against modernity, Niebuhr is actually no less critical of the kind of spiritual pride that might assume to out-narrate and dominate the intellectual arrogance he targets:

As soon as the Christian assumes that he is, by virtue of possessing this revelation, more righteous, because more contrite, than other men, he increases the sin of self-righteousness and makes the forms of a religion of contrition the tool of his pride (R. Niebuhr, 1941, p. 214).

The sin of pride, then, is a complex one to contemplate. It is rooted in insecurity (and the will-to-power response). But it can also lead to the self-deification of social groups: humanity and divinity can be easily conflated. The chosen people, nation or individual can all arise out of the 'collective egotism' that imagines itself to be godly. And even here, the churches can be vehicles for this kind of collective egotism. Here, Niebuhr sees this development as the invasion of the spirit by something less than the Holy Spirit: indeed, nothing less than the demonic (R. Niebuhr, 1963, p. 115).

It is worth pausing at this point in order to reflect a little more on Niebuhr's insights into the human condition. Whilst some might class his observations as caricaturing – and with the temporal and contextual limits of the mid-twentieth century to bear in mind also, since it must not be forgotten that he is writing at the very heights of power for both Fascism and Communism – the prescience with which he analyses the individual and collective challenges to humanity continue to have significant resonance. For Niebuhr, human beings are simultaneously bound and free; limited and limitless. This leads directly to the anxiety he narrates in *The Nature and Destiny of Man*: an anxiety that establishes the precondition for the escape into falsehood. Thus, there is an in-built temptation for individuals and groups to overstep limitations (which, Niebuhr holds, is a sin: 'trespassing'), which resides in human nature:

The ambition of man to be something is always partly prompted by the fear of meaninglessness which threatens him by reason of the contingent character of his existence. His creativity is therefore always corrupted by some effort to overcome contingency by raising precisely what is contingent to absolute and unlimited dimensions (R. Niebuhr, 1941, p. 198).

Arguably, the critique of the human condition and the excavation of the concept of sin is at its deepest in Niebuhr's writings when he turns his attention to the subject of sensuality. Here, he sees the inordinate focus on the sensual in late-modern societies as a destruction of the harmony within self. Various 'sins of excess' arise from this: human beings, having lost the true centre of their lives, are no longer able to maintain their own will as the centre of themselves. With absorption and distraction come disorientation and de-centring: humanity becomes lost in its own attempt at meaning-making. This prompts Niebuhr to pose a question:

> Is sensuality ... a form of idolatry which makes the self God; or is it an alternative idolatry in which the self, conscious of the inadequacy of its self-worship, seeks escape by finding some other god? (R. Niebuhr, 1941, p. 248).

He answers his own question by suggesting that sensuality is always an extension of self-love to the point where it defeats its own ends. It also represents some kind of attempt to escape the 'prison' of the self by finding a god in a process or person outside the self. And it can also be seen as some kind of endeavour to escape from the confusion which sin has created, into some form of subconscious existence.

Underpinning these kinds of observations, perhaps naturally enough, is Niebuhr's theological realism that refuses to relinquish a doctrine of original sin. For Niebuhr, sin is inevitable in the human situation itself. The self lacks the faith and the will to subject itself to God. There is an inevitable (empirically derived) tendency towards self-love which derives in turn from the primordial sin of a lack of trust in God. Correspondingly, its knowledge leads to an appropriate form of responsibility, which includes remorse and repentance. Of course, there is also the recognition that 'falling far short' may mean just that: I or we could have done better. But even here, Niebuhr presses the argument that there is something about humanity and sin – bound together – that requires more than greater endeavour or further refinements in human freedom. A doctrine of sin has to face the need for ultimate trust in God, and the conformity of wills and desires:

> We cannot, therefore, escape the ultimate paradox that the final exercise of freedom in the transcendent human spirit is its recognition of the false use of that freedom in action. Man is most free in the discovery that he is not free. This paradox has been obscured by most Pelagians and by many Augustinians. The Pelagians have been too intent to assert the integrity of man's freedom to realise that the discovery of this freedom also involves the discovery of man's guilt. The Augustinians, on the other hand, have been so concerned to prove that the freedom of man is corrupted by sin that they have not fully understood that the discovery of this sinful taint is an achievement of freedom (R. Niebuhr, 1941, p. 276).

Here, then, Niebuhr begins to express something of the heart of his doctrine of sin. True freedom is recognised in the bondage of the will. Interestingly, however, that bondage is not to the finite products of our freedom, but rather to the true source, absolute freedom itself – which is only found in God – and which thereby relativises all of the very products of our freedom. This is the truth that sets us free; but when we find our freedom, we also find our bondage, and the only true liberation that can be found within that. Reflecting on this in the second volume of *The Nature and Destiny of Man*, Niebuhr writes:

> The plight of the self is that it cannot do all the good that it intends. The self in action seems impotent to conform its actions to the requirements of its essential being, as seen by the self in contemplation. The self is so created in freedom that it cannot realise itself within itself. It can only realise itself in loving relation to its fellows. Love is the law of its being. But in practice it is always betrayed into self-love. It comprehends the world and human relations from itself as the centre. It cannot by willing to do so, strengthen the will to do good, the weakness is partly due to finiteness. The propulsive powers of the self, with its natural survival impulse, do not suffice to fulfil the obligations which the self as free spirit discerns. But the weakness is not merely one of 'nature'. It is also spiritual. The self never follows its 'natural' self-interest without pretending to be obedient to obligations beyond itself. It transcends its own interests too much to be able to serve them without disguising them in loftier pretensions. This is the covert dishonesty and spiritual confusion which is always involved in the self's undue devotion to itself (R. Niebuhr, 1941, p. 248).

What, then, is the Christian response to this? For Niebuhr, the true theological realism that addresses sinful nature lies in the realm of grace. It is only through baptism (the reproductive system at the heart of Christian practice) that enables humanity on its way. As Paul states succinctly in the *Epistle to the Galatians* (2:20), 'it is no longer I that live, but Christ who lives in me'. Christians are born of the Spirit, and in grace they find the sanctification and justification to ultimately overcome the sin that is indelibly a part of our human nature. Niebuhr comments that

> ... the new self is the Christ of intention, not of achievement. It is the self only by faith, in the sense that its dominant purpose and intention are set in the direction of Christ as the norm. It is the self only by grace, in the sense that the divine mercy 'imputes' the perfection of Christ and accents the self's intentions for its achievements (R. Niebuhr, 1941, p. 118).

As with baptism, so with the rest of Christian life: through death to the self there is birth, and it is there that we ultimately find new life, and the true promise of freedom that delivers our natures from slavery to sin.

To conclude, it is my contention that one of the unintended by-products of secularisation has been the gradual dissolution of the doctrine and grammar of sin from public life. This has reduced the capacity of more developed societies to reflect on human nature, whereby 'sin' becomes something that is mostly narrated as mere imperfection rather than being something much deeper, darker, denser and more destructive in our collective and individual lives. Churches have unintentionally colluded with this movement, and have bound up sin by nominating a contentious and narrow range of personal vices, which do little to help societies and individuals reflect on the nature and destiny of humanity in terms of sinfulness. Niebuhr's work, as we have seen all too briefly in this essay, has the capacity to help transform our understanding of sin and human nature, thereby enabling society to begin to engage with the complex and reticulate forces that both bind and blind our vision, which ultimately impairs our freedom and destiny.

Niebuhr achieves this through a well-grounded psychological understanding of sin, but one which is not merely individualist. There is also recognition of the institutional and collective nature of sin, which also throws some light on how secularisation has subtly impeded the contribution that the grammar and doctrine of sin might make to public life and social space. For example, his discussion of sensuality, and briefly discussed earlier, is a far more promising place to augment a discussion of sexual practice in contemporary society. By locating his reflections in the realm of the sensual, Niebuhr helps us to see that separation from God is not just a matter of personal choice; it is also through the subtle and insidious cultural forces (often unchallenged) that bind us. Pride and self-love, both of which spring from anxiety and insecurity, together with an investment in knowledge which exceeds its natural limits, combine to form a powerful alloy in which the cultural basis for many of our assumptions and much of our reasoning can be said to be intrinsically sinful. We are blinded by the spirit of the age.

That said, Niebuhr does not see the situation as one without hope. There is always the recognition of higher possibilities, and specifically the availability of grace that not only redeems, but also calls humanity to fulfil the possibilities of life. Our situation, therefore, in Niebuhrian terms, is something like this. There is the possibility of freedom, and the fulfilment of our God-given vocations: but this requires us to submit our wills and hopes to the higher destiny that God has for us. In service, there is perfect freedom. In the midst of this, humanity has to face the limitations and corruptions of all entities in all historical realisations. History cannot succeed in fulfilling this of itself. History, therefore, points beyond itself to God, who alone can fulfil the destiny of humanity:

> The mercy of God, which strangely fulfils and yet contradicts the divine judgement, points to the incompleteness of all historic good, the corruption of evil in all historic achievements and the incompleteness of every historic system of meaning without the eternal mercy which knows how to destroy by taking it into itself (R. Niebuhr, 1941, p. 212).

The death that flows from sin, then, is 'swallowed up in victory' (I Cor. 15: 54). Yet we live in complex times. In the midst of our late-modern societies, riddled as they are with pride, an abundance (or even excess) of knowledge, sensuality and consumerism, it is easy to lose sight of the prescient vision that Reinhold Niebuhr points us towards: one in which society faces and names a fuller range of thoughts, conditions and actions that are understood to grieve God. Only when this takes place can culture be truly challenged, and humanity slowly restored to the image of its maker. As Charles Taylor remarks:

> There is now something higher in one's life ... a dimension of longing and striving which one can't ignore .... Evil is capturing this for something less than, other than God. This is a tremendously powerful temptation. It is constitutive of human life as we know it that it has felt and succumbed to this temptation. Modes of life are built around this succumbing. The untransformed is endowed with some higher, even numinous power. So the self-feeling of power becomes pride, philotimo; but also the wild frenzy of killing, or sex, can be endowed with the numinous .... This is the fallen condition ... (C. Taylor, 2007, p. 668).

Yet this fallen condition is not without hope. But for the churches and societies to fall less short requires more than merely aiming higher. It means taking sin seriously; engaging constructively and humbly with the grammar and doctrine of sin, which otherwise continues to quietly shape the life, practice and ethos of individuals, communities and nations. Niebuhr would doubtless agree with Taylor's assertion that 'God's pedagogy' in the midst of this conundrum never ends. That pedagogy, which might do so much to reform our nature and reshape our destiny,

> turns on deepening our sense of the mysteries of sin and atonement; it never properly 'ends' at all: there is no era of satisfied graduates, who can look down condescendingly on the imperfect grasp of their less advanced predecessors (C. Taylor, 2007, p. 851)

Anything less than this is falling far short.

Conclusion

As we have hinted earlier, and following David Martin, broken or semi-structured religious symbols and meanings find their way into contemporary culture at almost every echelon. Hervieu-Leger (2000, pp. 163–75) and others have argued that we can see that the 'religious chain of memory' survives in post-traditional societies and post-institutional religion. It may be true that contemporary culture is now awash with many competing moral currencies, many of which are accepted within society, such that our moorings on sin and righteousness are difficult and delicate to hold on to. However, this is hardly a recent development; it has been so since the industrial revolution, and was true probably long before that, even though there can be no doubt that pluralism and globalisation have added to the moral mazes in which churches and religious groups now find themselves, struggling for a voice. Nonetheless, society remains saturated with religious symbols, ideals and sentiments. The canopy is intact.

By focusing on sin in this chapter – and its conceptual value in public life – we are effectively arguing for a more public and less private understanding of falling short. In turn, this should be balanced with an elucidation of faith, hope and charity, in which we are attempting to explore some alternative possibilities to the forms of religion identified and critiqued by Ulrich Beck (2010 – and here, quoting Friedrich Graf):

> In pluralist religious markets the winners are the providers with strong brands. Aggressive God-selling and the provision of a rigorous, hard-line religion generally enjoy greater success than the conventional marketing of products with a high degree of ambiguity and latitude of interpretation. If we take an example from the highly developed religious markets of the two Americas, it can be shown that a growing number of consumers show a preference for hard-line religious products. In the United States, the old mainline Protestant churches are among the losers. The winners are the unswerving conservative providers of the 'religious right'. An analogous situation is to be found in several societies of Latin America where conversion to charismatic groups and sects is depriving the Roman-Catholic Church of many members. The great success of such sects and, more generally, of the many charismatic Christian movements is probably best explained by the fact that hard-line religions have a lot to offer consumers. By demanding a high degree of religious commitment, thick-textured community spirit, the strict observance of moral norms and considerable financial support, they provide the people who congregate in them and who feel insecure in a pluralist, uncertain world with a strong, stable identity, a crisis-resistant interpretation of the world and the age we live in, well-ordered family structures

and thick networks of solidarity. The heaven of their authoritarian God the Father is a haven of irrefutable, self-evident truths where everything is clear and straightforward, a situation already anticipated in this world.[7]

By taking sin more seriously, the churches have an opportunity to sketch some new possibilities for a sacred canopy – one where an over-arching metanarrative can continue to offer discernment and direction in public life, and move beyond consumerism towards some sense of commonweal. To be sure, this is a demanding agenda. But it is not one the churches should shrink from, retreating into popular and individualistically gratifying forms of sectarianism. The task for the church is not to pander to popularity, but to engage more deeply with its vocation to the wider public. Faithfulness must be placed before success; serving all rather than pleasing a few. Placing sin – conceptually and actually – back on the public agenda, will not please everyone. But it may be one of the most cogent ways that the churches can serve society in the twenty-first century. Especially as capitalism and consumerism continue to deteriorate, and seem to offer little by way of guiding light to shape and direct any sense of the common good.

So this is about a recovery of nerve. One of the problems that churches face today in relation to nearly all aspects of culture, whether behavioural, social or as a production, is that its instinctive response is invariably one of fight, flight or fright. One of the tasks of theology in the future must be to place less stress on fleeing or policing culture, and more on discernment and understanding, and in so doing, rediscovering religion in the very fabric of the apparently secular. This is, ironically, a task that was probably all too familiar to earlier generations of Christians, and there is no reason to suppose that theologians need fear today's cultural complexities more than those of yesterday. Whilst it is true that the past is a foreign country, the cultures that Christians have had to engage with in the past – and with their variable socio-moral constructions of reality – were never less complex than our own of today. The more the churches can do to offer focus, articulation and meaning to the innate spiritual yearnings that are present in everyday life, including in an apparently secular culture, the greater the possibility of a genuinely emergent public theology becomes. Only then can there be a serious public discourse of sin, and new consensual forms of commonly-owned social censorship. Usually, it is better to light a match than to curse the darkness.

---

[7]   Friedrich Graf (2004), *Die Wiederker der Gotter*, Munich: Beck, pp. 28–9, and quoted in Ulrich Beck's (2010) *A God of One's Own*, London: Polity Press, pp. 171–2.

Chapter 6

Living with Pluralism: Public Faith and Human Rights

It is commonplace to imagine that the foundations of modern democratic states owe their shaping to modernity itself; that without continental revolutions, industrialisation and the Enlightenment, many people would still be living under feudal regimes or carefully ordered hierarchies of aristocracy. Yet the shaping of states and the emergence of democracy is often a tortuous and evolving process. One might say that overlapping canopies – constructions of realities – are elided with underlying foundations, in which religion can play an intricate and delicate role. Monarchies can live side by side with democracies, and both can claim divine sanction.

In this chapter, and building on the previous chapters in this section, concerned first with social Christianity, and then second with the discourse on sin in public life, we revisit a constantly recurring debate in the early years of the third millennium. The relationship between the churches, and the increasing emergence of human rights in public law and life, has pressed the claims of churches to be able to offer a socio-moral canopy that can in some sense be said to be both universal and high. Churches and denominations have found, to their cost, that their religious and moral proclivities have moved them to the margins. Changing social attitudes to sexuality in Britain, for example, have meant that Roman Catholic adoption and fostering agencies have found themselves out of step with legislation and practice on access and equality. Indeed, even ordinary people practising their faith privately in Britain – but in ways that have some bearing on public life – have come under legal scrutiny. Can an Evangelical Christian couple operating a bed and breakfast business refuse a same-sex couple hospitality? Can a Pentecostal couple be prevented from fostering children on the grounds that they hold a view that sexual relations should only take place between a man and a woman? So far, the law in Europe and North America seems to be in favour of progressive, liberal values – depending on one's view.[1]

---

[1] Since 2011, the Presidential administration of Barack Obama has stepped aside from the Defence of Marriage Act, and given equal rights to same-sex couples in the USA.

These initiatives have moved some churches – as moral agents, suspended above society, as it were – to ground level, and in something of a corner. At the same time, the issue of how to live together – as a society, and with some sense of public truth, whilst also respecting particular beliefs that may seem to be at slight odds with that same public – has pressed hard upon society. The assumptions that may have governed the religious and political cadence of the 'Elizabethan Settlement' (a rather good, though singular, kind of social and religious canopy) have needed to adapt to a more complex situation. In his 'Civil and Religious Law in England: a Religious Perspective' lecture at the Royal Courts of Justice, the Archbishop of Canterbury, Dr Rowan Williams opened up an intriguing debate on the place of Muslim Sharia Law within the broader context of public law. Commenting on how the two constructions of reality, or canopies, might peacefully co-exist, he noted how Muslim states were able to extend full citizenship to non-Muslims; that it was possible to have an overlapping consensus:

> … the free decision to be and to continue a member of the *umma Sharia* is not, in that sense, intrinsically to do with any demand for Muslim dominance over non-Muslims. Both historically and in the contemporary context, Muslim states have acknowledged that membership of the *umma* is not coterminous with membership in a particular political society: in modern times, the clearest articulation of this was in the foundation of the Pakistani state under Jinnah; but other examples (Morocco, Jordan) could be cited of societies where there is a concept of *citizenship* that is not identical with belonging to the *umma*. Such societies, while not compromising or weakening the possibility of unqualified belief in the authority and universality of *sharia*, or even the privileged status of Islam in a nation, recognise that there can be no guarantee that the state is religiously homogeneous and that the relationships in which the individual stands and which define him or her are not exclusively with other Muslims. There has therefore to be some concept of common good that is not prescribed solely in terms of revealed Law, however provisional or imperfect such a situation is thought to be. And this implies in turn that the Muslim, even in a predominantly Muslim state, has something of a dual identity, as citizen and as believer within the community of the faithful.[2]

Williams' irenic prose suggests that a society formed through an overlapping moral and social consensus is possible; even one with quite pronounced pluralism. However, such sentiments must also be weighed against the anxieties of churches

---

    2   R. Williams, 'Civil and Religious Law in England: a Religious Perspective', lecture at the Royal Courts of Justice,Thursday, 7 February 2008.

in coming 'under' legislation that may appear to threaten and weaken religious proclivities. Mention has already been made of English Roman Catholic adoption and fostering agencies: when the law changed to allow same-sex couples to adopt, the response of the bishops (note, not the agencies themselves) was to remove explicit Roman Catholic support. Thus, we find ourselves in a situation where the claim to public truth, for some faiths, has been re-narrated as private and particular. And the stance of the churches here, has (for some time) been puzzling to some:

> It is true that we did not consult the Churches about being regarded as a public authority or, indeed, any of the many other organisations which will be affected by the Bill. I have to confess that it did not occur to anyone in government that the churches would have any particular difficulty in playing their proper part in the enforcement of human rights in Britain. I therefore make no secret at all of the fact that, when this subject was raised in Committee, I was surprised by the suggestion that Churches and religious bodies should wish to be exempted from a Bill designed to enable people to assert before the courts of this country the basic rights and freedoms which they have enjoyed under the convention since 1953. I would have expected them to be as enthusiastic as any other body for the incorporation of the European Convention ....[3]

At first sight, a debate about church autonomy and human rights might seem unnecessary. After all, are churches not in favour of human rights? They are. Do they not campaign for justice and peace? They do. Are they not against racism and other kinds of discrimination? Generally, yes. Yet it is in this last area that the real problem can be located for churches in America, Western Europe and other parts of the world. Fundamentally, there is often a clash of cultures, between the values espoused by modern democratic states, and those held by religious groups who are attempting to present theocratic standards within a public domain.[4] For example, some Baltic countries, where Christianity is the national and established religion, and funded by the state, have not been able to privately debate the theological pros and cons of women priests or bishops, since the law of the land forbids discrimination on the grounds of gender. The issue of women's rights within the church is therefore, in effect, already to some extent determined by the state, not

---

[3] Lord Irving, the Lord Chancellor, *Speech to the House of Lords*, Hansard, London, 19 January 1998.

[4] It is taken as read that Bonhoeffer's resistance to the German state during World War II, or the tireless campaigning of many against the Apartheid regime in South Africa – both of which required opposition to a church that lent support to an abusive statecraft – are fine examples of individuals or church groups opposing a theologically legitimised state of affairs or social goal.

the church: they are 'forced' to accommodate. Similarly, in the Church of England, there are 'guidelines' on how a bishop or diocese may treat a clergyperson who is living in a homosexual relationship. Yet if that clergyperson is serving as a hospital chaplain, a position that is funded by the taxpayer, the National Health Service (NHS), as the employer of the chaplain, has a policy of non-discrimination in respect of sexuality, gender and the like. In other words, the 'employment' rights of a gay or lesbian priest are arguably better protected by the NHS than they are by an individual bishop, who may decide that a priest living an 'active' homosexual life is incompatible with the teachings of the church.[5] Here, there may be resistance.

Human Rights and the Churches of Britain

During 1998, representatives from British churches met with Home Office officials to secure an exemption for churches from the Human Rights Bill. The Bill, adopted by the Labour Government, became law in October 2000. The Human Rights Act (HRA) is concerned with making 'public' authorities accountable to the European Convention on Human Rights. The Act seeks to bring about equality and justice for all: it is an Act that gives 'further effect' to the 1953 Convention on Human Rights. So why would churches have been seeking exemptions from the Act? What would have been the effect of succeeding in securing such exemptions? Did members of churches understand sufficiently how they were being represented in this matter?

The pro-exemption voice appeared to be mostly inspired by a strong but small conservative lobby. In the case of the Church of England, it was alleged that one prominent conservative Evangelical churchman had been quick to galvanise like-minded lawyers into action, lobbying for exemption left, right and centre. Grist was added to the mill when it was suggested that a right-wing USA-based Christian pressure group was part-funding the legal costs of fighting the HRA and its incorporation in Britain. Typically, the concern of the Christian right over the legislation was that it would have meant churches being 'forced' to recognise (or even conduct) homosexual 'marriages', or Anglo-Catholic parishes 'compelled' to include women on shortlists for vacant posts. Such scenarios are, of course, a form of scare tactic. Clearly, in whatever form the Bill was going to be adopted, statute law in England still only recognises marriage between a man and a woman: any additional European legislation cannot change that. Equally, the rights of Forward

---

[5]   The clash of cultures becomes even more complex when competing religious convictions can be identified within debates about public space and the role of faith. For further discussion, see J. Haynes (1998), p. 128, and in *Daedalus* (Fall 2000), where several essays in this issue are of relevance.

in Faith parishes would always have remained protected, with the preferred particularity of an exclusively male priesthood for a small minority of churchgoers unaltered by an Act, Convention or the Bill.

The Bill has its origins in the *United Nations Charter* (10 December, 1948) which was a 'universal declaration' promoting freedom, justice and peace for all 'regardless of race, colour, sex, language, religion, political or other opinion, national or social origin, property, birth or other status'. The *European Convention on Human Rights* was signed in 1950, and came into force in 1953. The Human Rights Bill is, in fact, more about social aspiration and orientation than about specific prescriptions. The Bill states of itself that it is intended to 'give further effect to the rights and freedoms guaranteed under the European Convention on Human Rights'.[6]

For political and theological conservatives, the devil is in the detail. For example, Article 14 (of the Convention) states that 'the enjoyment of the rights and freedoms set forth in this convention shall be secured without discrimination on any ground such as sex, race, colour, language, religion, political or other opinion, natural or social origin, association with minority, property, birth or other status'. Yet the Convention is careful to avoid legislating for employment practice. (It protects a limited range of rights. For example, Article 4 prohibits 'slavery', but recognises that 'forced or compulsory labour' does not prohibit military service or 'normal civic duties'). Forward in Faith[7] parishes are not likely to find themselves guilty of sexual discrimination under law for refusing the ministrations of a woman priest (though this does not resolve the debate about sacralised sexism), and neither will religious schools be forced to appoint well-qualified teachers who are not sympathetic to the ethos of the education on offer. Such scruples are protected under Article 9 of the Convention, which guarantees freedom of thought, conscience and religion, whereby the liberty 'to manifest one's religion or beliefs shall be subject only to such limitations as are prescribed by law and are necessary in a democratic society in the interests of public safety'. Equally, Article 12 (Right to Marry) checks itself by offering it 'according to the national laws governing the exercise of this right'. It looks as though the conservative voice may be too reactionary, their fears being based on a false reading of the Bill.

Indeed, it is hard to see what churches have to fear from such a Bill. Yet there was a move to amend Clause 6, which is concerned with the definition of 'public authority', by adding churches, religious charities and religious schools to the list

---

[6]   *Human Rights: A Bill*, London, The Stationery Office, 23 October 1997.

[7]   I.e., 'traditionalist' clergy, laity or parishes opposed to the ordination of women as priests within the Church of England. Forward in Faith is 'catholic' in its culture. The evangelical equivalent within the Church of England is an organisation known as 'Reform'.

of exemptions. The effect of this would have been to excuse religious bodies from a clause that states that 'it is unlawful for a public authority to act in a way which is incompatible with one or more of the Convention rights'.[8] There is a further issue with Clause 10, which may eventually allow a Minister of State to challenge the General Synod, although assurances by the Lord Chancellor have been given on this. (However, concerned churches may still need to consider the wider and long-term implications of the Amsterdam Treaty in due course, especially as it affects legislation on discrimination.) Once again, it appears that conservative voices feared a liberal whitewash here. However, closer attention to the Bill (in the same clause) reveals that the clause does not apply if 'as the result of one or more provisions of primary legislation, the authority could have acted differently'.[9]

What the Bill does for the churches and religious bodies is include them as part of the public domain, whilst continuing to respect their particularities. At the same time, the Bill acts as a benchmark for public standards to which religious bodies must at least correspond with, but not necessarily conform to, most especially if they are already protected by primary legislation. The difference is crucial. The Bill invites all religious organisations to participate in a civil society by virtue of being a public authority. Whilst this makes them accountable to the public they serve, it also protects their freedom of expression.[10] To press for exemption was, therefore, to argue for religion being a private matter and not accountable to the public. It is still hard to see the missiological advantage in such a course of action for any church, let alone one established by law. If the maintenance of church identity is dependent upon decent public standards being excluded, then it is surely time to reconsider an established church claiming to exercise a public theology.[11]

One of the greatest challenges that faces the United Kingdom (not just the church), is how to modernise and adapt as a body in a third millennium that is more public and plural, globalised yet individualised, democratised yet privatised. The watchwords for a more forward-looking culture are now emerging: participation, modernity, opportunity, quality of life, radicalism, communication, possibility and flexibility. The public domain is deemed to be the crucible of a caring society.

---

[8]   Cf. the amendment tabled by Baroness Young, Lord Kingsland and Lord Henley in Second *Marshalled List of Amendments*, London: The Stationery Office, 21 November 1997, paragraph 40.

[9]   For a discussion of how the Courts would work to enact the Bill in cases of discrimination, see *The Council of Europe and the Protection of Human Rights*, Strasbourg, Conseil de l'Europe, 1993.

[10]   For further discussion, see D. Westerlund (ed.) (1996). The authors in this volume suggest various models of church-state interaction, which they refer to as 'policies of religion'.

[11]   See M. Hill (1999).

Small wonder then, that churches are being invited to participate afresh in the making of society, not just healing its brokenness or protecting its own interests.[12]

One of the dangers the churches faced, in attempting to turn their backs on the legislation, and perhaps succeeding in securing its exemptions, is that it would no longer be classed – at least in rhetoric rather than legal terminology – as a 'public authority'. Therefore, by definition, it may be perceived as a private and unaccountable body, at a distance from the centre of being in society. Loss of 'public' status is an unintended but self-marginalising strategy that might potentially vacate the socio-ethical arena. How, then, could churches speak with integrity on justice, discrimination and parity if they chose to be exempt from the very laws that bind the rest of society? Only, it seems to me, if they can claim that their morals are superior.[13]

Any moral claim of this sort would necessarily be open to public scrutiny. When the Roman Catholic report *The Common Good*[14] appeared in 1997, it was praised by media and churches, and was perceived as a significant contribution to public and political life. Yet it did not take long for politicians and other public figures to point out that the Roman Catholic church itself was not adopting the standards and measures for its employees that it was prescribing for the rest of society. If Trades Union representation and the rights of 'ordinary' workers are to be flagged up as concerns of the church for the common good of society, then presumably these same standards of justice and fairness are already being practised by the church on its clergy? Actually, they are not. Prescriptions for democracy from the churches do not translate into descriptions of their own theocracies.

Naturally, it was the fear of marginalisation that drove the pro-exemption lobby in the first place. If society and the majority of churchgoers embraced the Bill and its spirit as it did (the spirit arguably being the more important of the two), then objectors are left out in the cold. Yet had they succeeded, the vast majority of ordinary, civil-minded churchgoers would have been lumbered with defending a conservative agenda in the interests of protecting overall ecclesial particularity. And, ironically, the marginalisation would still have occurred, since the churches would have effectively voted not to be 'public' authorities. (Indeed, Ecclesiastical Courts were exempted from the Act in its final form.) For the Church of England, 'establishment' would mean morphological ties to a monarchy, whilst a connection

---

[12]   For a refreshing perspective and critique, see R. Furbey (1999).

[13]   See the discussion in R. Audi (2000), pp. 81–144, where the author argues for the separation of church and state. Religious convictions, according to Audi, cannot translate easily into secular reasons for laws and moral codes. Religious values, therefore, must become be subsumed as part of ethics if faith groups wish to share in the shaping of a civic society.

[14]   *The Common Good*, Catholic Information Office, Westminster, London, 1997.

with the sociality engendered by the democratic and elected State would at the same time wither.[15]

To be sure, there were and are grounds for churches being cautious about embracing legislation that ties churches into society as 'public' and 'accountable'. Bonhoeffer would doubtless have had plenty to say about this. As would Desmond Tutu on the Dutch Reformed Church in the Apartheid era.[16] (Having said that, the South African churches played a significant role in peacekeeping and monitoring in the transition from Apartheid to democracy, and, through the subsequent administration on the Truth and Reconciliation Commission, are offering a visionary model for 'public' theology.) Any church closely identified with society risks obviating its 'difference', and therefore the very point of belonging to what should be an alternative community. Pulling down all the social and moral frontiers of the church would be a mistake: the unbounded is soon the empty. People do not flood into bodies without definition: they flood out. But nonetheless, the situation of the Act was different to those that were once at home in Germany or South Africa. Churches were not being asked to sanction crude nationalism, and nor were they being asked to keep silent in the face of anti-Semitism, racism or its modern-day equivalents. Nor were the churches being asked to entirely conflate or lose their identity with the 'public' realm under some kind of utilitarian principle.

On the contrary, the distinctiveness the churches can offer is being invited afresh to participate in society as salt and yeast. The Human Rights Act offers the opportunity for churches to recover their public role, and rediscover their prophetic voice in the political realm. In this sense, churches need to move beyond a simplistic dialect in which they either say an uncritical 'yes' to the Act, or seek to secure a potentially damaging legal exemption. A wiser approach to the culture of rights enshrined in the Act would be to go with the flow of the legislation, with a combination of passion and coolness, recognising that it is only when public participation has been assented to that the prophetic can flourish where it is needed. In other words, I am suggesting that churches can only be the social form of the truth (or the social transcendent body) if they ensure that they remain public bodies.

This form of engagement is, of course, a risk, but no more so than the incarnation itself. Whilst some would argue that this is an invitation to weld together secular liberalism with select Christian doctrines, our argument nonetheless stands. Pursuing this agenda is about being prepared to see Truth being embodied socially, contextually and temporally, in order that grace may abound. In such a situation,

---

[15]   For a fuller discussion, see P. Edge and G. Harvey (eds) (2000).

[16]   For a very different perspective on Christian opposition to the state in another African nation, see M. Schoffeleers (1999).

the church cannot guarantee its own power absolutely, neither be sure of entirely protecting truth, nor be certain of the outcomes of its intercourse with society. But it can at least be there, and continue to speak as of right as a public body, and as a social incarnation of transcendence, mystery and morality. Put another way, the task of Christians is not to guard an empty tomb, but rather follow a risen Lord, and serve society.[17]

Conflating Secular and Sacred Cultures: Paradigms of Civil Religion

Bhikhu Parekh – the first Hindu peer in the House of Lords – has outlined a new paradigm for a relationship between religion and the State (1997, pp. 7ff). First, he argues that instead of marginalising religion (as many secularists might have), its distinct contribution to public life should be recognised, and faith given a stake in maintenance of a free and open society. He is aware that religion can sometimes do the opposite of this, but suggests that the more openly dialogical a religion becomes, the more it is able to foster moderation and respect within itself: society can 'civilise' the church. Second, when religion enters politics, it has to accept the constraints of political life. This includes speaking in a 'public' language that is intelligible to all citizens, and accepting 'the burden of public judgement' which sometimes requires people to live with deep disagreements. Third, religion plays an important and direct role in moral life, and the community therefore has a deep and collective interest in the well-being of churches and their beliefs. For this reason, religion should be taught in school in the same way that children are politically educated. The teacher is neither to subvert or convert, but discuss beliefs in an open, respectful, comparative and analytical manner, recognising that religion is a distinct form of human consciousness and experience.

To give Parekh's arguments a slightly different turn, it could be argued that being a Christian in the twenty-first century cannot simply be about belonging to a church, but should rather be seen as equally consisting of being a certain type of citizen within society. 'Civil religion', therefore, becomes something significantly more than 'social glue' or 'the spiritual dimension' to society. Rather, it also becomes bound up in the actual aspirations of society which are themselves

---

[17]   Of course, how this is done will vary from one Christian tradition to another. For a critical and theological perspective of the human rights agenda, see J. Lockwood O'Donovan (1998, pp. 52–65). O'Donovan identifies three dominant conceptual elements in the tradition of rights theory: property right, contract, and freedom of choice. For O'Donovan, there is a question as to why Christian thinkers have been willing to 'adopt a child of such questionable parentage as the concept of human rights'.

related to the common good. Andrew Shanks takes this a stage further, when he argues that:

> A genuinely 'open' church ... would be an open forum: reproducing within itself, the full range of (thoughtful) moral conflict characteristic of the surrounding world; excluding nothing except intolerance; and differing from the world only in the exemplary manner in which it tried to process these conflicts ... (A. Shanks, 1990, p. 90).

Shanks continues by contending that the church must move beyond simply providing pastoral remedies for personal sin, which he says can no longer make the church, priest or pastor a focus for communal unity. Instead, the clergy needed to be gifted in tackling the phenomenon of structural sin on behalf of the community: they need to be issue-raisers, prophets and protagonists. In this respect, he sees the Christian Spirit as being invested in a new form of mission:

> ... the stage which Christianity has now reached is to recognise that the church-phase of its development is over, and that the Christian Spirit has entered into its ethical, or political, maturity ... the innermost essence of Christianity drives it out beyond the Church; it has to seek embodiment in nothing less than the body which encompasses the entirety of human life, namely the state (A. Shanks, 1990, p. 114).

Yet Shanks, like Parekh, knows that churches need to be maintained as distinctive bodies, independent of the state and the public, if they are to be the yeast and salt of the Kingdom of God. The church is there to help fund civilising strands within society. But it does not own society, and neither does it entirely own all the moral strands that might guide and make sociality.[18] As Coleridge suggested almost two centuries ago, the Church of the nation is not quite the same as the Church of Christ, yet it is there to secure and improve the moral cultivation of its people, 'without which the nation could be neither permanent or progressive'.[19] The church is therefore not a world to come, but another world that now is, whose role is to combat political evil, not just institutional defects.

---

[18]   Recent research on Sector ministry in England (i.e., prisons, hospitals, the armed services and higher education) has shown a modest expansion in the number of non-Christian chaplains that institutions are employing, although the situation remains far from perfect. See J. Beckford and S. Gilliat-Ray (1998), S. Gilliat-Ray (2001), and H. Orchard (2000).

[19]   S.T. Coleridge (1976), originally published 1839.

Whilst this may be true of churches in Britain,[20] and perhaps more generally of Western Europe,[21] the parameters of civic religion within civil society follow very different contours in the USA. The fundamental breach between the ruled and the ruler, coupled with the need of large post-Enlightenment states to win the willing assent of the governed, and achieve a degree of consensus on the normative foundations for legitimising authority, have always posed a problem for nations where religion is not established. Writers such as Jean-Jacques Rousseau (1712–78) argued that religion should play a key part in the legitimisation of the state but, at the same time, it does not follow that this leads to a re-established church. For Rousseau, Christianity was a religion of inward devotion – a spirituality that was vital for individuals, but which had no obvious or organised political shape, except insofar as it could contribute to what he famously dubbed as 'civil religion':

> Now, it matters very much to the community that each citizen should have a religion ... Each man may have, over and above, what opinions he pleases, without its being the Sovereigns business to take cognisance of them; for, as the Sovereign has no authority in the other world, whatever the lot of its subjects may be in the life to come, that is not its business, provided they are good citizens in this life .... The dogmas of civil religion ought to be few, simple and exactly worded, without explanation or commentary. The existence of a mighty, intelligent and beneficent Divinity, possessed of foresight and providence, the life to come, the happiness of the just, the punishment of the wicked, the sanctity of the social contract and the laws: these are its positive dogmas. Its negative dogmas I confine to one, intolerance ... (Jean-Jacques Rousseau, 1973, pp. 307–8).

It is not difficult to recognise these idealised seedlings of religion embedded in American civil society – within Rousseau's words. Indeed, the notion that a form of religion somehow shapes modern American life in a non-controlling way is a thesis with a long track record. Ernst Troeltsch (1966) has argued that liberal democracy is a product of religious forces. Similarly, Talcott Parsons affirms liberal American democracy, but not as a secular creation, but rather as the

---

[20]   More accurately, it is the 'Christian culture' of a society rather than simply specific churches that produce civil society, although the two are normally closely related. It is also worth noting that many societies, guilds, companies and other associations, with Christian or other religious roots, also help to produce a civil religion and civil society culture. The Freemasons are, in Britain at least, one obvious example. See P. Clark (2000).

[21]   See D. Herbert (2001).

institutionalisation of Protestant values. For Parsons (1963), American democracy is a child of Protestantism, not a secular competitor. George Jellinek (1979) has further argued that the American concept of inalienable rights (and toleration) is traceable to the radical religious movements that were expelled from Europe, and were early settlers in America. To an extent, many Americans have derived a degree of comfort from the creation and sustaining of such a culture.

However, this picture of almost benign support – civil society and civil religion living off one another in gentle symbiosis – has changed markedly as American culture has rapidly developed in the postwar years. In America, as in other, Western European, countries, the supposedly inclusive nature of a civil society has been challenged by religious groups that claim their spiritual or cultural rights are not being respected. This may include pressing for legal exemptions in respect of attire (e.g., Muslim girls wearing headscarves in France, or British Sikhs wearing turbans but not crash helmets), to defending female genital circumcision. Equally, Roof and McKinney (1987) point to the influence of black churches on American politics, and the advancement of civil rights through appealing to the white Christian conscience. Far from being benign, religious values are now commodities that are very definitely mobilised.

Similarly, the New Christian Right has also gained prominence, becoming increasingly active in politics.[22] In recent years, the New Christian Right has become suspicious of 'tolerance' as a general principle of civil religion. Indeed, there are now many religious lobbying groups, highly organised and well-funded within the USA, which seek to directly influence the shaping of American life as well as the foreign policy of the USA. Writing in 1967, Robert Bellah noted how 'pluralised' civil religion was being made up of an eclectic mix of symbols, beliefs and ideals. Granted, these performed a similar legitimising function to the one Rousseau had in mind, insofar as they provided a fairly simple creed that supported civil society. Yet Bellah has also observed how the very foundations of postwar American civil religion are themselves now threatened by vapid individualism.[23] The present parameters of the debate are perhaps best described by Richard John Neuhaus. On the one hand, Neuhaus (1984) maintains that an American civil society cannot exclude religion from shaping public life and discourse. On the other hand, he also argues that religious traditions can only inhabit such space

---

[22]   For a fuller discussion, see R. Wuthnow, 'The Political Rebirth of American Evangelicals', in R. Wuthnow and R. Liebman (eds), *The New Christian Right: Mobilization and Legitimation*, New York, Aldine Publishing, 1983, pp. 167–85.

[23]   See R. Bellah, 'Civil Religion in America', *Daedalus*, vol. 96, no.1, pp. 1–21, 1967, and *The Broken Covenant: American Civil Religion in a Time of Trial*, New York, Seabury Press, 1975.

on the condition that they respect the rules of open public debate, and do not themselves become tyrannical and autocratic. In other words, we are back with Parekh: religion being offered to society, rather than imposed upon it. This is the new paradigm of civil religion within so-called secular cultures.

However, there are many different ways of following this recipe, and the transition from the Clinton-Gore years through to the Presidency of George W. Bush, and onwards to Barack Obama, will test Neuhaus' thesis as much as it confirms it. Within weeks of assuming power, for example, Bush launched an initiative that encouraged 'faith-based' social programmes to supplement or replace government social welfare programmes. In Britain, collaboration between churches and government in urban renewal programmes is well established, although under some strain as debate continues over responsibility and funding for David Cameron's Big Society project.

However, the earlier American equivalent of the Big Society project – the Office of Faith-Based Welfare – had an entirely different feel to it. Marvin Olasky (2000) was, arguably, its guru – an ex-communist who espoused a philosophy of 'compassionate conservatism', a less than subtle blend of politico-religious concerns, which was partly responsible for shaping the moral tone of Bush's presidency. No less influential was Myron Magnet and his work (1997), with President George Bush describing his bestseller as 'the book which influenced me the most, second only to the Bible'.[24] The triumvirate of Bush's religious advisors was completed by Chuck Colson, the former assistant to Richard Nixon jailed for his part in the Watergate scandal. Colson was known for his dramatic conversion to Christianity during his seven-month prison sentence,[25] and for his subsequent advocacy of prayer ministry in prisons as an aid to correction and transformation. Colson was the founder of the Innerchange Freedom Initiative Charity, which actually runs some prison wings in American jails, and claims that the rates of recidivism are lower in those that the charity manages.[26] This development arguably represents a stage beyond civil religion, at least in the sense that Rousseau might have meant it. 'Civil' has become elided with 'public', and in the process, and correspondingly, faith is now more sharply defined and narrower in its outlook.

But what does this all mean? In what sense can religion of this kind create or inhabit public space? It is ironic, since in essence it suggests that the very 'public space' that religion once nestled within is now deemed to be empty of

---

[24]   See E. Vulliamy, 'The Power of Prayer: America's Moral Crusaders', in *The Observer*, 4 February 2001, p. 17.

[25]   See C. Colson (1984).

[26]   E. Vulliamy, ibid., p.17.

values, or, alternatively, full of competing convictions that need policing. Thus, religious groups that are so minded now no longer see their values as 'private' or as individual, but rather as qualities that may transform an allegedly vacuous and over-liberalised democracy into something more like a theocracy. It is perhaps an inevitable consequence of the individualism identified by Bellah, coupled to the pluralism and modernity of the postwar years, which has eroded the original concept of civil religion and that has led to this loss of confidence in the generous and inclusive shaping of public space.[27]

Conclusion

The very concept of public space is one of the more challenging frontiers that churches find themselves engaging with at the beginning of the twenty-first century. With public space atomized into increasingly determined domains – leisure, sacred, secular, political and so forth – the identity and meaning of such spaces is ironically contested as never before. Churches, in the context of the increasingly pluralist and inclusivist domains of the developing world, have tended to tread hesitantly and warily rather than confidently. Indeed, the problem of how religion takes its place in society and shapes public space is an issue now faced by many of the world's major faiths. The 'Arab Spring' of 2011 was as much about a clarification of the role of religion in socio-political spaces as it was about an assertion of individual rights and democracy. The protests against capitalism around the world in 2011 were, of course, related to the events that took place in North Africa and the Middle East. The Occupy Camp set up outside St. Paul's Cathedral in London represented a farrago of claims and counter claims that questioned the values and ideologies shaping public life. The many tents of the protesters, mirroring the single dome of St. Paul's, was an unintended irony, to be sure. But the multiple canopies of the protesters do suggest a range of questions directed towards *any* sacred canopy. What kinds of critical interaction does the church have with capitalism? To what extent can the church move beyond being a kind of shop steward for the welfare state, and begin to articulate a genuinely confident and rich public theological leadership, that shapes national public life

---

[27]   On the transition from civil to public religion, see W. Swatos jr and J. Wellman jr (1999), *The Power of Religious Publics: Staking Claims in American Society*. In a way, the subtitle says it all. The fact that 'claims' are now 'staked' shows how the implicit religious values of America – 'invisible religion', to borrow from Thomas Luckmann – have been transformed into a much narrower set of explicit claims, which will divide as much as they ever unite. Many of the essays in the volume reflect these concerns from a confessional perspective.

and social values? Such questions are at the heart of our commonweal. And such questions perpetually call the church to a more intentional public theology, in which rights, values and spaces are re-located under an inclusive and generous canopy of theological dialogue and moral discourse.

The collapse in civic confidence that is prevalent at present, coupled to the identification of the canopy of 'social space' as something 'public' that can be filled by various interest groups (including religious), does seem to confirm Nazila Ghanea-Hercock's thesis that 'no ultimate solution can be found to this question of on what to basis to resolve all conflicts that are ever to emerge between human rights and the endless wealth and diversity of religious or other beliefs' (N. Ghanea-Hercock, 2000, p. 221). However, there may be hope. She notes how religious and secular cultures can change; world-views are not 'frozen'. This fact alone, she argues, ought to encourage dialogue between religions and the proponents of human rights upon the areas where they don't see eye to eye. It may be that seemingly intractable disagreements about sexuality, gender or personhood can be resolved. She suggests two interim understandings that may help this process along. First, mutual respect between the traditions of human rights and religious traditions must recognise that 'all traditions and practices have to pass the test of some sort of universal moral code'. She cites An-Na'im in support of this contention:

> Traditional culture is not a substitute for human rights; it is a cultural context in which human rights must be established, integrated, promoted and protected. Human rights must be approached in a way that is relevant and meaningful in diverse cultural contexts (A. An-Na'im, 1992, p. xiii).

The second interim understanding recognises that human rights are a 'man-made' code. As such, it can do no more than register the highest moral values that any society presently perceives. Again, this suggests that religions may have a part to play in contesting or supporting such values, even as they are themselves supported and contested. This is an important insight, for it recognises that churches, if they wish to argue for a particular stance on gender or sexuality, must do so in a way that requires them to be accountable to civil society, if indeed a religion wants to be regarded as public, or make public claims. This dynamic affects all faiths.

In his recent *Islam and Liberal Citizenship* (2009), Andrew March asks how Muslims can be both good citizens of liberal democracies and good Muslims. He is mindful that some Muslims would argue that separation of religious loyalty and political loyalty is not part of the Islamic tradition, and therefore participation in an open and pluralist society is not possible. Other Muslims – perhaps more extreme

– might argue that all believers should oppose non-Islamic forms of government, and strive to implement Islamic law.

Yet using the theory of John Rawls (1993), March argues that there is a tradition that is both consistent with orthodox Sunni Islam and also compatible with modern liberal citizenship, which is rooted in the idea of 'overlapping consensus'. This, suggests March, might be found in the synergy between a public conception of justice, and religious or ethical outlooks. Indeed, he argues that the more religious traditions are engaged with, the more likely it is that consensus with public concerns will be found. There can be, therefore, an alliance of interests between secular and sacred. Indeed, through engagement with public life, religious traditions may not only shape society: they may also discover some deeper truths on how they in turn are shaped.

Of course, one can be left with a precarious equilibrium. So a primary task for the churches must be to contribute to a kind of peaceful openness, which will be the foundation of a civil society. The prospect of church autonomy and human rights co-existing within a culture depends upon this. However, this may still be perceived as alienating by some cultures and religious groups within society. Laurence Sager argues wisely for civil society when he states that 'the regime of liberty is premised on protection rather than privilege' (2000, p. 206). In other words, a civil society does not attempt to dole out advantages or exemptions to groups or individuals on the basis of their beliefs. Rather, it aims at parity, and therefore takes an interest in religions or cultural practices only when the rights of individuals or groups are being impeded or eroded.

The key to moving forward here may be for the churches to recover a richer reading of contemporary culture. The issue of the so-called Occupy Protesters outside St. Paul's cathedral, and mentioned earlier, is a case in point. The protest began as a nascent grumble against the power of capitalism, with the alleged excesses of the banking industry and financial sectors forming a particular focus for antipathy. Yet the protest was a more occluded affair than it might at first appear. The tents outside St. Paul's inevitably resembled a modern art installation, and drew parallels; somewhat quirky, and with a multiplicity of meanings, some of which may be quite deep. The protesters originally intended to be outside the London Stock Exchange, and it was only by accident that the ground they eventually camped upon was shifted from the secular to the sacred. Was the installation of the tents an act of figurative art, or something more abstract? Or was it, perhaps, a synergy of the two – abstract-figurative, in other words – the bringing together of two opposing styles of art by taking strong references to the real world, and synthesizing them with departures from reality? If so, the protesters are merely engaged in a form of artistic mimesis – copying the abstraction and figuration of what they now see in capitalism itself. And in so doing, the protesters indicate capitalism as an economic and social system, questioning its capacity to provide a meaningful canopy under which individuals and societies can flourish. Perhaps the tents, as temporary installations, carry some meaning. Is this a case of money, pensions and financial services – all we thought reliable and permanent – turning out to be transitory? Here today, gone tomorrow; much like the tents. Their proximity to the dome of St. Paul's – a more enduring sacred canopy – is not without significance.

Four centuries earlier, Richard Hooker committed himself to a vision of church and society that kindly prefigures such debates. That is to say, he saw civil society and civil religion as a matter of progressive growth and mutual interdependence, with church and society providing one another with life and health. Organic approaches to ecclesiology recognise the heterogeneity of congregations and churches, and their deep need to be reconciled in a common, if complicated broader social life. For Hooker, the church was a living body that was rooted in society, and sometimes in their operations, the two could not be distinguished:

> The stateliness of houses, the goodlines of trees, when we behold them delighteth the eye; but that foundation which beareth up the one, that root which ministereth unto the other nourishment and life, is in the bosom of the earth concealed: and if there be at any time occasion to search into it, such labour is then more necessary than pleasant, both to them which undertake it, and for lookers-on. In like manner the use and benefit of good laws, all that live under them may enjoy with delight and comfort, albeit the grounds and first original causes from whence they have sprung be unknown, as to the greatest part of men they are' (Book 1.I.2).

In Hooker's mind, sociality is supported by two foundations (or perhaps exists under two overlapping 'sacred canopies') – 'a natural inclination, whereby all men desire sociable life and fellowship' and 'an order expressly or secretly agreed upon, touching the manner of their union in living together' [Bk 1.X.1]. The ideal order is described by Hooker as 'the law of a Commonweal'. Significantly, the concept of an original agreement makes the order similar to a social contract. Just as all types of law derive from divine laws, all authority derives from ultimate authority, which is from God. And yet Hooker does not abuse this lineage by demanding slavish obedience. For Hooker, laws are public, and all truth is in a kind of common trusteeship.

The use of Hooker – only alluded to here very briefly – suggests that the tension between church autonomy and human rights need not be so sharp. Hooker argues for the upholding of a civil society, because he sees this as a guarantor of both humanity and religion. Moreover, a public religion, even if it had to be compromised in certain of its aspects to become and remain public, was better than a private faith. Or, put another way, an extensive and intensive private religion – even one where the number of adherents may be growing all the time – does not offer the same benefits to society as an open civil religion. Hooker understood that the images of God contained within a civil religion may both subvert and legitimise political authority or the values within a prevailing culture.[28] The socio-sacred canopy, in other words, may continue to be both rich and viable. This much is matter of hope.

---

[28]   Cf. D. Nicholls (1989).

PART III
Charity and Church

Chapter 7

Context and Catholicity:
An Anglican-American Dilemma?

What an interesting year 2008 turned out to be. The world witnessed an election for the US presidency, in which Barrack Obama won a pretty handsome majority in senate and congress, and also won the popular vote by some margin. And just a few months before, the world's media was also invited to be both spectator and speculator on a Lambeth Conference for Anglicans, which passed off more or less peacefully, even managing to avoid the consequences of various ecclesial manoeuvres in the American Episcopal Church (TEC) from overly distorting the agenda. But what is the connection between these two events? Quite simply, I want to suggest that some of the current crises in Anglican identity are partly rooted in some of the un-surfaced cultural and contextual assumptions that shape American life.

That said, this chapter is not intended to be a mere list of gripes and grumbles. It is, rather, an invitation to begin critically exploring the relationship between catholicity and enculturation, and sketch some of the dilemmas facing global Anglican polity. I should say at the outset that the choice of the word 'dilemmas' is itself deliberate: I do not say 'problems'. A problem is something that can be solved. Dilemmas are, however, arenas where issues and values can only be balanced. And I believe that part of the crisis facing Anglican polity at present is rooted in the inability to distinguish between problems and dilemmas. But I am ahead of myself already, so let me begin at the beginning.

One Event, Two People and Several Issues

With the inauguration of President Obama now many moons ago, it may seem a little strange to some observers looking back on the event that quite a bit of the focus was on Rick Warren, the pastor of Saddleback mega-church in southern California. Obama had chosen Warren to give the invocation on 20 January– conferring the kind of status on a pastor normally that would normally be reserved for the likes of Billy Graham. The other noteworthy person present at the inauguration was the Bishop of New Hampshire, Gene Robinson, who led the prayers. Robinson was elected bishop in 2003, and, as a divorcee and gay man, has seen his elevation to the episcopacy become a focal point for the divisions in global Anglican polity. To some, he represents the ascendancy of imperialistic Episcopalian liberalism. To others, he is a prophetic forerunner – a champion for gay rights, who is challenging the innate homophobia of a church that is resisting both modernity and equality.

In choosing both Warren and Robinson to participate in the inauguration, Obama appeared to have selected two Christian leaders to represent the right and the left, and in so doing achieved some creditable political and religious balance. Here, perhaps, was the wisdom of Solomon in action? Yet I want to suggest that both Robinson and Warren have much more in common than might appear to be the case, and that this arguably highlights a problem in the relationship between catholicity and context. So let me say more, and begin with Warren.

It was Warren who hosted the first debate between Obama and McCain that kick-started the presidential race. Warren is a well-known exponent of conservative Christian values on all the cornerstone issues that currently unite and divide evangelicals: gay rights, abortion, and so forth. So selection of Warren to give the invocation is not without controversy. But what exactly was a black northern liberal doing inviting a white southern conservative to preach? Cue the predictable banshee cries and wailings of protest from the political left.

The choice of Warren, however, represented a more interesting conundrum in contemporary American life. Warren's books, such as *The Purpose-Driven Church* (1995),[1] have sold hundreds of millions. The sentiments express that unique American recipe: the subtle and seductive fusion of religion and pragmatism; of manna and mammon. The ambiguity of this fission is printed on every dollar bill: in God we trust. So techniques in marketing and any kind of general organisational theory are imported into belief and practice, so that the potential of faith is maximised in its service of the consumer. Cue abundance: happiness and self-improvement is within the grasp of any faithful believer.[2]

In the USA, user-friendly forms of Christianity are a dime a dozen. The common DNA that unites them all is the promotion of religion as a panacea: something that will solve problems and improve the lives of individuals. It is a rather functional, pragmatic attitude to faith. And when it ceases to work, one simply discards and moves on.[3] There is bound to be something better in the spiritual marketplace for

---

[1]   See also *The Purpose-Driven Life* (2002).
[2]   See, for example, Thomas Lynch and his critique of American culture – 'McFunerals, McFamilies, McMarriage, McValues' etc. (1998, p. 25).
[3]   For an illuminating discussion and critique, see Barbara Ehrenreich (2009). Ehrenreich suggests that the positive thinking has, amongst other things, powerfully

the restless consumer. Something more 'me'; a faith that is even more effective and affective than the last. This is, after all, a faith-land where Jesus might be Lord, but the customer is actually king. (And, by the way, like any other customer, always right.)

However, the kind of Christianity espoused by Warren expresses both the problem and the opportunity that the Obama presidency faces. For with the collapse of confidence in capitalism, the dawning realisation that growth cannot be indefinitely expediential, and that not everyone can be a winner, comes the haunting sense that some deeper values may have to come to the fore in shaping the America of the next few decades.

To be frank, the pursuit of happiness and self-improvement, accompanied by a thick spiritual veneer, will not easily survive the ravages of a new Great Depression. Or for that matter, the new emerging world order. Something more substantial will be needed for the long road ahead. A collective vision for discipleship will be required, one that is rooted in challenging American values as much as affirming them. Locating a vocation that will serve others, and not just be about sustaining one's self, will be a priority.

What, then, of Robinson's role in the inauguration? As the Bishop of New Hampshire, he is the first openly gay man to be called by an Anglican diocese to such a position. Despite the fact that Robinson was chosen by a two-thirds majority of the local electors, his elevation to the episcopate has caused a tsunami of international debate and disagreement, even threatening the unity and identity of the Anglican Communion. The resulting hullabaloo – even by Anglican standards – could be comfortably described as a hurricane of controversy. Indeed, as ecclesiastical tempests go, this particular one appears to be almost off the barometer scale.

Given that Robinson would be rendered culpable by some for creating the recent inclement ecclesiastical weather that has dogged so much of Anglican polity, even the title of his book seems open to the charge of hubris. Can it really be appropriate to infer that there is any calm place left in which to reflect on the nature of the gospel and the church, whilst in the midst of such heated exchanges on sexuality and biblical authority? Yet in his recent book, *In the Eye of the Storm* (2008), we find a temperate, measured lucid and composed writer – a rather touching irenic memoir, in fact, from a man who despite being at the centre of such controversy, and held responsible by many for the potential dismemberment of the Anglican Communion, is nonetheless keeping his cool.

---

infected religious belief and practice, turning demanding discipleship into forms of consumer-focused spirituality that meets individuals at their point of need.

Indeed, Robinson's book should be understood as a kind of quintessentially Anglican polemic: the very embodiment of fervent detachment – a delicate fission of biblical, personal, ethical, theological and reflective material. And the substance of the text ranges far and wide, covering a familiar litany of topics that are near and dear to the hearts of your average North American Episcopalian. Chapters concentrate on sexuality and justice; faith and life; diversity and exclusion; politics and inclusion; and ending with communion and identity. This familiar terrain is, however, addressed in a manner that is simultaneously moderate and ardent, capturing something of the heart of Anglican polity (at least in style) – as well as neatly expressing its current dilemma (in substance). Here is a cradle Anglican expressing his mind and heart; baring his soul for the world to read.

However, the book cannot escape the production and reception of its underlying context. Anglicanism has never considered itself to be a sect or denomination originating in the sixteenth century. It considers itself to be both catholic and reformed, and with no special doctrines of its own. Yet there is something about the style of Anglicanism – its cadence and timbre – that gives it a distinctive feel. Whilst one can never generalise – there are, after all, several kinds of Anglican identity – there is nonetheless a unifying mood in the polity that rejoices in the tension between clarity and ambiguity, decisions and deferral, to say nothing of word and sacrament, or protestant and catholic.

Caught between extremes, critics of Anglican polity have often ruminated that Anglicanism cannot escape its Laodicean destiny. So neither too hot nor too cold – just warm. In other words, the classic *via media*: tepid – and proud. And because Anglicanism is born of England, just like its climate, the polity often struggles to cope with extremities. Anglicanism is mostly a temperate ecclesial polity: cloudy, with occasional sunny spells and the odd shower – but no extremes, please.

Temperature, then, is an important key to understanding the very context from which Robinson's book has emerged, as well as its content. For his work has materialised out of the new ecclesiastical climatology witnessed at the beginning of the twenty-first century, which just like the rest of the planet, now finds itself exposed to extremities. Normal and temperate weather configurations seem to have given way to immoderate and excessive patterns of behaviour that are driving a new agenda. The sense of 'furious religion' has returned. Cool, calm religion – that beloved export of Europe for so many centuries – is giving way to hot and sultry expressions of faith that despise moderation and temperateness. And Anglicans of all hues are caught up in the new extremes of spiritual weather. Ecclesiastical global warming has arrived.

So, whilst *In the Eye of the Storm* offers us a telling *apologia* for calmness and centred-ness, in which Robinson acknowledges the weather around him, he inevitably abrogates any real responsibility for the conditions that have drawn so many into the subsequent hurricane of controversy. In many ways, he is probably right to be so coy. The turbulence that regularly erupts in Anglican polity has been around for many centuries, and has only recently found expression in the new debates on gender, politics, scripture and ecclesial order. Sexuality was never going to be any different; the storm merely points to the endemic weakness and strength embedded in Anglican diversity.

But what *In the Eye of the Storm* cannot help Anglicans with, is how precisely to face and resolve the divisive dilemmas that seem to threaten the very future of the Communion. Some churches, of course, thrive on intensity and heat; it is a sign of vibrant life and feisty faith. But others who are of a more temperate hue find this disturbing: heated exchanges, anger and passions seem to dismay more than they console. Anglicanism, then, as a *via media* expression of faith, finds the soul of its polity profoundly troubled by excess. For it strains to embody what one distinguished Anglican has described as 'passionate coolness'.

'Passionate coolness' is a typically Anglican phrase: framing ecclesial identity within an apparent paradox. So I suppose one could say that what currently afflicts Anglicanism is not this or that issue – but the heat and intensity that often accompany the debates – because Anglicans are used to temperate, cool disputations. What Anglicans have in the sexuality debate is hot passions mixing with cool reserve: heated exchanges suddenly being expressed in a traditionally temperate climate. And when heat meets coolness, a storm can brew. Robinson is in there of course – and right at the centre too.

But this book is, as I say, a model of mild yet ardent temperate Anglican polity. And ultimately, that is the only grounded future where Anglicans will truly be able to face one another with their manifest differences. So perhaps this is where some of the hope lies for the Anglican Communion, and indeed for the wider world. For surely now, and in the immediate future, what societies need are robust models of breadth that can genuinely live with difference and diversity, and offer a passionately moderate polity that can act as a counter-balance to religious extremism and narrow forms of exclusion that vilify and divide.

Context and Catholicity

Given these opening remarks, I am aware of the risk of relegating a hurricane to the status of a storm in a teacup. Robinson's appointment is a serious matter for Anglican polity, to be sure. And confidence in the resilience of Anglicanism – as a robust and discrete culture that can ride out some aggressive and intemperate weathering – is only part of the reality that Anglicans face. There is no question that the danger of schism is serious. Wars, as wise folk know, can be started at any time of one's choosing; but the author cannot choose the time and manner of ending. So it is little wonder that the early church fathers, when faced with a choice of living with heresy or schism, always chose the former. Doctrine and practice can be corrected over time. But schisms are seldom mended; ecclesial fractures do not have a record of healing well.

That said, Anglicans could now look back at the 2008 Lambeth Conference with some degree of satisfaction. In general, the verdict seems to be that for the most part, it passed off peaceably. Of course, much ink was spilled in the run-up to the Conference, writing off Anglicanism, attacking the leadership of the Archbishop of Canterbury, or pointing to the gathering forces of conservatism in movements such as Gafcon (Global Anglican Futures conference) and FOCA (Fellowship of Confessing Anglicans). The media reporting prior to the conference was mostly gloomy and doom-laden: as helpful as a phalanx of Job's comforters staffing the telephones at your local branch of the Samaritans.

But Anglicans hardly need the media to provide the dubious comforts of depressive consolation, for they are very good at squabbling amongst themselves. Mired in a culture of blaming and mutual castigation, Anglicans seem to have all but lost the knack of cultivating and practising the virtues of tolerance and patience amidst their differences and diversity Moreover, the last few decades have seen an unholy and viral trinity of individualism, impatience and intolerance unleashed. This has rapidly spread to very different quarters of the Anglican Communion, yet with unsurprisingly similar results. So now, each part of the worldwide church, whether liberal or conservative, white or black, can claim to be true and right, whilst expressing their individuality, irritation and annoyance with all those they disagree with.

I suspect the only antidote to this plague of rashness is an old Anglican remedy: the recovery and infusion of those qualities that are embedded in the gospels, and in deeper forms of ecclesial polity. Namely, ones that are formed out of patience, forbearance, catholicity, moderation – and a genuine love for the reticulate blend of diversity and unity that forms so much of the richness for Anglican life. But in the woof and weave of the church, these virtues have been lost – or rather mislaid – in a miscibility of debates that are marked by increasing levels of tension and stress.

There is support for this kind of polity. For example, in Kenneth Locke's recent book we find a subtle and careful exploration of the ambiguities that help form Anglican identity. Although be pays due and patient attention to some of the inherent weaknesses in this type of complex ecclesial formation, he is also clear about the depths and riches that make up Anglican life. Chapters cover authority, episcopacy and ecumenism – with some excellent comparative reflections drawing on Lutheran, Roman Catholic and Orthodox sources. The chapter on Anglican ecclesial authority is as illuminating as it is sobering (Locke, 2009). Locke recognises that rich and dense ecclesial communities are also complex; so it is not so easy to be simple and clear, as some may hope.[4]

Yet if this sounds like too much of tangle for some, it is interesting to note that when Jesus reaches for metaphors that describe the kingdom of God (and, by implication, the possibility and potential of churches), he often uses untidy images. 'I am the vine, you are the branches' comes to mind. No stately cedar tree of Lebanon here; or even an English oak. Jesus chooses a sprawling, knotted plant that requires patience and careful husbandry. And one that is hardly pretty to look at either. (But the fruit and what it produces, interestingly, is another matter for taste and looks.) In another short parable, he compares the kingdom of heaven to a mustard seed – one of the smallest seeds that can grow into 'the greatest of all shrubs and sprouts large branches' (Mark 4: 30–32). The image is ironic, and possibly even satirical. One has every right to expect the kingdom of God to be compared to the tallest and strongest of trees. But Jesus likens the church to something the sprouts up quite quickly from almost nothing, and then develops into an ungainly sprawling shrub that can barely hold up a bird's nest.

So then, what exactly is the problem? If Anglicans could settle for a little less clarity and simplicity, and embrace complexity and catholicity, would all be well? Yes and no. Part of the problem for Anglicans, at the moment, lies in our inability to discern the underlying issues that are causing tensions, and squabbling about the presenting issues. Or, put another way, dealing with symptoms, not causes. Sexuality is a classic example of the dilemma that Anglican polity faces at present, and I want to suggest that finding a new conciliation and peace in the Communion will rest with discovering and addressing some of the deeper cultural pulses that are causing similar kinds of problems for other denominations, institutions and societies.

There are some encouraging signs that some Anglican commentator and scholars have also perceived this, and Bill Sachs is one such.[5] True, many Anglicans could be forgiven for the almost audible inward groan that emanates at the mere mention of homosexuality and Anglicanism in the same sentence. Surely Anglicans have had quite enough of the issue? Worn out by the divisive debates and debacles, is it not time for the Anglican Communion to move on, and perhaps tackle something a little less contentious – such as mission and ministry, or justice and peace?

The answer to these questions is, of course, 'yes'. But that should take nothing away from Bill Sachs' remarkable, indeed peerless book, which surveys the terrain of one of the knottier problems to have arisen in Anglican polity for many a year.

---

[4] See also Rowan Williams (2004).

[5] See William L. Sachs, *Homosexuality and the Crisis of Anglicanism* (2009).

His thesis will repay careful reading, and is well worth the time one might invest to ponder how a crisis such as this assumed the proportions it did, and where any hope for the future of the church might lie.

There cannot be many Anglicans who don't hold an opinion on the subject in question. But as Sachs points out, eloquently, Anglicans across the globe, whether liberal or conservative, traditional or progressive, are often caught between their biblical, doctrinal, ecclesial and legalistic frameworks on the one hand, and their experiential, contextual and pastoral concerns on the other. Indeed, one of the great strengths of this book is the lucid articulation of emerging contextual theologies and the ways in which they compete with hitherto unarticulated but assumed notions of catholicity, homogeneity and more complex forms of global belonging. The local, indeed, is both one of the strengths of Anglican identity; but also a potential source of weakness when attempting to speak and act on a global scale. Sachs articulates this potentially problematic dynamic beautifully and clearly, and without recourse to party-based sniping. There is no siding with liberal or conservative slants. Sachs knows too well that the Anglican Communion and its somewhat patchwork polity is far more complex than it seems. Anglicans all agree on what the bible says; we are just spending quite a bit of time – and acrimoniously, on occasions – figuring out what it means, and where, why and when to apply texts in the twenty-first century.

Sach's narration of the crisis begins by outlining the defining moments of the debates, which brought an issue that was bubbling below the skin of Anglican polity and identity boiling right to the surface. As Sachs suggests, even with regard to the elevation of Gene Robinson, and the proposed elevation of Jeffrey John to the episcopate, the ensuing divisions in the church were in fact already emerging. Tensions on sexuality existed long before 2003, and caused significant difficulties at the Lambeth Conference of 1998, and had already coloured and clouded the arch-episcopacy of George Carey.

Sachs, as a contextual theologian, then locates these difficulties and disagreements in the wider milieu of ecclesial polity. Tensions, for example, have always existed in the contention for the shaping of early Christian unity. Ideals and realities can also be conflictual, as are the concentrations of power (in the centre or on the periphery, and between local and catholic) in the formation of a global polity. Sachs contends that the key to understanding the debate is the realisation that indigenous Anglicanism is both the foundation of its global polity, as well as its nemesis. Drawing on writers such as Michael Sandel and John Tomasi towards the end of his thesis,[6] Sachs shows that the kind of activism which promotes rights – vindication through political processes – rather than seeking tangible social and

---

[6]   See Sandel (2009) and John Tomasi (2001).

communal harmony as a whole, and for the greater good of all, is bound to be deficient for a church, where there are higher goals to reach for.[7]

Sachs is in no doubt that there are difficult days ahead for the Anglican Communion. One way of resolving its future would be to plot a more assertive course; to chart a pathway, in effect, that was directive and hierarchical. This would have its champions, to be sure. Another way forward is to capitulate to despair, or simply to 'walk apart' – in effect, to cave in to endemic consumerist individualism. But there is another way, and Sachs carefully expounds this in his conclusion.

Taking respectful issue with Philip Turner's and Ephraim Radner's recent *The Fate of the Communion* (2006), Sachs suggests that unity will need to continue to be progressed through careful listening and speaking, and recognition of the blend between interdependence, intra-dependence, independence and dependence. All Anglicans dwell within this framework, and have to work through the consequences of practising 'contextual reliance on the authority of Spirit without the balance of a wider collegiality' (p. 247). This is an issue for Sydney as much as it is for New Hampshire.

Sachs believes that the future of the Communion lies in recognition of multiple contexts that partially form ecclesial polity, even though these same realities may need challenging and addressing from time to time. Many Americans, for example, operate quite happily and unconsciously within a 'spiritual marketplace', leading to an individualist and consumerist mindset that picks a tradition or combination of traditions that suits lives at particular points in time. The result is that the local congregation tends to express and interpret the wider tradition for individuals, but at the expense of the broader and deeper adherence to a given denomination. Local congregational life, therefore, and for the purposes of constructing meaning, value and concepts of wider belonging and catholicity, is now far more dominant than it used to be.

That said, the 'Communion' of the future must entail a readiness to be in fellowship with one another, but without this necessarily meaning 'agreement' on all things, or ceding authority to one another. As Sachs points out, 'no position on homosexuality could embody the whole of (the) Anglican tradition' (2009, p. 249). I am sure that this is right. However, the argument for the future of Anglican polity doesn't necessarily hinge on dissenting from this kind of view. It might rest, ironically, on accepting that some positions – amongst traditionalists, progressives, conservatives and liberals – whilst being faithful expressions of a localised contextual theology, are nonetheless not easily able to fully commune within a body that is seeking to rediscover its catholicity.

---

[7] See Sen (2009).

I suspect, then, and following Sachs, that the roots of current crises in Anglican polity lie not with sexuality (at least in the long term), but rather with some of the deeper cultural drivers that shape American life. These largely un-surfaced assumptions are exported the world over through Americanised versions of capitalism and democracy: the complete right to choose and self-determine; the intrinsic goodness of (almost unlimited) consumerism; the basic rightness of rights that lead to happiness and the pursuit of individual freedom and purpose, thereby subordinating a broader catholicity and sociality; and finally, that the ends justify the means.

Americans might be surprised at this short list. They may complain, with some justice, that these are by no means found and held exclusively on their continent, and they would be right to do so. Yet I think what is at issue here is this particular concentration of un-surfaced assumptions in American culture, which can be found in the marketplace, public sphere and in the media. Take, for example, the majority of American television programmes and series that concentrate on crime, justice and police work. Almost all of them uphold the rightness of the law; so justice is served. Yet many will also express something beyond this. Namely, that when justice is seen to fail or fall short, the righteous can take the law into their own hands. The law, in other words, is contingent, not absolute. Whilst this is clearly a generalisation, 'the ends justify the means' would serve as adequate subtitle for many episodes for most American police, legal or crime dramas.

Small wonder, then, that whenever the American sense of liberal idealism in church polity is challenged by another power, Americans tend to react in a way that is true to their theological and cultural instincts. Are there not choices for all? Did this course of action not seem right us at the time? Have we not done the right thing in moving forward now? Why then, should we be stopped? Local democracy becomes an apotheosis. It is the Boston Tea Party all over again. Don't argue and debate – it is time-consuming. Take control of your life: act now.

Were proof needed of this, I need only recall chairing a seminar some years ago in the USA. We had taken as our topic the fall-out from the Gene Robinson affair, and were exploring Anglican patterns of mediation, and, in particular, the irenic polity advocated by Richard Hooker. But this was too much for some. In the plenary that followed, one questioner exploded: 'We voted for this! What can be wrong with that? They voted for the creeds at Nicea. It's just the same!' Except it isn't. One group of voters in New Hampshire is not on a par with an ecumenical council that drew together the entire Christian world as it was then known.

Read like this, the cultural and contextual difficulties currently plaguing Anglican polity need some unmasking.[8] Sexuality is clearly an important issue. But it is also an unnecessary distraction – exactly not the issue that the church and the wider Communion should be focusing on. Yet that Anglicans have become so hopelessly and helplessly distracted in recent years is hardly surprising, for it is also part of the wider cultural milieu and malaise. The playwriter David Hare has characterised the last decade as a decade of distraction. Instead of looking at the issues and situations that truly need examination, many Christians have looked away and focused on other matters, allowing ourselves to be distracted by simple pursuits rather than wrestling with complexity.[9] Thus, when 2,948 people from ninety-one nations die in the Twin Towers of New York, the response is to invade Iraq – pursuing the wrong suspect for the crime. Afghanistan is also invaded. But most of the 9/11 hijackers, it turns out, are from Saudi Arabia.

In the church, with much angst and anxiety about declining church attendance, the response is interestingly not to reinforce the front line of mission (parish and established sector ministry), but rather to pour millions of pounds and resources into specious missiological schema that go under the nomenclature of 'fresh expressions' or 'emerging church'. Which, ironically, simply turn out to be ways of manoeuvring faithful Christians into lighter forms of spiritual organisation that do not carry heavy institutional responsibilities or broader-based ministerial burdens. The Christian consumer entering the new world of 'fresh expressions' or 'emerging church' can enjoy all the fruits of bespoke spiritual engagement and stimulation, but with almost none of the tariffs incurred through belonging to an ordinary parish church.

As the oft-quoted saying goes, 'if you don't want to know the result, look away now'. Alas, many Christians do. Unwilling to do their sums and calculate the cost of weaning a new generation of Christian consumers on light, carefully targeted spirituality, the churches simply end up losing some of their brightest and best potential leaders to projects that are essentially a form of distraction. And who otherwise could bring much-needed energy and effort into helping shape the broader institution. Distraction is endemic: fed by consumerism, choice, and the need to keep people engaged, fulfilled and happy, it is rife in the churches – to the left and right, amongst conservatives and liberals, traditionalists and progressives.

---

[8]   For a useful discussion of American culture and ecclesial polity, see Colin Podmore (2005). Podmore explores how decisions are taken in the Church; the roles of synods, bishops and primates; how the Archbishop of Canterbury's ministry should develop; what does being 'in communion' and 'out of communion' mean; and how significant are diocesan boundaries in an age of globalisation?

[9]   David Hare, 'The Decade of Looking Away', *Guardian Magazine*, 17 October 2009, pp. 5–7.

It is a tough time to be an ordinary church member; but happy the person who has found their cultural and contextual home in a new 'fresh expressions' or form of 'emerging church'. One where there is little to bond the person to the messy contingencies of long-term institutional commitment, but where all the rewards of organisational membership are replete and immediate. As David Lyon warns,

> Max Weber once commented that one effect of the rise of Protestantism was that religion strode confidently into the public square of worldly affairs, slamming shut the monastery door behind it. As modernity developed further, however, one might say that religion kept moving. It may now be found in the consumer marketplace, the shopping mall, the TV screen, and the website – even in Disneyland …. Religion has expanded into spheres less visible than the institutional and public ones it occupied in Weber's day. Thus, it takes its place alongside other meaning clusters available in the so-called private sphere. There, people are free to choose on their own what to do with their time, their homes, their bodies and their gods…. (D. Lyon, 2000, p. 81).

This may seem harsh. Yet I want to return to the suggestion that a good deal of the present issues that seem to be destabilising Anglicans (and other denominations) at present are in fact symptomatic rather than underlying and causal. To be sure, many of the attempts to return polity to its truer or truest state are full of sincerely held beliefs and worthy goals. But the common denominator is the lack of deeper ecclesial comprehension here, resulting in a real failure to read the cultural and contextual forces that are shaping polity at deep and profound levels. The consequence of this is that the churches tend to miss the moment.

Christianity does indeed face dangers in the developed world. But they are not, I think, secularisation or industrialisation. Plenty of people will turn aside from such things to embrace faith and meaning if that is all society can offer. The real threat comes from both within and without. Within, it is the uncritical absorption of individualist, consumerist assumptions that corrode catholicity and bonds of belonging. This moves the church, effortlessly, from being an established institution or body that faithfully replicates and transmits trustworthy and historic values, to being a series of attenuated organisations that have more short-term and utilitarian goals, including competing with each other for numbers, truth and vindication.

The threat from without is also one of comprehension. Christianity is intrinsically 'foreign' in any context. Every believer is a citizen of somewhere, but also of heaven. We are in the world, but not of it. Yet the foreign-ness of Christianity in the modern world has now begun to assume a new identity: alien. Whereas foreigners may speak other languages, learn yours, and otherwise mingle, aliens are unwelcome, treated with suspicion, and often repelled. Seen as invasive and intrusive, they are frozen out rather than welcomed in.

To some extent, 'fresh expressions' or 'emerging church' movements have tried to stem this tide. But all too often, and in so doing, many have sold the pass, culturally. By becoming too relevant they have lost the necessary otherness religion brings to society. Fearful of being alien, the foreigner has gone native. In the same way, liberals have sometimes been guilty of treading the same path. Many conservatives, on the other hand, have disengaged, and whilst succeeding in protecting their own identity, have only made an enclave for themselves, from which to make occasional and specious forays into the wider body politic. Each time this happens, the foreigners take one more step down the road to becoming aliens.

So, what's to be done? The risk of un-policed and uncritical enculturation has always been absorption – into one's self and into the society one is supposed to be transforming. As we have seen, it happens with respect to numerical growth in congregations, where the church all too easily elides apparent success with faithfulness. Failing to read the signs of the times, the church can quickly become absorbed by power, prestige and possessions (the three temptations visited upon Jesus in the wilderness), and assume that by demonstrating numerical fecundity, the church can compete in a world of choice, capitalism and consumerism. But the tide may be turning. It may be time to resist the presumption that unlimited growth is an inherently desirable goal. As David Hare explains in his play *The Power of Yes* (2009),

> (Not everything can grow all the time) ... Once Bradford and Bingley became a bank, I remember taking an immediate dislike to a new non-exec who said, 'I want one thing from this company'. He said, 'What I want is regular, incremental growth'. In other words, he was saying '*This company must grow every year*'. Now that we all know that nothing in the world shows regular incremental growth. You know that. I know that (p. 37).

And if there are warnings about enculturation on something as (simple) as capitalism and consumerism, then there is every sign that the church needs to develop a similar wisdom for discerning culture on matters of sexuality – both the secondary and the symptomatic. Here, the Anglican Communion, like all churches, needs to engage in two simple tasks of discernment. First, to figure out the constraints and opportunities afforded by balancing local contexts with catholicity.

Second, to discern the potential for a higher vision of cultural transformation that theology and mission might rightly seek.[10]

Theodore Roszak, in *The Making of a Counter-Culture*, suggests that the agenda before those who seek to transform society is not centred on organising, managing or repairing reality. It is, rather, about asking 'how shall we live?':

> 'The primary aim of counter-culture is to proclaim a new heaven and a new earth ... so marvellous, so wonderful, that the claims of technical expertise must of necessity withdraw to a subordinate and marginal status...' (2000, p. 13).

But what might it mean for 'technical expertise' to withdraw to the sidelines? In a church absorbed by the apparent rewards of Mission Action Plans, tactics and strategies, technical expertise is, of course, very much to the fore. Yet the pursuit of productivity and success – even in mission and evangelism – has a long, if marginal history. Gibson Winter, writing over fifty years ago, chided the protestant churches of America for their failure to understand their responsibility in the expanding metropolises of the postwar era:

> The problem of emptiness is the pressing issue of modern life. Even ex-urbanites confess that the emptiness which led to the exodus remains with them. In the final analysis, the over-developed society discovers emptiness and despair at the end of its struggle for productivity. Productivity without meaning is empty. The churches, too, are experiencing emptiness. Struggling to preserve their position in the metropolis by frenetic building programmes, their congregational life remains hollow (Winter, 1961, p. 175).

Winter recognises that the churches will not fulfil their mandate by further withdrawal into homogenous enclaves. Nor will competing with the inchoate values of metropolitan and suburban culture bring any reward either. Growth for the sake of growth, and development for the sake of development, risk simply heaping emptiness upon emptiness. In terms of ecclesiology, churches may therefore need to be a little more cautious of Mission Action Plans, and strategies for evangelism and growth and the like. On one level, this might sound odd to some – unnecessarily cautious, and perhaps even antithetical to the gospel. After all, who would vote against action plans and strategies for growth? Yet in sounding a warning note here, I simply wish to draw attention, again, to the problem of distraction discussed earlier.

---

[10]   For further discussion, see Colin Podmore (2011, pp. 12–37).

Mission Action Plans, for example, tend to take little account of the macro-social shifts that shape church growth and decline. Deep social changes and upheavals – urbanisation and industrialisation, for example – produce conditions that shape and delimit religious affiliation. Strategies and tactics that try to act independently of deep cultural pulses, or simply fail to comprehend them, may find that formulae such as Mission Action Plans, despite their honourable intentions, ultimately engender disenchantment and cynicism rather than vision and hope. Moreover, apparently neutral ecclesial formulae that are rooted in the inchoate capitalist values of productivity and growth may need to begin some serious self-reflection and evaluation. Do Mission Action Plans really produce substantial and measurable growth differentials? Or is their promotion and presence in the church something more akin to a candy-coated placebo? (We feel all the better for swallowing the pill, but can't really say why.) Perhaps what the churches in the developed world might need to do in the twenty-first century is step out of capitalist values and logic – even those that currently saturate our missiology – and focus on quality, not quantity; and offer transcendence and stillness, rather than familiarity and frenetic programmes. In other words, to cease competing with the world on its own terms, and take seriously the simple demand to follow Christ – independent of how this might look to the world. The gospel has some warrant here, cautioning against our tendency to compare and compete. In a rather comparative and competitive vein, Peter once said to Jesus, 'but Lord, what about this man?' Only for Jesus to reply to Peter, 'what is that to you? Just follow me' (John 21: 21–22).

So the church might not be about holding our own in the world, but rather recognising that we are to become a radical form of counter-culture. T.S. Eliot's vision for a Christian culture is not one where right has triumphed over left, liberals have achieved ascendancy over conservatives, or traditionalists and progressives have battled to a creditable stalemate. It is, rather,

> '... a society in which the natural end of man – virtue and well-being in community – is acknowledged for all, and the supernatural end – beatitude – for those who have the eyes to see it' (1939, p. 42).

Here, if Anglicans could find the grace and humility to conduct their debates with this kind of higher vision in mind, we might be able to see that present difficulties and differences are also our opportunity. For if we can find a way forward to live with diversity, and yet in unity, we shall have held up to the world such an example of polity that the wider public sphere and body politic might itself seek the renewal of its mind and heart, as surely as Anglicans earnestly seek this for themselves.

Conclusion

The Anglican Communion, then, might take some comfort from the present problems it is experiencing. It may need to get beyond them too, and see that the presenting, besetting issues are not as serious as the stubborn and underlying cultural trends that have given them such force and identity.

The church, meanwhile, might take some comfort from the lips of Jesus. Like the mustard seed, the church can continue to be an untidy sprawling shrub. Like a vine, it can be knotted and gnarled. Neither plant is much to look at. But Jesus knew what he was doing when he compared his kingdom to these two plants. He was saying something quite profound about the nature of the church: it will be rambling, extensive and just a tad jumbled. And that's the point. Jesus seems to understand that it often isn't easy to find your place in neat and tidy systems. And maybe you'll feel alienated and displaced for a while. But in a messy and slightly disorderly church, and in an unordered and rather rumpled institution, all may find a home.

At the same time, and to mix our metaphors for a moment, Jesus did not feed the storm. In one gospel, he apparently slept through the maelstrom, only stilling it when roused by his disciples. But calm it he did. So, despite the current storms that bedevil the worldwide Anglican Communion, I predict that the outlook is ultimately calm, and the long-term forecast remains moderate. Indeed, this is the best hope for religion in the modern world. One of hospitality and charity – even if a certain restlessness is bound to continue, forged as it were in the testing furnaces of truth and justice. Yet I dare say we might discover that, when we look back in, say, a century, that Bishop Robinson's role in the eye of this particular storm will have emerged as something more complex and ambiguous than many currently suppose.

The irony of the present debacle is that it reminds us of how significant current cultural and contextual bearings have on theological and ecclesial disputes. Americans are in love with choices. And this is the one American Anglicans now face. Whether, on the one hand, to go with a catholicity that will be experienced by many as constraining. Or, on the other hand, to capitulate to the endemic context of consumerism, which is sometimes at the expense of a broader catholicity. Or, put another way, the local against the global.

At this point Americans will doubtless remind themselves of their sacred duty – to uphold democracy, and not to give in to intimidating third parties; so no climb-downs. Yet the track record of American foreign policy does not paint such a neat picture. As many small nation states have found to their cost, in Central and South America, and in the Caribbean, democracy is fine – just so long as the right choice for Uncle Sam is made. That said, not all controversy, dis-ease, debate and difficulty is bad. Anglicanism is inherently 'open' and provisional. And as Bruce Reed's work reminds us,

> Biologically, (ecclesial) life is not maintenance or restoration of equilibrium, but is essentially the maintenance of dis-equilibrium, as the doctrine of open systems reveals. Reaching equilibrium means death and decay (1978, p. 147).

So, to return to the inauguration with Warren and Robinson present, Obama is on stronger ground than many of his predecessors. His choice of these two ecclesial paragons, on one level, reaches out to both the right and the left, and implicitly calls for a pause in traditional liberal-conservative hostilities. It challenges the old cold-war impasses of democrat versus republican, or traditionalist versus progressive. The old ways of trench-war debating will not suffice for the twenty-first century. Obama's campaign was framed on calling his country to higher and deeper principles. But what might these be rooted in?

Obama's strength lies not in the bewitching power of the new, but rather in the renewal of the old. His campaign, and much of what he stands for, is rooted in the original vision of the founding fathers of America. That freedom is an inalienable right – but only worth something if all can enjoy it. And that out of diversity comes a genuine and collective strength. From the outset, America was birthed not in one dominant ideology, but rather a whole farrago of Christian expressions that forged a nation rooted in diversity, and still later was to become a more complex alloy of competing and complementary faiths.

So perhaps it now falls to Obama to inaugurate a new kind of presidency, in which religion plays a different role. This will undoubtedly be one that displaces the old hegemonies and rivalries that have characterised the country in the postwar era, and promises to establish new kinds of conversation that are generative and constructive for the common good. For a country that normally likes to keep religion and the state well apart, Obama's vision for the nation is already turning out to be one of profoundly deep Christian visualisation and realisation.

It is still far too early to say if President Obama will have been ushering in a new age for American politics and religious rapprochement. Or for the culture that chose him. And Anglicans cannot yet know the true causes of their present difficulties. But in time, the malevolent forces that have brought such instability into Anglican polity will be unmasked. And I suspect we shall see that sexuality and gender are mere symptoms of dis-ease, and not causes. Indeed, we may be surprised at the root and branch problem: perhaps it will be the assumptions we make about choice, individualism and the nature of institutions – all of which have eroded our sense of catholicity and moral responsibility for the parts of Christ's body we seldom see or know? We cannot tell. But what can be said with some certainty, is that the consumer age we have grown up with is now passing, as all ages must. In God we trust.

Chapter 8

An Incorporate Body:
Church and Culture

One of the emerging concerns in this volume has been the growing shadow that is cast over the church by the twin towers of secularisation and consumerism. The impact, however, as we have seen, is somewhat ambivalent. Secularisation is not always the threat it appears to be: and often little more than a farrago of assumptions and assertions that amount to a less-than-nuanced description of the place and role of religion in contemporary culture. Consumerism – which emerged as a concern in the first three chapters, and in the previous one – causes the church to mutate in a variety of ways, not all of which are inimical to its identity and mission. The church is a resilient body. It will always struggle – on the line, as it were – between being culturally relative and culturally related. It cannot avoid being rooted and grounded in its contexts, as much as it cannot avoid being rooted and grounded in Christ. The incarnate nature of the body of Christ, the Church, is an expression of the incarnation: specific in time and place, yet eternal and mystical. As the *Book of Common Prayer* expresses it (in prayer of consecration) 'we are very members incorporate in the mystical body of thy son': heaven and earth; body and soul; chronos and kairos. The church remains, in the midst of this, and to borrow from Philip Larkin's poem 'Churchgoing', a serious place on serious ground – and one that cannot grow obsolete, since many of the compulsions that drive humanity and reach for destiny need the kind of sating that only religion can provide.[1]

There is something of a double-bind here. It is not just that consumerism takes place with respect *to* religious institutions. It now also takes place *within* them. It is not merely the case that religious consumers locate and choose their individual institution of faith-preference. Once inside, they continue to exercise choices. The days when people's church membership indicated what they believed and practised, and were socialised into the same, are over. Religious diversity has grown not just between churches, but within them. Believers and belongers increasingly expect to be able to have the right to decide for themselves what to believe and practise, whilst also exercising their rights as members. A change of religious belief no longer means a change of religious affiliation. Official and

---

[1] See Philip Larkin, *Collected Poems*, London, Faber, 2001.

operant religiousness are therefore increasingly out of synch, with at least one consequence being that the role of clergy becomes more challenging: managing increasing religious diversity within the bodies they preside over, whilst their own authority is simultaneously relativised by those whom they serve.

To be sure, this thesis should not be allowed to mask or in any way underestimate the forces arranged against the church. Consumerism and secularisation (as well as secularism) are alive and well inside the church. To press the bodily metaphor a little more, we might see these as viral or bacterial forms that are essential for the production of antibodies. In the right quantities, forces inimical to the church prompt the production of the means of defence. Overwhelmed by such forces, however, and the church can find itself weakened and enfeebled. Or, put another way, and with a more metaphorical slant, the issue in the parable of the sower – in whatever synoptic form it is encountered – is not with the seed *per se*, but rather with the quality of the soil. The gospel has a consistent power and potency; for it comes from the constancy of God. The issue is not God's nature or constancy, but rather the context for reception, which is variable across times, places and cultures. Moreover, the context has a significant bearing on how the seed flourishes or diminishes; atrophies or etiolates; lives or dies. For that reason alone, the synergies that emerge between faith and culture are vital to understanding the origins of theology and ecclesiology, and their present practice. Indeed, attempting to treat culture and faith as somehow as separate and distinct entities is something that this book, and the previous two volumes in the trilogy, has sought to resist. Which is why, for example, the concept of 'terroir' – discussed in the preceding volumes – is such a helpful and illuminating motif for ecclesiological enquiry.

The Gallic word 'terroir' is derived from the word *terre*, meaning 'land'. It is in commonplace use for wine-making and the cultivation of tea and coffee plantations, and is the single word used to denote the special characteristics that the geography, geology and climate of a certain place bestowed upon particular varieties of grape (wine), leaf (tea) or beans (coffee). The term recognises that whilst vineyards or plantations may share apparently similar soil, weather conditions and farming techniques with near neighbours, the type and taste of the wine, tea and coffee can differ markedly from place to place – even when they are geographically close, or even proximate. 'Terroir' recognises that local conditions – natural and human – can have a significant bearing on the production of difference and distinctiveness.

Used in ecclesiology, the term can helpfully illuminate and explain why no two churches are ever quite the same, even though there are many similarities in terms of types.[2] Just as there are red and white wines, Burgundies and Bordeaux,

---

    2   See Lawrence E. Jones (1965), *The Observer Book of Churches*, p. 191: 'no two churches are alike, and it is this fact that makes visiting them such a joy...'.

so there are churches, denominations and forms of local distinctiveness that mark out one church or congregation from another. One of the key tasks of ecclesiology, therefore, is to give an explanatory account for the unity and diversity of Christian ecclesial life. Yet this should be done not only with reference to the claimed theologies that shape and order ecclesial life, but also with reference to the cultures, micro-ecologies and contextual conditions that account for why churches emerge with particular social imaginaries and structures. Indeed, these are the shibboleths[3] of faith – the distinguishing practices of one's social or regional origin that find theological and linguistic expression in ecclesial life. There is one church, one faith, and one Lord, to be sure: but many dialects, perspectives and particularities that identify one part of the body from another.

Of course, there can be no real question that the church is an incarnate and incorporating body. Central to the concern of this trilogy of books on ecclesiology has been the shape of the church: the relation between the fluid and the concrete church (volume one), implicit and explicit theology (volume two), and in this third volume, the ideal and the real. *Terroir*, as a term, is illuminating for ecclesiology since it allows us, analogically, to consider new ways of opening up the Church-Culture debate. Similarly, the concept of 'topology' may also provide a complementary form of illumination in ecclesiological study. It was George Steiner who initially developed the idea of 'topologies of culture'. Topology is, strictly speaking, a branch of mathematics that deals with the fundamental properties of shapes, which remain the same, even though they may be bent or distorted: as, for example, drawing a square on a flexible surface, instead of stone or slate. A square drawn on, say, a large plastic sheet, can be bent, possibly twisted, or even rolled. In such a scenario, the shape remains the same, but the distance between the points of the square now differs, and their intra-relationship changed. But this is only temporary, since the shape can eventually be returned to its original condition when the surface becomes stable.

The analogy hardly needs much further exposition. The church has a distinct shape and identity, over space and time. Its fundamental role and purpose is given and known. Yet the surfaces it rests upon and are embedded in are malleable. Culture changes. And the shape of the church – in its ideal and real forms – is bent first in one way, and then in another. This is not necessarily a weakness. If the church is a resilient body, then one would expect a combination of flexibility and

---

3   See Judges 12: 5–6. The Hebrew word refers back to grains within a stalk of wheat, and, in different contexts, streams – conveying the sense again of unity and diversity. In the Book of Judges, however, the word 'shibboleth' is also an instrument of ethnic cleansing. The victorious Gileadites ask refugees from a battle to say the word in order to secure passage across the River Jordan. The accent or pronunciation of the word by refugees allows the Gileadites to identify the Ephraimites, and exterminate them.

reflexivity, coupled to the inviolate and utterly solid. The resilience of the church can be sometimes best found in forms of pliability that seem to have an almost unlimited capacity to stretch and bend. At other times, the resilience is expressed in uncompromising solidity: concrete hardness. Topology – as an interpretative key – enables fresh illumination in the study of ecclesiology in contemporary culture.

For example, and staying with squares for the moment, one might consider the Anglican Quadrilateral in this topological light. The Anglican, or Lambeth-Chicago Quadrilateral, as it is sometimes also known, is essentially a four-point articulation of Anglican identity, which owes its origins to an 1870 essay by William Reed Huntington, who was an American Episcopal priest. The Quadrilateral is often cited as encapsulating the fundamentals of the Anglican Communion's reference-point for ecumenical discussion with other Christian denominations, and for resolving its own intra-ecclesial disputes. The four points are: 1, the Holy Scriptures as containing all things necessary to salvation; 2, the historic creeds (specifically, the Apostles' and Nicene Creeds), as the sufficient statement of Christian faith; 3, the sacraments of Baptism and Holy Communion; and 4, The historic episcopate, locally adapted. It is the last of these, and the notion of 'locally adapted', that has tended to signal to Anglicans across the globe that culture – including regional or local culture – has a bearing on ecclesial belief and practice.[4] On matters of sexuality and gender, what is appropriate or permissible in the developed world may not be received in quite the same way in the developing world.

A topological approach to ecclesiology helps us to get beyond the binaries of the ideal and real, and the concrete and fluid. Instead of a 'flat geometric' approach to ecclesiology, a topological interpretative approach helps us to discern the interplay between the dynamic and static properties of Anglicanism, and the cultures in which it is embedded, and see that the shape of the church does indeed, on one level, remain; and on another level, is also bent and distorted. The key to the approach is to see that the surface – in this case the culture or context in which a church is immersed – will both actually and apparently change the shape of the church, yet not necessarily permanently. Thus, on one level, the Anglican Communion can be spoken of as 'stretched', or possibly even at risk of tearing.

---

⁴ See also David Bebbington's *Evangelicalism in Modern Britain: A History from the 1730s to the 1980s* (1989), in which he proposes a simple quadrilateral understanding for Evangelicalism, in which he identifies the four main qualities which are to be used in defining evangelical convictions and attitudes: 1, Biblicism – a particular regard for the bible; 2, Crucicentrism – a focus on the atoning work of Christ on the cross; 3, Conversionism – the belief that individuals need to be saved; 4, Activism – the belief that the gospel requires particular expression.

Yet on another level, the shape is intact, since the ideal and concrete forms and relations remain as they are. One can also see that the distortions in shape emerge out of a complex nexus of competing convictions. Many proponents of theological and ecclesiological vision within the Anglican Communion assume or argue for a certain pliability. Some, equally, argue for solidity and fixedness. The lines do not run neatly through 'Liberal' and 'Conservative' dispositions. 'Conservatives' may argue for a loosening of structures and pliability in regulations and ecclesial order. 'Liberals' may argue for upholding structures and depending on their apparent solidity, whilst arguing for greater pliability in some aspect of moral reasoning or ethical probity.

Topology, conceptually, suggests that spatial relationships and geometric properties can remain fundamentally unaffected, despite apparently continuous distortions in both size and shape. Moreover, we note that whilst geometry tends to deal quantitatively in terms of fixed lengths or proportions, topology utilises and expands geometric concepts in a qualitative manner – permitting stretching and bending, but without tearing or breaking. Put another way, ecclesial relations defined geometrically are fixed, stable and robust – but also limited. Ecclesial relations defined topologically are pliable and dynamic – but still have a clear and recognisable shape. Of course, churches, and systematic expressions of ecclesiology, are not asked to choose between these two visions. Rather, the invitation is to recognise that both 'models' are pertinent and valid, and that the church lives, believes and practises on both these dimensions – and indeed more than these. The church is not a single dimension of being. It is, rather, one in which solidity and fluidity coexist; in which pliability and concreteness interact; in which the propositional and relational spark; in which the ideal and the real form fascinating synergies of vision and practice; in which kairos and chronos, church and kingdom, compete and complement. This should not surprise us, since the central metaphor for the church in the New Testament – namely the body of Christ – is both a geometric and topological model. It is the combination of flex and stretch with bounded-ness and solidity that makes the body what it is. Sinews and bones; flesh and blood; skin and shin. The Anglican Quadrilateral, therefore, is not an inflexible model or shape that is about to crack or tear. Because the shape exists in more than one dimension, and is bound to have topological qualities as well as those that are geometric. To be sure, there are always challenges to the shape, just as there is pain in the body; and there can be wounds too. But it is a mistake to see all apparent ecclesial problems in only one single dimension.

To put this another way, the 'core' of Christian identity and practice is, if you like, already established. Luke 10: 27 states that what is required of the church and its members is to love the Lord your God with all our heart, soul, mind and strength, and our neighbours as ourselves. In one sense, everything that flows after that is a matter of locally and temporally adapted tactics. So given these remarks, we now turn to three critical issues of incorporation in the church, which explore the ambiguities of ecclesial life conceived of through a more topological vantage point. The three issues are all ones that have already received attention in the preceding two volumes: education, formation and vocation. And in each section that follows, we shall explore aspects of contemporary culture that have a particular bearing upon and significance for pedagogy, ecclesial practice and Christian identity.

Education

If consumerism poses a particular set of issue and threats to the churches, then it follows that comparable challenges will be located in other forms of institutional life. The sphere of higher education is one such, where a movement towards a consumerist foundation for education – traceable in many of the world's developed economies – is already shaping attitudes to pedagogy. The influence of market forces in education should, on one level, not surprise. And any critique of the marketisation is not intended to be a criticism of choice or accountability *per se*; nor a defence of the arcane. However, the influence of consumerism and market forces runs deeper than merely opening up wider choices. Steadily and increasingly, education has found itself corralled into a world of rhetoric and grammar that first subjects and then ultimately strips learning of its deep trajectory and ultimate dignity. Education is, ultimately, about wisdom, trust and the enlargement of our understanding of life. But subject to the 'anti-poetry' of 'aims', 'objectives', 'outcomes', 'pathways' it becomes mechanistic rather than organic. In the name of the clear, rational and progressive, it loses its heart and soul.

The rationalisation of education is part of a wider and deeper political attempt to control thinking and constrain enquiry, and privilege acquisition and individual personal wealth over and against an informed and on-going political debate about the nature of society and the common good. As Sue Gerhardt notes, 'a society which sustains individualism ... at the expense of collective interests and the needs of the social group as a whole' is in trouble (Gerhardt, 2010, p. 13).[5] By focusing on the 'goals' of education – and making students active consumers in the marketplace of higher education – the deeper purposes of pedagogical formation, and the cultivation of wisdom, are lost to the sating of the more immediate demands of market forces. Yet education of any kind is ultimately a bound hostage to such forces. Very few forms of education can clearly and demonstrably 'repay' their

---

[5]   See also Sue Gerhardt (2006).

investment. Yet we know enough about education that ignorance is even more expensive. The roundedness of education is not simply about the subject to hand, but also about the hidden curriculum.[6] For example, what is learnt in a seminar is not merely a little more about the set text in question, but also how to listen respectfully, to debate strongly yet inclusively, and to learn to combine emotional intelligence with more specific forms of learning. It is virtually impossible to 'cost' this exercise – one that happens every day, in every university. And the grammar or rules of such engagements are seldom explicitly disclosed or taught – yet remain a fundamental part of learning, and one that resists the atomisation and acquisitiveness of more market-driven education.

Indeed, we may go further here, and say that education is somewhat incompatible with marketisation. Ultimately, students are not customers, and teachers are not 'service providers'. The logic of student choice is also highly problematic and questionable. There are parts to most curricula in most subject fields that are less exciting than others. Yet covering these areas – so that the student is grounded and rounded in a subject or discipline – is essential for the integrity of the pedagogical enterprise. In the case of theology, it may well be argued that a seminarian, paying for their own education and formation, and taking responsibility for their 'career' in the church, may not like, say, the study of the early church, and should therefore not have to do this. But the omission of patristic education would leave the door open for some heresies or doctrinal errors to re-emerge in later preaching. Education, therefore, has to steer a line between specialisms and preferences, and covering all the necessary ground that is essential for the discipline and field. There will always be a tension between what is desirable and essential; but the marketisation of education risks capitulation to the unformed desires of those who have yet to learn. Bread and circus is entertaining and absorbing; but not necessarily educational. What marketisation has done to higher education is move it from something that served the common good to being a desirable commodity that the individual now purchases. In such a move, something fundamental has been lost; the market drives out the deeper rationales for education, namely the pursuit of wisdom, and the building up of our common life.

In terms of theological education, the stakes are much higher, since what is at issue is the cultivation of virtues, the education of desire, and the forming

---

[6]   See John H. Westerhoff, in Westerhoff (ed.) (1972), pp. 64–5): My conviction is that this hidden curriculum, this unconscious learning, is so important we cannot afford to let it remain unconscious. We need to look at the total learning experience of people and bring as many aspects of it into our conscious, deliberate, systematic, and sustained efforts. That is what it means to make learning education.

of character. Theological education cannot be about a set of tasks mastered, programmes undergone, doctrines merely understood. As Stanley Hauerwas pleas,

> It is not enough, in other words, that those called to the ministry refrain from or do certain things; it is necessary that they be the kind of persons, that they have the character, to sustain them in the ministry …. It is not enough that a person is not 'immoral'; neither should they be vain, proud, intemperate, cowardly, ingratiating, and unloving. Moreover, it must be asked whether a person exhibits the patience and hope so necessary to the ministry. For without patience and hope there is little chance a person will have the constancy to sustain him or her through the disappointments and betrayals so often involved in the ministry.
>
> I can think of no virtue more necessary to the ministry today than constancy. From the crucible of patience and hope comes the fidelity to task that makes the ministry not a burden but a joy. So finally we must ask of those in ministry whether they are capable of joy; if they are not they lack a character sufficient to their calling. For a person incapable of joy will lack the humour necessary for the self-knowledge that that character requires (1998, pp. 135, 143).

Market forces, and crude or instrumentalist attempts to measure, rationalise or control the formation of God's people – whether as laity or as clergy – miss the vital elements and essential gifts that theological education brings to the world of the seminary, and to the wider world. To be sure, instrumental and organisational pedagogies are in the ascendancy; but they are not neutral tools, and they carry with them aspirations and assumptions that have a profound topological bearing on the shape of the church, and on the contextual *terroir* in which the seed of the gospel is expected to grow and flourish. William C. Spohn articulates this by stating that spiritual practices in education

> … train the *affections*, the deeper emotions and dispositions. It is important to distinguish the affections from feelings. *Feelings* are transitory occurrences that may be genuine or not. The affections behind the Christian moral life are not simply spontaneous, like feelings. They can be tutored and evoked, for example, by the language of prayer or the rhythm of ritual. They can also be deliberately shaped by specific practices like hospitality, caring for the sick, sharing possessions, and forgiveness.... These practices are regular, concrete activities that tutor Christians in the ways of Christ. Embodied spirituality, therefore, links the content of the story of Jesus to lives that express the gospel. The practices of Christian spirituality provide pedagogical avenues by which, under the power of

God's spirit, the transformation called for by the Gospels is able to occur (1999, pp. 13–14, 41, 48–9).

This kind of pedagogical understanding of theological education for ministry recognises that change and development of character may be more important than the acquisition of skills. Unable to make the lengthy (indeed, perpetual) journey into the wisdom of God, theological education for ministry risked becoming thin and technique-orientated; satisfying 'criteria', and meeting milestones consisting of aims, objectives and outcomes. Pandering, in other words, to narrow, associational and organisational views of the church, and failing to comprehend the beauty and depth of God's purposes for a complex institution – an organic body that both formed and was formed by the people of God within it. And whilst the instrumental views of education, training and formation flourished, the actual ecclesial identity and density of the church suffered slowly, yet incrementally.[7] As Rowan Williams puts it

> Within and beyond all the debates about the detail of theological education and ministerial formation these days, the largest question still remains too often unanswered: what is the shape and unity of the Christian view of creation itself? What is the comprehensive story we tell? This is not a question about having more 'doctrine' in a course, but about how the whole process of ministerial education makes us natives in the landscape into which Jesus has invited us, and gives us some of the tools for celebrating how God has acted to introduce us into this place. We are not called on to give a bit more room to one module among others here, but to see this actual and present world joyfully and consistently in the light of God's being and doing, in the light of the Trinitarian life and the incarnation of the Word (2004, p. 13).

However formation is facilitated according to local need, of critical importance across the church is the safeguarding and enabling of institutions that can best serve the needs of the church for the formation of the clergy. These will need to

---

[7]   One could say that, characteristically, the majority of recent approaches to Anglican formation, training and education for ministry – at least in the Church of England – have tended to favour 'functionalist' rather than 'behaviourist' approaches. Much of this is 'applied' in both tone and orientation: blueprints, aims, objectives and anticipated outcomes. Most of these fail to read or understand the complexity of the church in its dense and extensive catholicity, or comprehend the kind of local variables that can be located in disparate parochial life. For a useful critique, see Denham Grierson, *Transforming a people of God*, Melbourne, Joint Board of Christian Education of Australia and New Zealand, 1984, pp. 14–27.

be places that foster not only education and training, but also those characteristics that pertain to institutions focused on formation, cultivating educational caritas, pedagogies of love and spaces for spiritual discernment, wisdom and intuition.[8] That will require continued investment in places where those clergy training for ministry can be engaged in the subtle modes of formation that are common to nearly all colleges and courses: worshipping, learning and eating together, and in so doing, being formed through implicit as well as explicit curricula. It will require continued investment in forms of training that continue to offer something quite distinctive.

Given these remarks how do we make informed and intelligent choices about the shaping of theological education and ministerial training in today's culture? Although skills (or ministerial arts – training) and knowledge (theology – education) may be regarded as the two chief curricular components of preparation for ordination, there is a another that is, arguably, a no less significant common denominator in Anglican theological colleges and courses: formation.

Formation

Because the shape of ecclesial life is to some extent determined by the contextual ground in which it is located, and as the socio-sacred synergies grow and develop over time, so we discover new patterns of polity emerging that could not have been easily foreseen. Moreover, these new and emerging patterns require careful explication and explanation. What seems apparent on the surface often requires some kind of deeper reading in order to understand something of the shape and dimensions of ecclesial life. Consider, for example, how capitalism and individualism shape ecclesial horizons. In the USA, church and state are separated. Religion is a vital component in public life, but the expectation of most Americans is that their faith is matter of personal choice. The entitlement to choose, to be free, and to not have the state interfering in one's personal religious beliefs, is seen as an inalienable right. The USA also has a complex history with respect to Socialism. Apart from a brief period in the first half of the twentieth century, socialist thinkers have made little headway in public life. Socialism is, in most American minds, only a heartbeat away from Communism. Both are regarded as forms of control that are interventionist and oppressive, and inimical to freedom – especially the freedom of the individual. Thus, the politics and culture of the nation play out in the multiplication and diversity of churches. Catholicity and control is replaced by consumerism. American highways are littered with experiments in

---

[8]   On this, see Nel Noddings and Paul Shore (1984), and Nel Noddings (2002).

ecclesial diversity – denominations and difference are expressions of the same market impulses that forged the nation's identity and continue to shape its political landscape.

The second largest economy in the world, however, has a different *terroir*, and its churches an entirely different topology. The churches of China are rooted in soil that is a fusion of both Communism and Capitalism, but both ultimately subordinate to the hegemony of Chinese identity, which stresses the collective over and against the individual. Whilst this is clearly a caricature of sorts, the contrast between the ecclesiologies of China and the USA are instructive for our purposes here. In the USA, the individual and the congregation are the primary repositories of power and order. In China, a form of state-ordered (some would say 'controlled') catholicity has been adopted, in order to prevent multiplication, denominational diversification, and, ultimately, individualism. Just as the roots of American ecclesial life lie in the American Revolution of 1776 (the right to self-determination, and non-interference), so the character of Chinese ecclesial life is embedded in history and identity.

Officially, there are just two kinds of church in China – Catholic and Protestant. The Roman Catholic Church is subject to some state control – especially in the choosing of its bishops. Whilst this has produced tensions with the Vatican, the Chinese Roman Catholic Church is undeniably recognizable in polity and practice, doctrine and orders. The Protestant Church of China – also known as The Three-Self Patriotic Movement – is a single body, rather than an ecumenical expression. The Three-Self Patriotic Movement (TSPM) was begun in 1951 by a Cantonese Christian named Wu Yao-tsung (1893–1979) and promoted a strategy of 'self-governance, self-support, and self-propagation' (hence 'Three-Self') in order to remove foreign influences from the Chinese churches and to assure the Communist government that the churches would be supportive of the newly established People's Republic of China under Mao. Wu's own background has a bearing on the emergence of a single Protestant body for China: he was a member of a Congregational church in China, worked for the YMCA, attended Union Theological Seminary in New York, and was a proponent of the social gospel throughout the 1920s. Mao's Cultural Revolution (1966–1976) repressed and banned active Christianity – even the TSPM. The Chinese government restored the TSPM in 1979, – partly in order to counter the trend of the 'unregistered' meetings of the growing House Church Movement, which are still subject to degrees of harassment and hounding.

What then of topology? How does the *terroir* of the USA and China shape ecclesial horizons? We have already noted that American assumptions about ecclesial life are shaped by those that condition culture more generally: the right to freedom, self-determination and individual choice. China, in contrast, is a nation where Communism and Consumerism are in a delicate relationship, but, I would argue, ultimately subordinate to a Chinese sense of oneness. There are five time zones in the USA, stretching from Hawaii to New York. China, which is just as large, has only one time zone. The United States of America rejoices in its diversity and many tongues. China has a single official language, and although regional differences and ethnicities are obvious, nonetheless seeks to speak and act as a single body. A unity of states is different, arguably, from a single country.

It is the hegemonic culture of China, therefore, that conditions the topology of Chinese Protestantism. The desire to be one supercedes the impulses towards diversity and choice. The TSPM expresses Chinese Protestant Christianity in two distinct ways: first, its accountability and relation to the state, and second, its purposeful unity and singleness over and against diversity and choice. Unity is prized above freedom; the common good and collective over and against individualism. This has an impact not only on Christianity, but also on other faiths too: the state 'recognises' those that build up common life or contribute to culture. But it has no need to take serious account of those that do not do seem to contribute in this way.[9]

In effect, Chinese culture has produced what the European Ecumenical Movement could not engineer – a visible oneness in which 'styles' of churchmanship (e.g., Anglican, Methodist, Baptist, etc.) are subordinated within a single Protestant movement of equality and mutual respect for otherness. True, critics will say that this is 'state-controlled' (but 'sanctioned' is arguably a better term), and that this has consequences for the Chinese House Church Movement – persecution even. However – and this is perhaps unfashionable to say – *all* unsanctioned movements in China are seen, not only by the government, but also by wider Chinese culture and society, as potentially inimical to Chinese oneness. The apparent threat posed by the House Church Movement lies not in its theology, or even, necessarily, in its witness, but in rather in what it represents in terms of individualism and consumerism, which are seen as the potentially deeper problems.

It is not easy to mediate between these *terroir*-type and topological differences. At a recent church service in Shanghai – in a TSPM church that was in fact a Methodist building before Mao came to power in 1951 – what was striking was the vibrancy of the worship, and the freedom of the worshippers. The normal service I attended (one of eight on offer that Sunday), were each packed with over a thousand worshippers. Each service had a 'style' (Anglican Choral Evensong was being offered at 6pm; something rather more Presbyterian in character earlier

---

[9]   For a fuller discussion, see Hu Yingqiang, 'Protestant Christianity and Chinese Religions: An Ecumenical Perspective', in *Chinese Theological Review*, vol. 22, pp. 25–41, 2010.

in the afternoon), yet the TSPM was a single and unified congregation. I sat next to some Americans, who were dumbfounded by the experience. After expressing surprise at the number of worshippers and the effervescence of the service (testimonies, prayers and exuberant singing), they stated that they had anticipated that the churches would be empty – 'as all state-controlled churches are, like the ones in Europe'. They then went on to surmise that the number of worshippers was probably an elaborate charade – something the government had engineered to impress the visiting tourists. Christianity, they said, could not be Christianity unless there was a full and complete right for the individual to exercise their freedom of choice. And as you could not do that in China, *ergo*, this could not be proper or authentic Christianity.

The conversation that followed represented a clash of cultures more than theologies. Of two languages unable to understand one another: an encounter of mutual incomprehension. The Americans assumed that any form of socialism or communist society suggested that the church-goers were likely to be closet atheists. The Chinese could not get especially excited about a synergy of individualism, consumerism and seemingly limitless freedom so beloved of the USA, even if it was the result of democracy, and that the Americans present espoused as 'God given'. Neither understood the *terroir* of the other; neither, therefore, could comprehend the ecclesial topologies of the other. The Americans could not conceive of a form of Christianity that challenged their own socio-cultural values. And a socialist, state-sanctioned, anti-consumerist and non-individualist form of faith did precisely that.[10]

So what does ministerial formation look like in relation to the complex *terroirs* the church finds itself immersed in, and the complex topological challenges it faces? Formation, as a process, refers both to the character and virtues of the individual, and to the nature of the institution that helps to infuse individuals with formational values. More often than not, such values are implicit rather than explicit. They will centre on the way the seminary, community, course or college practises common life; realising, for example, that how it eats, learns and worships together may be as important as the explicit curricular content.

Formation is a subtle (and some may say nebulous) concept, yet its presence as a key element in all forms of Anglican ordination training should not be overlooked. Anglicans, in their open and provisional ecclesiology, are often better able to express their theology by pointing to what their practices actually consist of

---

[10]   For a discussion of the shaping of Chinese Christianity in a developed world context, see Kwong, P. (2011), *Identity in Community: Toward a theological Agenda for the Hong Kong SAR* (Explorations in Intercultural Theology, volume 9), New Jersey, Rutgers University/Transaction Publishers.

rather than to their beliefs – although training and education remain closely linked. Yet it is the formational aspects of training that frequently shape the cadence, timbre and character of believing and practising.[11]

So, from the outset, some kind of deep comprehension and wisdom as to what kind of *body* one is serving is required. The shape of training will be rooted in prior theological and ecclesiological visions. In turn, they will be shaped by the perceived needs and challenges of the prevailing culture and context that the minister is immersed in.[12] Reading and discerning culture, therefore, becomes a key task in ecclesiology. Unless there is understanding of the ground – the *terroir* – that shapes the fecundity of the seed, it is likely that the church will continue to struggle in comprehending its life and witness. Ideologically-formed blueprint ecclesiologies will continue to be produced that purport to address the present and shape the future of the church. But if the topological challenges that face the church are not also understood and weighed, such initiatives will struggle to succeed. Indeed, such ventures, though well-intended, and seeking to inspire, may ultimately be more inimical to the body of Christ.

Vocation

Given these remarks, we now turn to the nature of vocation – and in particular to consider the nature of leadership in the church. Again, the focus is on Anglican polity, although most of the comments in this brief section will have a putative reach across to other ecclesial traditions. The Anglican church is not unique in struggling to define and clarify what it needs from its church leaders, and what kind of church it aspires to be: it is typical in our culture of late modernity – replete with secularism and pluralism – many denominations have sought to consolidate and clarify their identity within an era of considerable cultural fluidity. It cannot be surprising that recent Anglican theology has invested more time and energy in deliberating on and defining episcopacy than any other generation. Indeed, and understandably, there have arguably been more deliberations on the nature, function and identity of episcopacy in the twentieth century than all those that

---

[11]   The German term *Bildung* is often regarded as an equivalent, or perhaps stronger term, for defining formation. The term dates to 16th century Pietistic theology, according to which, the devout Christian should seek to cultivate (*Bildung*) their gifts, competencies and dispositions according to the image of God.

[12]   See M. Percy, 'Sacred Sagacity: Formation and Training for Ministry in a Church of England Seminary', *The Anglican Theological Review*, vol. 90, Spring 2008, pp. 285–96.

were penned from the reformation to the end of the nineteenth century. So there appears to be no escaping questions of task, role and identity.[13]

But what, if anything, is the generic *terroir* of the Church of England? One key insight here is to recognise that the church is an institution, rather than an organisation. The distinction between an organisation and institution is a classic sociological paradigm.[14] Philip Selznick, argues that organizations exist for utilitarian purposes, and when they are fulfilled, the organisation may become expendable. Institutions, in contrast, are 'natural communities' with historic roots that are embedded in the fabric of society. They incorporate various groups that may contest each other, the institution, values and the like. Clearly, in Selznick's thinking, a church is an institution, requiring leadership, not mere management. So the church, when treated like an organisation, can only be managed. And such management will, inevitably, be somewhat deficient, since the church is an institution in which only certain types of management will be possible.

Paul Avis puts it quite sharply when he states that 'If the gospels are any indication, Jesus Christ showed scant regard for modern management wisdom … he was not looking for managers, but for learners and leaders – disciples and apostles' (1992, p. 96). Yet, as Avis reminds us, many theories of leadership seem to be 'unfashionable' in the church. There is a certain kind of squeamishness around the urgent ecclesiological and hermeneutical task that may face the church in this respect. Because bishops are 'given' to the church, ideally having the necessary Christian character to occupy the role (e.g., sacrifice, commitment, exemplary discipleship; or perhaps the characteristics listed in 1 Tim. 3: 1–7; or the ordinal, etc.), and are in one sense there by grace rather than through merit, there is a characteristic reticence in overly prescribing the attributes needed for the role. Avis suggests that 'leadership demands outstanding intellectual ability and outstanding intellectual application' (1992, p. 97), which of course on one level is true – but it is arguably not always right for the church.[15]

---

[13] See M. Percy (2009), p. 148. One thinks immediately of Kenneth Kirk's *The Apostolic Ministry* (1946); or more recent reports that have concentrated on senior leadership or episcopacy in relation to contemporary organisational issues: see, for example, *Resourcing Bishops* (London, Church House Publishing, 2001); *Working as One Body (The Turnbull Report)*, 1996, and *Talent and Calling (The Pilling Report)*, 2007.

[14] See Philip Selznick (1957). (Cf. Avis, 1992, pp. 107ff).

[15] Avis also considers the bishops as a collation of leadership in the church. Drawing on Medhurst and Moyser (1988), Avis points out that bishops and archbishops are inevitably drawn into irenic behaviour patterns (as peacemakers and reconcilers, etc.), but that this may risk 'cloaking sullen acquiescence' or mask alienation and its longer-term consequences. Thus, Avis argues, 'the occasional (intellectual) gadfly among the bishops to

We might go further here, and suggest that the fundamental issue for the Church of England is not so much identifying and enabling its leaders, but beginning with a prior exercise, namely clarifying identity. Leading a diocese, as a bishop, of course requires some understanding of a theology of episcopal orders, with imagination, vision and courage, together with other traits and gifts in leadership that will enable the individual to operate well in public life, and engage with all the many congregations and parishes in his or her care. But the complex task of episcopal leadership also requires a deep understanding of what a diocese is. It has organisational aspects to it; but is primarily an institution. It speaks a language of vision and aspiration; but much of the role is about managing multiple and complex needs, including many anxieties.

Of course, there is no 'answer' to the vast majority of these, so the episcopal task is to 'hold' the people of God. Or, put in more secular idiom, leading by managing of concerns, issues and tasks. But there are ironies here too. Dioceses often talk about 'structures', 'systems' and 'processes' as though these things actually exist; but forgetting, in fact, that this language is mostly in the realm of metaphor, and refers to a more idealised construction of reality. The socio-ecclesial imaginary projects a kind of 'ideal' organisation in which everything is ordered, clear, accountable and can be rationalised. In truth, most dioceses do not have much in the way of actual systems, processes or structures. The church is, rather, a body of people; a somewhat inchoate collation of relationships, with most people giving their time and energy voluntarily, and therefore without the usual bonds of obligation (i.e., not compulsory) that one might expect within an organisation. The church is primarily an institution. So there are limits to the amount of organisational theory or practice it will comprehend or tolerate – despite the fact that many clergy now find themselves wrestling with more and more of the attributes of organisational ethos: aims, objectives, outcomes, and so forth.

A diocese is, manifestly, not a conglomerate organisation– or at least that is not how it is experienced by most who identify with a diocese.[16] A diocese is, rather, agglomerate in nature: a bundle of competing convictions; a multiplicity of congregations, parishes, organisations, expectations and so forth. 'Leading' an agglomeration – especially one that is rooted in institutional identity rather than organisational in character – is highly complex, and requires the leader to hold together a number of roles and perform a number of tasks, which will, at times, place the person at odds with themselves, the body or person they are ministering to or with, and therefore seemingly lack the very constancy of which we spoke

---

ask the awkward questions and to bring conflicts into the open' (p. 100) is to be encouraged within the broader composition of collective Episcopal leadership.

[16]   Except, of course, for fiscal, legal and related purposes.

earlier. But unless the actuality of the diocese is discerned and understood, with its specific *terroir* and topology, it will prove difficult to lead.

Conclusion

Ultimately, this chapter is an invitation to consider more deeply the variety of ways in which culture and context shape the church. Class, race, gender, ethnicity, culture and local history all form the crucible in which the church is refined. And until the social conditions and forms of ecclesial life are understood, it is hard for theological vision, or strategies of various kinds, to gain significant purchase within the body that they seek to re-shape and recalibrate.

It is for these reasons, perhaps, that many who embark upon the course of episcopal leadership quickly find themselves in managing mode – but all the while cloaked in the rhetoric of leadership. And, perhaps more problematically, administering sedatives and stimulants in equal measures; pacifying and animating simultaneously. There is, of course, no shortcut to growth; visionary leadership or new, revolutionary formulae do not easily work in agglomerate bodies. To try to lead like this is to potentially expose the body to the risk of ecclesial or missiological steroids: but muscle and mass quickly gained do have serious medium- and long-term consequences. As many leaders have learnt in the church, the best kinds of growth are of the slow, deep and steady kind – and those same leaders often possess the humility and wisdom to know that they will seldom see the fruits of their labour. But their successors might.

In view of this, Avis suggests that leadership requires a fundamental reconciliation of its roles and tasks. First, it has a symbolic role. In ecclesiological terms, the leader is a primary bearer of the institution's values, as well as someone to inspire faith in the common purposes of the institution. Naturally, this means that leaders will need to be attentive to the projections and unconscious assumptions that are placed upon the role by those within the institution. Second, the leader's priority is to focus the energies of the institution on its primary tasks. This may require the articulation of vision, identifying policies, exploring and implementing strategies, and engaging in tactics. Third, the leader will need to be a problem-solver. This requires the wisdom to distinguish between problems and dilemmas (the latter cannot be solved, usually – they express an endemic tension in the institution); determination to overcome contextual, environmental or institutional issues that inhibit the institution from flourishing; and identification of those factors that need addressing and the issues that need resolving. Of particular concern to Avis is the 'cognitive myopia' that can develop within institutions: 'responding only to the immediate, the visible, the palpable, rather than searching for the deeper, long-term causes and attempting to deal with them'.[17] So vision remains the issue. But not merely in terms of the fruits of our imaginations, whether they are illusory or delusory, or revolutionary. Vision is, ultimately, about clear sight: seeing not only what is right in front of you, but also being able to see what might be some way ahead; and perhaps what might be even beyond that.

---

[17] Avis (1992), pp. 107–18.

Chapter 9

Communion: Faith, Hope and Charity

One of the more subtle temptations for the church – faced with pluralism, yet equally resisting a resort to fundamentalism or relativism – is to find solace in privatisation and specialisation. To become so bound up in itself that its language, practices and rubrics begin to take on the air of a body that unintentionally excludes the very people and communities it is for. Yet mission is 'not simply the self-propagation of the church by the putting forth of its power which inheres in its life', as Lesslie Newbigin argued (1978, pp. 62–3). To accept that picture, suggested Newbigin, would be to sanction an appalling distortion of mission. Mission is not just something the church does, but is something, rather, that the Spirit does, which changes both the church and the world. The initial legacy of Jesus to his disciples was not a book, creed, system of thought or rule of life, but a visible community. The community did not develop around an idea or practice; rather, the ideas and practices developed out of a new community – and it was, initially, gradual and provisional. It took time to take shape; and it still takes time to take shape. It is never full or complete (Newbigin, 1953, p. 32). Some years ago I was asked to fill in a questionnaire for a survey organised by some local schoolchildren. One question was this: 'what is the church?' My answer was as follows:

Partly a building
Partly people
Partly an ideal
Partly complete

The idea of partiality to describe the church is fascinating, especially when compared to the Kingdom of God that might be glimpsed on the other side: 'the heavenly city, coming down like a bride, complete ...'; or, 'in my father's house there are many rooms ...'; so no need for extensions, then. It is enough; it is finished. But as though we need reminding, we as a people are not; we remain incomplete. We await the fullness promised – 'when we shall no longer know in part, but full ... and see face to face'. Neither is our church ever the finished product. And yet God accepts us, and continually beckons us to his house – the heavenly place where there is room for all.

Philip Sheldrake states that a 'theology of place must maintain a balance between God's revelation in the particular and a sense that God's place ultimately escapes the boundaries of the localised' (2001, p. 30). He argues that God in Jesus becomes committed to and redeems all humanity, including the places that are marginal, excluded and unacceptably 'other' to humanity. The very idea of body of Christ is about God remaining – dwelling with us – such that we are always in, under and surrounded by the grace of God, and there is no space and place that God is not in and over.

As we noted earlier, the sacred canopy identified by Berger is struggling to retain its' place and power in late-modernity. It is perhaps no longer intact, at least in terms of providing a shared over-arching meta-narrative. It arguably persists in only two senses. First, as that which individuals may continue to interpret, but not necessarily with any shared agreement on ultimate meaning. Second, as a micro-canopy that need only work for the subscribing or ascribing individual or group, so does not necessarily require a shared understanding in order to acquire its validation. The prevalent individualism of late-capitalism and postmodernity ensures that any claim for a sacred canopy is prey to the forces of pluralism, relativism and consumerism. Moreover, a sacred canopy that has lost sight of its religious origins and aspiration for commonly held stories, together with forms of authority and shared values, will surely cease to be an overa-arching canopy that can be sustained for our age. This applies to capitalism as much as it might to religion.

Which is why, to help counter this dynamic, the ecclesial canopy, and for which we have been arguing is both a calling of the church, as well as a theological and metaphysical description of God being Lord over all. Where we are rooted and found, God is also to be encountered in, around, over and amongst us. As Isaiah proclaims, 'He sits enthroned above the circle of the earth, and its people are like grasshoppers. He stretches out the heavens like a canopy, and spreads them out like a tent to live in' (Isaiah 40: 22). This space, then, as an embodiment of the life and manifesto of Jesus, is a place of faith, hope and charity. And in its totality, it is as comprehensive and inclusive as God's saving plan for humanity already is. This is the place for all; the space that seeks to leave no-one excluded or marginalised.

Speaking of room for all, we remember, too, that this is the vision behind what it means to be a parish church. The word 'parish' is never used in the New Testament, but it is, interestingly, an ancient Greek word, which literally means 'those outside the house': not the insiders, but the outsiders. The Greeks used it to refer to the areas of a city where the non-citizens lived – those with few rights, who were non-Greeks, and therefore excluded. So a parish church, in an ideal world, is not an exclusive place, but an inclusive place for the local stranger; for those who don't know the way, the truth and the life; for those who don't know they have a place in the heart of God, and who are ignorant of their room reservation in heaven. It is the inside place for the outsider; the only club that exists for non-members, as William Temple once quipped.

The notion of an ecclesial canopy, although inviting, is not without its complexities. In the Introduction, we drew attention to John Milbank's essay 'On Complex Space' (1997), which, like much of his work, is substantially attractive in many respects, but less so in terms of style, tone and ethos. Milbank obviously believes in the inevitability of complex social space, but has consistently sought to out-narrate liberal or secular perpetrations of diversity and difference over and against a universal or catholic understanding of society. I have some sympathy with him here. For example, our local comprehensive school – now here is a complex space replete with competing interests and ideologies – has a fairly functional reception area for receiving visitors. On the walls one can see recent artwork from pupils, photographs of recent school music and drama productions, and sports activities. The statement of school beliefs and values is, however, a more permanent feature of such displays. What does the school articulate here? Respect for all; no bullying; and recycling to care for our planet. The complexity of social space here, and the overlapping and competing religious identities present in the school, has, in other words, reduced the value and belief systems to the blandest set of principles possible.

But this is only a caricature of 'the poverty of Niebuhrianism', as Milbank might call it (1997, pp. 233–56). The kind of ecclesial canopy that I have sought to articulate need not capitulate to the basest, most vapid kinds of liberalism. On the contrary, the dynamics of faith, hope and charity – fused with a deep Christian vision for both generosity and the intelligent, articulate and passionate expression of apologetics – can infuse the space and the canopy with a richness that can glory in the social variegation that we find ourselves immersed in. In the midst of considerable diversity, there is simply no need to collapse into a kind of flaccid reductionism. Rather, the task of theology and the church is to seek the overlapping areas of consensus; work honestly at the differences; and also seek to live with and under a canopy of faith that provides shelter; a sense of both openness and containment; identity and capaciousness. The church, I think, can live like this, and offer this. An ecclesial canopy can indeed provide the necessary and adequate resources for holding together diversity, and maintaining unity, through the articulation and practice of values, and the consistent witness to the transformative narratives that have hitherto shaped society.

It is in precisely this vein that Daniel Izuzquiza's *Rooted in Jesus Christ: Toward a Radical Ecclesiology* (2009) sets out to shape a spirituality of ecclesiology rooted in a more contemporary catholic theology. Engaging with the Radical Orthodox

School of theology and writers such as Milbank,[1] Izuzquiza acknowledges that the church has suffered much in contemporary culture through secular reasoning, becoming, in effect, a private, marginal and compressed space within an over-arching secularist sphere. A social construction of reality, if you will, in which the secular domain is an imagined meta-space, into which religion falls as a mere 'sub-product' – a private set of beliefs and practices that are merely part of a larger set of values and more convincing, shared meta-narratives. Milbank, of course, rejects this construction of reality, and proposes a theology that is rooted in creation and providence, which then re-locates the secular within the paradigm of theology, rather than being an emancipation from it.

Izuzquiza, whilst critical of aspects of Milbank's theological approach (and especially his *style* of argument – see pp. 46–7), clearly shares some common concerns. Izuzquiza finds Milbank's interpretation of secularisation problematic; his critique of positivism (and especially the status of the social sciences) overbearing; and the political implications of his theology imperialist, noting here the powerful reassertion of a superior pre-modern Christianity in a postmodern context. Izuzquiza rightly identifies Milbank's ecclesiology as a delicate fusion of conservatism and socialism, and of nouveau-Anabaptist communitarian polity flecked with strong high-church and Anglo-Catholic accents. He does not find this adequate, and suggests that it remains strangely abstract and disembodied as a vision. Instead, Izuzquiza proposes a radical ecclesiology that is rooted in a theology of the body of Christ:

> The body of Christ speaks about communion, inclusive relations, unconditional welcoming, union-in-difference, incorporation in a common reality. The body of Christ talks about the Eucharist, about our Lord Jesus and his healings, the cosmic Christ and the final recapitulation of every body, caress, hug, and tear of human history. The body of Christ builds up the church as a real and visible alternative to the system. The body of Christ shows that another world is actually possible … (Izuzquiza, 2009, p. 109).

Thus, and under this capacious ecclesial canopy, there will be cooperatives, credit unions, houses of hospitality, farming communes and shelters for the homeless. This place, in other words, will be the specific practice of Christian space – the kingdom of God in action. Not a utopia, of course; but quite possibly a monastery, convent, church or faithful gathering that is rooted and grounded in the Christian story, and knows that under the sacred canopy, God sees all. No sparrow

---

[1]   See, especially, John Milbank (1990).

falls to the ground without God seeing; the hairs of our head are numbered; all desires known, the thoughts of our hearts weighed, and no secrets hidden.

There is some sense, then, in which Izuzquiza is articulating a vision that is resonant with the *Rule of St Benedict* – the ordering of community life as a school for the Lord's service, promoting hospitality, hope, faith and charity. Izuzquiza roots his ecclesial vision in a rich reading of Paul's notion of the body of Christ, which, he argues, consists of four inter-related ideas: the bread, Christ's body, the church and the body of the Christian. The personal and communitarian aspects are therefore richly related, and irreducible. For Paul, therefore, there is no distinction between private and public, or corporate and individual. The term, like the vision, is comprehensive (p. 139). Closely related to these four inter-related ideas are four models of the church. First, a purity system (anthropological), in which differences and defilement are named, challenged and overcome. Second, it is a physical space (archaeological), in which the physical plant becomes the site of practice for God's kingdom, with a focus on celebration and sharing. Third, it is an economic programme, including acts of hospitality, alms-giving and the redistribution of wealth. Fourth, it is a political alternative to the prevailing powers and authorities, in which Jews, gentiles, men and women, slave and free can co-exist in mutual love and interdependence.

For Izuzquiza, the key to understanding the body of Christ is rooted in the inter-relationships that now form a new social reality. Indeed, the social-sacramental life of the church is formed in the bread, Christ's body, the church and the body of the Christian. A deep experience of the body of Christ will be one without division (though it may have much diversity), of unity (though this is not the same as uniformity), of common purpose (though there are varieties of gifts), which leads to a truly deep social transformation. When this occurs, the body of Christ cannot be broken (by which we mean atomised), and his power limited, since a life rooted in Jesus Christ will have powerful and radical consequences in all areas of reality (pp. 138–52). This is the body of Christ in both its corporeal reality and its mystical state: 'the ecclesiology of the church as (a) radical sacrament' (p. 160). As Izuzquiza says,

> … Ecclesial communion generates social communion. A life rooted in Jesus Christ means a radical transformation of all reality. Eucharistic dynamism embraces each Christian's personal life. It embraces ecclesial life. It embraces the world's life. United to Jesus Christ, we believers are called to be the body of Christ, to be a sacrament of communion and liberation for the life of the world (2009, p. 165).

But what might this mean more practically? Now, in our final section we turn to work this through the context of Anglican belief and practice.

Anglicanism – the Communion as a Charitable Canopy

The idea of the Anglican Communion as a Big Tent, or as a capacious space which all may inhabit, has a long an august history in the practice of polity, ecclesiology and the spirituality of the church. Yet in times of crisis, that sense of space can quickly evaporate. What was previously experienced as gracious and capacious can quickly become licence and disconnectedness. Atomisation follows, accompanied by a sense of compression and alienation. Yet the recovery of this sense of God-given space and grace lies at the heart of the Communion, and having the wisdom and patience to wait for its re-emergence will undoubtedly serve the church well. Oliver O'Donovan contends that waiting and striving for this moment will ultimately serve the church, and the gospel, well:

> There are no guarantees. There never are in the Christian life. But that is not a reason not to try. And seriously trying means being seriously patient. Anyone who thinks that resolutions can be reached in one leap without mutual long exploration, probing, challenge, and clarification has not yet understood the nature of the riddle that the ironic fairy of history has posed for us in our time (O'Donovan, 2008, p. 119).

If the Lambeth Conference can be said to have passed off relatively peacefully in 2008, the years since then (not many of them, granted), seem to have been a little less kind to the Communion. Debates on sexuality have returned to haunt the Instruments of Unity and the Provinces; and the Church of England has had some turbulent debates on women bishops. Moreover, there seems to be no sign of these difficulties disappearing. The fractious nature of the debates appears to be as polarising as before, and the Communion under some strain and duress. Writing almost half a century ago, Stephen Bayne observed that

> ... the Church of England, alone among the churches of the Anglican Communion, has its unity given to it. That unity is given from the outside. It is given by the establishment of the church, by the formal identity of the church and the nation. The Church of England does not need to be held together by the voluntary loyalty of its members ... [yet] this is not an unmixed blessing. But it has succeeded in giving to the Church of England – and in turn, to all the rest of the churches of our Communion – an extraordinary liberality of spirit and

gentleness of mind, which tolerates wide differences of opinion and variations in theological outlook, within the working unity of the Catholic church of the land ... this is one of the most precious gifts. And I rejoice to find it transplanted ... to North America, to Japan, to Central Africa, to Brazil, to any other part of the world you can mention. It was given to the Church of England, because of its hopes and necessities as a national church, to discover a profound secret of unity – that the unity of the church does not consist of people thinking alike but in people acting together ... (Bayne, 1964, p. 181).

There is nothing, perhaps, remarkable about such sentiments; except, perhaps, to note two profound changes in recent times. The first is that the Church of England is moving rapidly towards a culture where it is 'held together by the voluntary loyalty of its members'. And second, and linked to this, like-mindedness becomes a more important characteristic in such institutions, which paves the way for narrower and more sectarian modes of ecclesial existence.

The contrast between European and American religion is an important one. In the USA, it is the congregation rather than the parish that is the core unit of religious life. Congregations are more flexible than parishes: they have the capacity to migrate geographically, and can also mutate socially, allowing them to respond to changing needs more easily than parishes. Congregations do belong to denominations (rather than state churches); but they also tend to sit light to denominational affiliation, since the primary unit of power and authority is the local congregation. So American religious life gravitates towards the local and the individual; and European religious life to the collective and national. The right to a degree of 'self-determination' in ecclesial polity is something few Europeans imagine; but something most Americans assume.

Whilst acknowledging these cultural shifts and tensions, and their impact on the wider Communion, I nonetheless see no reason to despair at this juncture. Our hope, after all, is not rooted in political compromise, but in the gospel. It is grounded in the virtues and character that all Christians are called to. Which is why, I suspect, we shall rediscover as a Communion something deeper in our calling to develop bonds of affection, and in the kind of story-swapping and listening that is encouraged through the ongoing Indaba process. The content of the stories and experiences exchanged and reflected upon in the Indaba process is, arguably, not the issue for Anglicans.

Rather, the key question is, can we listen to one another attentively, and patiently – mindful that this is God's time, God's church and God's future – and not ours to possess and shape to suit our own requirements and proclivities. Can we, as a mature Communion, develop levels of intellectual and emotional composure – fashioning a deeper kind of ecclesial intelligence – that comprehends the subtle relationships between content and mood, style and substance, the now and the not-yet? Can we, as a Communion, place our trust in God for each other, and commit to acting together for the sake of the gospel and God's kingdom, even if we know we cannot be like-minded? I strongly suspect that the Anglican Communion will, through patience, forbearance, courage (and perhaps a little fear), rediscover its bonds and unity, even amidst its differences.

This will also mean a more charitable understanding of conflict in the life of the Communion. Too often, we assume that conflict is a sign of weakness; that difficult arguments point to eventual fragmentation. Yet it need not be so. The history of the Christian church rests in contending for creeds, articles of faith, the canon of scripture and actual doctrines that began their life in the most acrimonious of debates. Luis Bermejo SJ argues that there are four stages to a cyclical process in ecclesial life (*The Spirit of Life*, 1989): communication, conflict, consensus and finally Communion. Issues in the Anglican Communion tend to get refracted through this four-fold process. Bermejo argues that this is how the Holy Spirit moves the church – it is not the case that only the last of these stages is 'spiritual'. The Holy Spirit can also be manifested in gifts and fruits: tested, pruned and refined in conflict. Yet the problem remains: the catholicity of Anglicanism is more geographical than theological. That said, Anglicans need not fear the arguments that appear to divide, or their causes and consequences. Rather, they should see that conflict is a phase of life in the church in which the Holy Spirit moves. Indeed, the Spirit is present in the conflict; it is part of the gestation of the church. And, indeed, its vibrancy, with occasional ruptures, may in fact be a sign of maturity, rather than problematic.

Correspondingly, this can point us to the imperative of continuous scriptural reasoning for the church – a process of reading the bible together, recognising that the diversity of scriptures (note the plural) is where we discover both our unity and diversity, and our plurality and commonality. This means waiting upon the Lord together, sitting under the word of God together, and continuing to share in the common sacramental life that God has given us:

> The book, the Bible reveals the self-revealing God along with the way the world is, the way life is, the way we are. We need to know the lay of the land that we are living in. We need to know what is involved in this Country of the Trinity, the world of God's creating and salvation and blessing .... The text is not words to be studied in a library but a voice to be believed, love and adored in workplace and playground, on the streets and in the kitchen. Receptivity is required .... Spiritual theology, using Scripture as text, does not present us with a moral code and tell us to 'live up to this'; nor does it set out a system of doctrine and say

'think like this and you will live well'. The biblical way is to tell a story and invite us to live like this (Peterson, 2006, p. 113).

The Anglican Communion manifestly lives under the scriptures; they are what help shape and form the ecclesial canopy. By continuing to enter into and under the word that God has given us, the body of Christ is nourished and transformed by new understandings. Yet even when these do not immediately emerge, the mode and manners of sharing and being together have a deep impact on the formation of our common life. Sometimes, living righteously is more important than being right. Being good and charitable more important than having our perspective vindicated. Embodying faith, hope and love more of a witness to the Truth than winning a debate.

Indeed, one might profit further from pondering and praying with George Herbert's poem, 'The Holy Scriptures' (parts 1 and 2), and taken from *The Temple* (1633).

Oh Book! infinite sweetnesse! let my heart
    Suck ev'ry letter, and a hony gain,
    Precious for any grief in any part;
To cleare the breast, to mollifie all pain.
Thou art all health, health thriving till it make
    A full eternitie: thou art a masse
    Of strange delights, where we may wish & take.
Ladies, look here; this is the thankfull glasse,
That mends the lookers eyes: this is the well
    That washes what it shows. Who can indeare
    Thy praise too much? thou art heav'ns Lidger here,
Working against the states of death and hell.
    Thou art joyes handsell: heav'n lies flat in thee,
    Subject to ev'ry mounters bended knee.

II

Oh that I knew how all thy lights combine,
    And the configurations of their glorie!
    Seeing not onely how each verse doth shine,
But all the constellations of the storie.
This verse marks that, and both do make a motion
    Unto a third, that ten leaves off doth lie:
    Then as dispersed herbs do watch a potion,

These three make up some Christians destinie:
Such are thy secrets, which my life makes good,
    And comments on thee: for in ev'ry thing
    Thy words do finde me out, & parallels bring,
And in another make me understood.
    Starres are poore books, & oftentimes do misse:
    This book of starres lights to eternall blisse.

Herbert's poem provides an instructive and meditative framework for Anglicans contemplating their common identity and authority. First, we note that Herbert (properly) refers to 'scriptures' – the Bible is a collation of sacred texts, not one single book. It has both a unity and a plurality. Herbert also expresses the different ways that scriptures can be read – some verses are to be sucked for their sweetness; others mend and heal as we look into them; others refresh deeply; others instruct, or convict. Scriptures are to be approached with reverence, for God speaks through them and to us.

It is the second stanza, however, where Herbert offers the idea of scriptures as a canopy – 'starres lights' in the heavens – that again suggests the idea of a unity and plurality. One canopy, but many lights; one heaven, but many stars that shine; one sky, but many constellations. As Herbert says, each verse makes a motion to another – there is an intricate inter-connectedness in it all:

Oh that I knew how all thy lights combine,
And the configurations of their glorie!

Herbert's vision for his church is rooted in his understanding of scripture. If the scriptures are like stars within a heavenly canopy, then the church too, can reflect this sacred canopy. To live and reason scripturally is to see the connections between the constellations, and to own before God that the canopy we sit under is more than we can ever take in.

Charity, then – as an ecclesiological characteristic – is both a value and a virtue. In contemporary culture, we are often tempted to view charity with mild pity; it comprises gifts and donations that mend gaps that should otherwise not be there. Giving to charity is, all too often, an exercise which prompts either parting with loose change; or perhaps something more planned and systematic. Yet charity, properly understood, is something much richer and deeper than this, and should form one of the well-springs that sustains the church; or constellations that guide it. The word has roots in the Latin term 'caritas' – 'costly esteem and affection' – there is a warmth and tenderness to charity. It is a word that resonates with 'cherishing' and 'benevolence'; the one who is charitable is the one who sees the other as dear and valued – esteeming highly, and loving. There is diligence and duty here, to be sure; but also a deep and compassionate love for the other that is Christianity at its best. Wycliffe used the word 'charity' in his translation of I Corinthians 13 in order to (slightly) draw out the contrast with love; charity is active, and it also has a mood – a cadence and timbre, if you will. It is not just an act, but a tone of engagement.

In the same vein, hope is a leap[2] in expectation; it is a wish, dream and anticipation of what is to come. Just as faith is trust, confidence, reliance; and the living out of what is believed. To be charitable, ultimately, and to live charitably, is to both imagine and see the world benevolently and mercifully – as God might see it. This not, I must stress, a new vision for pastoral theology. The idea of faith, hope and charity being the very foundations for an attentive, loving, compassionate pastoral theology should not surprise us. And that such love and compassion have political implications – for society and ecclesial polity – will hardly be news. William Paley, in a treatise on morality from 1785, states that

> I use the term Charity neither in the common sense of bounty to the poor, nor in St Paul's sense of benevolence to all mankind: but I apply it at present, in a sense more commodious to my purpose, … charity [is] promoting the happiness of our inferiors. Charity, in this sense I take to be the principal province of virtue and religion: for, whilst worldly prudence will direct our behaviour towards our superiors and politeness to our equals, there is little to set beside the consideration of duty, or an habitual humanity which comes into the place of consideration, to produce conduct towards those who are beneath us, and dependent on us … (Paley, *The Principles of Moral and Political Philosophy* [1785]. Foreword by D.L. Le Mahieu (2002, p. 12).

But here, charity is not a gift, as we have been describing it. It is a duty, and conferred on those 'who are beneath us'. Yet true charity would be a form of gift. It would be the giving of something that could be kept or, in turn, given away – so the gift is significant in scale and scope. And the gift should also, to be a true gift, raise the status of the recipient – otherwise it is merely a distraction or some sort of sop. Charity should ultimately dissolve social barriers and boundaries, not perpetuate them, or merely try to negotiate difference, without challenging divisive diversities rooted in class, wealth and other forms of discrimination.

Lest this sound too abstract, we may do well to remember that the ministry of Jesus is rooted in God's charity – a radical commitment to challenging

---

[2] Some etymologists suggest that hoping is indeed connected to hopping: leaping forward.

divisions, and bringing about forms of equality that amounted to a nascent form of politically-led pastoral theology. The early Christian church took this to heart, and extended the articulation and practice of the body of Christ to include the widows and orphans, gentiles, slaves, women, children and foreigners. The call was for universal brotherhood. The reason for driving out the money-changers in the temple was a fundamental expression of his rejection of a 'gifts-for-God' spiritual economy. Charity, for Jesus, was freedom from any kind of bondage – and all with equal access to his Heavenly Father. Later, Christians in the Middle Ages, like Bernard of Clairvaux, would take this message to heart, and practise the richness of their relationship with God through a deep solidarity with the poor.

Alms were there to empower and enable, not merely to provide additional help and support but with no prospect of deliverance from economic or social bondage. Martin of Tours (died 397) is one of the early saints who are defined by a charity that is both politically radical and also daring in its implication for ecclesial polity. Martin, a serving solider in the Imperial Roman army, had a vision of a cold and naked beggar. In his vision, he cuts his cloak in half, and gives half to the beggar. In a subsequent vision, he sees Christ wearing the same cloak, rejoicing in the gift. Martin, in serving the beggar, has served God. His charity is one that Christ recognises, and affirms. At the same time, it appears that Martin has understood from the outset that charity is not simply being moved to act through pity. It is also passion – dear and costly love for, and compassion for, the other. Charity is a fusion of pity, passion and compassion. It is something well beyond filling in the gaps; it is an extravagant, excessive passion for equality. It is a practice, not a theory.

The concept of practice has recently received significant interest in organisational circles through the work of Etienne Wenger. Wenger analysed workplace habits, and then attempted to develop a social theory of learning. It is this that gave birth to the concept of communities of practice, which Wenger defines as '... groups of people who share a concern or a passion for something they do and learn how to do it better as they interact regularly' (Wenger, 1998).[3] Even if participants in such communities are innocent of their membership and unaware of their practices, the very idea of

> a concept of practice includes both the explicit and tacit. It includes what is said and what is left unsaid: but is represented and what is assumed. It includes the language, tools, documents, images, symbols, well-defined roles, specified criteria, codified procedures, regulations, and contracts that various practices make explicit for a variety of purposes. But it also includes all the implicit relations, tacit conventions, subtle cues, untold rules of thumb, recognisable

---

[3]   See also Etienne Wenger, McDermot and Snyder (2002).

institutions, specific perceptions, well-tuned sensitivities, embodied understandings, underlying assumptions, and shared worldviews. Most of these may never be articulated, yet their unmistakable signs of membership in communities of practice are crucial to the success of the enterprises (Wenger, 1998, p. 47).

Wenger sees one of the primary functions of communities of practice as the formation of identity. And identity, according to Wenger is negotiated through the shared membership of social communities, and that '... practice defines a community through three dimensions: mutual engagement, a joint enterprise, and a shared repertoire' (p. 152). His approach remains realistic throughout – identity is not something we construct in our heads intellectually or in our imagination, but rather something that is constructed by our day-to-day practices.

In terms of the practice and identity of the church, the trinity of faith, hope and charity is complex. The disciples do not easily 'read' the nuance of what is being asked of the church by Christ. Identity and practice are bound up in complex gestures, symbols and inferences. Perhaps an obvious example of this is when Jesus begins to prepare his body for crucifixion and burial, and is anointed with precious oil by a woman. John 12: 1–8 names the woman as Mary, and the text assumes her to be Mary, a sister to Lazarus, as the text also identifies her sister as Martha. However, the iconography of the woman's act has traditionally been associated with Mary Magdalene, even though there is no biblical text identifying her as such. According to the Mark 14: 3 the perfume in his account was pure and expensive. Many biblical commentators assume that this story occurs only a few days before the crucifixion, due to the numerous events that followed in Luke's gospel. This seems the most logical timing to me, not least because of the discourse that follows the complaint from the disciples that the oil could have been sold, and the money put to better use to feed the poor (charity?). Jesus, however, replies that 'the poor you have with you always ... but I am only with you a little while' (faith?). And Lewis Hyde says of the issue of hope in the story,

> As usual, they [the disciples] have been a little slow to catch on. They are thinking of the price of oil as they sit before a man preparing to treat his body as a gift and atonement. We might take Jesus' reply to mean that poverty (or scarcity) is alive and well and inside their question, that rich and poor will live among them so long as they cannot feel the spirit when it is alive amongst them (Hyde, 1983, p. 119).

This is, I am sure, a subtle and sound reading of the story. The implication is that faith, hope and charity cannot be understood apart. It is only when they are brought together in conversation, structures, constructions of reality and theology, and in the church, that the wisdom of their intra-dependence, and under God's supreme love (the ultimate, connected canopy), can they be fully appreciated and understood.

Coda: Faith, Hope and Charity – Applied Anglican Polity

Education is what is left – the residue – after we have forgotten all the things we learnt. The challenge for Anglicans, then, and in their polity, is to recover some real sense of and the actual practice of *charity* in relation to faith and hope, and under love. To develop a charitable imagination that is not rooted in pity and perceived need, but rather in a rich and generative appreciation for the other – valuing them as dear, cherished and beloved. To 'live in love and charity with you neigbour', as the *Book of Common Prayer* puts it. Such a way of living requires both warmth and coolness; acts of faith; and the practice of hope. This may seem just too liberal and unspecific for some, but I think the tone of the church matters very much, not just for Christians in their churches, but also because it is part of the wider and deeper way in which ecclesial polity shapes society. As Will Hutton remarked on the eve of the 2008 Lambeth Conference,

> Anglicanism is a liberal tradition central to the very conception of Englishness, but it finds itself under mounting threat .... The genius of the Church of England is that because it is the official church it has to include the universe of all the English – Christian, agnostic and atheist, of whatever sexual orientation. It represents the cultural heartbeat of the country, and as the country has become more progressive so has it .... This is not just a precious institution at individual moments of crisis. Anglican priests are bulwarks for a cluster of values – tolerance, mutual respect, kindness, altruism, redemption – wherever they go in the communities they serve. I've never met one I did not respect enormously. In some social housing estates they are the only decent non-official figures people encounter. And even if God is only a hypothesis, it is crucially important that the country's leading religious institution is liberal.

> (Rowan) Williams understands this. The popular view is that he is an ineffectual, hand-wringer who is risking the break-up of the Church of England. I disagree. He obviously has a responsibility to try to keep the worldwide Anglican church together if he can. But he has a greater responsibility to the genius of Anglicanism – its capacity to reconcile Christian faith with the lived lives of the

English and in so doing transmute religion into a powerful liberal, rather than reactionary, force.[4]

In a similar vein, one of my predecessors at Cuddesdon used to describe Anglicanism as a matter of 'passionate coolness'. I rather like this stylistic interpretation of the Anglican mood, since it suggests an actual energy for temperate ecclesial climes. But it has a weakness too, which is that people can often dwell on the actual comfort that the accommodation and temperance bring. And temperance can be an over-rated virtue, if it is allowed to dictate moderation and exclude the excess of passion. If it sets the tempo all the time, then the radical of excess, which drives religion, is inhibited.

One of the characteristics that marked out early Christianity is that it understood faith to be an expression of passion and deeply held convictions. Faith, in terms of discipleship, is often not reasoned coolness. It is passion that spills over; the love that is stronger than death. Yet excessive, passionate faith is not the same as extreme faith. The former is intemperate and immodest; but it abounds in energy because it springs from the liberty of God. It is released as a kind of raw energy, precisely because it breaks the chains of inhibition, and springs forth from spiritual encounters that can border on ecstasy. But this is not, as I say, extremism. It is merely passion resulting from encounter, conversion, conviction, resurrection and transformation.

Yet our passion and energy as a Communion is also to be linked to our call to temperance and self-control – the kinds of virtues listed by Paul in Galatians. Yet temperance and self-control are not about control from without. The modelling of such virtue is, rather, the deep spiritual exercise of restraint for the sake of the self and the other. It is a spiritual discipline and a character that can only be exercised in proportion to the energy and passion that wells up from the same source. It is a steely and willed act of moderation or self-control that emerges out of passionate convictions, grace and love. That's why the list of the fruits of the Holy Spirit from Galatians is so important. Love, joy, peace, patience, kindness, self-control, humility, gentleness and faithfulness are all rooted in the passion of Christ – a putting to death of our desires, and seeing them reconfigured through the Holy Spirit into the heart of God. So excess and abundance are of God; extremism, however, is of the flesh.

In terms of Christian discipleship, these observations are important for several reasons. First, spiritual passion is not just about the expulsion of energy. It also has another meaning in religion which is concerned with the absorption of pain,

---

[4]   Will Hutton, 'Rebel Anglican bishops threaten the very heart of our liberal traditions', the *Observer*, London, 6 July 2008, p. 25.

sacrifice and suffering – like the passion of Christ. Here, passion is absolutely for the other; but it is passion that is almost entirely configured in its receptivity. Much like the passion of a parent or a lover, God's passion is sometimes spoken in eloquent silence; in sacrifice and in endurance. In solidarity and in suffering; in patience, kindness, self-control, humility and gentleness.

Second, it is perhaps important to remember that the example of the early church – those people that inspire us in our faith – is often to be found in the delicate combination of passion, practice and reason. One of the qualities I sometimes look for in candidates for ordination is the initial inability to contain their passion – for the church, for Christ, and for others. There are not many laurels or crowns being dished out in heaven for being slightly left-of-centre and (merely) politically correct. Discipleship is not about being liberal, conservative, or even somewhere in the middle. It is about knowing your place before God, and being passionate for the possibility of the kingdom.

Third, the temperance Anglicans might seek should not be allowed to blunt the energy and enthusiasm that flows from living the gospel. To be sure, orderliness and calculation have their place. But if they are allowed to control and marginalise passion, then there is a great danger that temperance can become totalitarian. Religion in moderation is, arguably, a contradiction in terms. It should offend, cajole, probe and interrogate. More colloquially, and to mix metaphors, one might say that a faith that does not get up your nose is hardly worth the candle.

The call, then, is to consider the radical nature of commitment, and to call others to this radical discipleship. This is a faith that revels in the excessive, but is not extreme. It is passionate; and yet com-passionately held in such a way as to be persuasive rather than repellent. I happen to think that the Church of England, and indeed the wider Anglican Communion that Bayne says is born of the same ecclesial DNA, might just be on to something here. It is often far too easy to despair of the apparently tepid nature of Anglican polity; and its interminable vacillations and argument. And yet, I find it strangely full of the fruits of God's Spirit – exactly the kinds of abundance and generosity listed by Paul in *Galatians* 5. Indeed, let me say a little more at this point.

I love the Church of England because it is patient. It does not expect the world to change in an instant, or to be bludgeoned into belief, because it knows that certain things take centuries. I love it because it is kind. It is kind enough to welcome strangers, whatever their beliefs, and shake their hands, and offer them a coffee after church. I like the fact that it is neither envious (of more flamboyant, more attention-seeking and more successful-at-proselytising religions), nor boastful. I like the fact that it is not normally arrogant or rude. I like the fact that it does not insist on its own way, but is genuinely tolerant of other religious beliefs – and none. I like the fact that it does not rejoice in wrongdoing, but quietly presents an ethical framework of kindness. I like the fact that it believes in the values of the New Testament, and of St Paul's description of love, which I've just paraphrased, but also believes that it is more important to embody them than to quote them.

I like the fact that it doesn't speak like a child, think like a child, or reason like a child. I like the fact that it is mature enough to value faithful doubt. I like the fact that it is mostly calm. I like the fact that it recognises that the religious impulse is here to stay, and that the more you try to crush it, the stronger it will become. And that all human beings, irrespective of their beliefs, have yearnings for the transcendent. And I like the fact that although secured in scripture, tradition and reason, it is not afraid to seek and find God in our wider culture – in art, literature, nature and in society. Indeed, this is faith, hope and charity.[5]

As Paul says of the fruits of the Spirit, there are no laws against such things. So one can truly celebrate this part of Christ's body – the Church of England – into which God has been gracious enough to cultivate an abundance of fruit to savour. Anglicans can afford to listen to one another attentively, and with graciousness. For 'the unity of the church does not consist of people thinking alike, but in people acting together ...', as we noted earlier. So unity is not inimical to diversity: it is, rather, essential for what unity is fully meant to be, in its meaning and truth. Diversity does not mean division: it is, rather, the core of what preserves the intention of faith, hope and charity which creates and sustain diversity. So, hope faith and charity are once again to the fore here, and an ecclesiology rooted in these virtues and practices will surely not be far from what Christ might have intended for his body. This is body that is comfortable in its own skin. It will not be anxious about its growth or profile. And it will be one that has the sense to value the quality of wisdom, holiness and discipleship above any measurability that prioritises seeking value through quantification. As one theologian puts it, living like this would mean that in the church

> We have a gift to share that will enlarge any culture because without a scriptural vision of covenant and justice, mercy and fidelity, generosity in personal relations and political structures alike, we shall find ourselves and our cultures becoming less and less human, less and less sustainable, less and less liveable. This is a vision of a gospel that seeks to be at home in the human world, yet reshapes it more radically than we could have imagined.[6]

---

[5] This meditation is adapted from an article by Christina Patterson ('Thank God for the Church of England'), originally published in the *Independent*, 25 July 2009, p. 13.

[6] Archbishop Rowan Williams, *Sermon*, Service to celebrate the Bicentenary of the British and Foreign Bible Society, St Paul's Cathedral, Monday, 8 March 2004.

Indeed. This is what it means to be the yeast in the dough and the salt of the earth. This is what it means to try to re-shape the world; to imagine a spiritual topology for the created order. To imagine the kingdom of God, which in blessing the world is something like the ecclesial canopy we always seek: one of faith, hope and charity.

Conclusion

Faith in the Canopy: A Forward-Looking Critical Retrospect

In the work of Peter Berger, the 'sacred canopy' serves as a cipher for the construction of reality under which a society lives (1967, pp. 3–4). In Berger's thinking, and despite apparent secularisation, the social construction of reality is nonetheless pervasively (and perhaps innately) religious. But can there be any serious claim to an ecclesial canopy? By which I mean, any sense in which the church offers a capacious and transitional space for encounters with God, a place enabling both transformation and dwelling, and for confronting the suffering and joy of human life? Many would argue not, but as we have progressed through the three sections of this volume – broadly concerned with faith and consumerism, Christianity and public life, and finally ecclesiology – we have at least gained some sense of how the church continues to offer a meaningful canopy and space that provides a significant transitional and transformational space: one where holding and releasing, challenging and affirming, and the pastoral and the prophetic can co-exist.

The canopy of which we speak is, of course, both an allusion and illusion. We allude to something that can be difficult to articulate; and the illusion imagines something that is plainly real, yet not within reach. Overarching canopies that are above us are ways of speaking and imagining the world we live in – a cosmology not of planets and atmospheres, but rather of values, ideas, stories, myths, symbols and practices. The ecclesial canopy, such as it is, is something that is both part and apart from the other kinds of canopies that provide shelter and communal space both within and beyond modernity. A canopy provides the space for containment, community and configuration. Religion not only survives, but can also flourish in modern pluralistic societies, by being embedded in an assortment of cultures and subcultures by providing adherents with beliefs and practices that offer morally challenging and satisfying modes of being and belonging. The groups that flourish best will be those that are able to engage with modernity, adjust with times, and offer clear distinctions from, and significant engagement and tension with, the forces and facets of modernity that represent significant challenges to faith communities. Or, to express this in a more analogical and cosmological framework, the religious groups that will flourish in the future are those that possess the greatest capacity to live within the various 'spheres' of modernity, be they secular, consumerist, pluralistic, and so on. The 'ecclesial canopy', as a sphere, dwells within a competitive set of spheres. And its future strength lies in both maintaining its distinctiveness from and ensuring its full engagement with modernity. Here, values and practices will be need to be defended and refined; protected and adjusted.

So what of our present time, and of Christianity in contemporary culture? And what of the threats to the capacious and transformational spaces that the churches aspire to be? Here, the problem that the church now faces turns out not be one of secularisation so much as competition for time and energies, and consumerism. I do not only mean by this the erosion of Sundays – through competing leisure or consumerist activity. The problem is perhaps deeper than this. We are not, as people, time-rich. Ironically, one of the problems of our age is that more has turned out to be less. Technology and other means of production have meant that communication and reification is instant. We are impatient if delayed.

As Zymunt Bauman notes, we have 'taken the waiting out of wanting' (2000, p. 76). And if not affected by rampant consumerism, our attention is caught in other ways. We are saturated by information and news, and have enough gadgets to provide us with all manner of communications and connections in an instant. But in so doing, our attention-span has been lost. We have somehow lost our capacity to fix our minds on one thing; to gaze with awe, or to be still, and know. Swept away by the apparent relevance and power of current affairs, the breakfast news has become Matins, and the evening news our Compline.

Underneath this technology lurks a deep social suspicion – that we are permanently on the verge of some sort of crucial transformation or secular epiphany that will change the way we think, act, behave, react, eat, relate or dress. The moral question – not 'what can this new piece of technology do *for* me, and further enhance my life?', but rather 'what is this technology doing *to* me as a person, and shaping my life inimically?' – is drowned out by the incessant demands of mobile phones, e-mails and other forms of prompting. Knowledge replaces wisdom; social network sites replace real relationships; technology drives out humanity.

Yet the critique offered in this volume is not so much of capitalism *per se*, as to simply remind ourselves that the fiscal metrics that judge the success of capitalist exploits do not necessarily have a care or heart for the consequences of relentlessly driving towards profit. The crisis in the developed world is the worship of success and mammon and the illusory freedom this buys. It fails, as all ideologies ultimately do fall short, because it lacks a larger vision for human flourishing which is not rooted in personal gain, but rather in seeking the common good. The welfare and best interests of my neighbour are, in other words, things that matter very deeply to social wellbeing. David Cameron's Big Society, like

George Bush's Faith-Based Initiatives before it in the USA, need to acquire a vision for society that is not rooted simply in a neuralgic response to economic meltdown or a desire to shrink government. So, for a true and deep form of social flourishing to take place, religion (or, more particularly, the church) might have to rediscover its nerve.

The recovery of such a nerve is something that lies well beyond mere absorption with the temporal aspects of simply being 'established', or, for that matter, of concordats; or, indeed, of alternative models of ecclesial polity that are communitarian, sectarian and disestablished. It is, rather, a hope and expectation that the church can be broadly and deeply incorporative within its given social context, providing the necessary shape, ethos and purpose for life that enables true flourishing, and enables the horizons for social flourishing to be elevated beyond our collective interest. Put another way, the church can be the place that enables the ordering of the world in a way that makes common sense; but without losing the humility that must accompany worship and mystery.

I do not find it surprising that religion continues to flourish in a capitalist, consumerist and technologically shaped society. True, the forms of religion that now flourish may not be quite what the churches might have hoped for. Spirituality, in all its mellifluous forms, continues to abound. Churchgoing – indeed, any kind of committed, regular and obligated bonding to an institution – is still under considerable pressure, and subject to on-going challenges in contemporary culture. But it survives, and can sometimes flourish. Not only in the effervescent neo-fundamentalist forms (including Pentecostalism and Conservative strains of faith), but also in 'classic' forms such as cathedral worship. Indeed, it is not unfair to suggest that the 'types' of religion that flourish today are forms of practice: pilgrimage, memorialisation and celebration. The living and the dead, the married and the new-born, can still bring many together in ritual and practice – purposefully, and with a sense of mystery in the presence of divinity. The 'liturgy' for memorialisation and celebration is a vehicle that takes us briefly from kingdom of this world to the kingdom of God. Liturgy literally means 'the work of the people': it is the dramatic script we both perform and are performed by, as it retells and enacts the story of our redemption. Liturgy moves us, literally. And still with movement, pilgrimage, too, offers an event that is seminal, yet is a journey that has a clear beginning and end. The word pilgrimage comes from the Latin *peregrinus*, referring to a person wandering the earth in exile, in search of a spiritual homeland. So when people do actually come to church, what might they find? J. Robert Barth suggests that

> The search for the numinous that is expressed in symbol is at the same time more
> than a search. It is an encounter; it is a search that is already in some measure

successful. The 'search' is a struggle to articulate what has already been grasped without words – what has been felt in the bones, and what has been dreamt, what has been glimpsed in vision. The search is for word, words to express this numinous 'other'. The search is to articulate an encounter, and encounter with the sacred, which has already taken place and yet which still takes place around the symbol ... (1977, p. 121).

It is, of course, not ultimately possible to accurately predict how religion will shape society and be shaped by it in the future. Movements come and go; intensity usually slides into eventual extensity (e.g., bureaucratisation and routinisation in the case of charismatic renewal), but this is not about secular forces dissipating faith. One lesson that the late twentieth century has taught us is that yesterday's fanatics are often tomorrow's government. Religion, like life itself, goes through cycles – and is constantly changing and renewing itself. The period of late modernity we generally regard as the 'secular age' may just be a blip on the landscape: just a phase in the long, complex history of humanity and its evolutions of society.

But are there any clues as to what might become of the ecclesial canopy in the twenty-first century? Secularisation, as a theory, has largely run its course. Secularists, for all their avowed atheism, do not seem to be gaining in number. For all the talk of the church running out of steam, we may yet find that at 2,000 years old, we are still rather young – perhaps in our infancy. No-one can assume that any of the problems facing today's church are terminal. Yet the churches cannot afford to be complacent either, since patterns of believing and belonging, as we have discussed, are subject to consumerism and individualism as never before. The signs, in other words, do not point either to a strong or weak future for the churches. The evidence, such as it is, seems contrary at times, and difficult to weigh and judge. The sifting and discernment that needs to take place for todays' church to flourish is an on-going project, and one that requires the church to ponder a range of tactical adjustments, resisting and adapting to contemporary culture in equal measure. And there is perhaps one particular recent moment, and a place, that somehow sums up this complex ambivalence and challenge for the churches – the debate surrounding the Spirit Zone in the Millennium Dome – and to which we now turn, to offer a final explorative sketch.

The Spirit Zone

The Millennium Dome was a project that began its life in 1996, and was intended to capture the 'Millennium experience' in a series of segments, one of which was devoted to religion and spirituality. The controversies surrounding the content of what came to be known as the Spirit Zone do not need further elucidation here, save only to say that pluralism, the extent to which Christianity could be explicit without appearing triumphalist or conversionist, were all hotly debated at the time.[1] What can be said with some certainty now is that the Spirit Zone took seriously the claim (which is contestable) that everyone is spiritually innate. Pathways in the Spirit Zone took people on journeys through community and culture, in which scriptural quotations and symbols merged together with children's voices in a montage on spirituality. The paths diverged, with one taking a specific Christian route on the history of Christianity, and also looking at 'living icons' or 'witnesses' to the faith in the past, focusing on justice, healthcare and politics. Another path provided focus on common human experiences (e.g., death, birth, marriage, etc.) through the eyes of different faiths.

The paths began to converge again when religion was addressed as a source of conflict and cooperation. In turn, this led to a kind of 'Graffiti Wall' of images and quotes, dealing with life-choices. Near to this was a modern honeycombed 'Prayer Wall' (for placing actual scrawled prayers in), and a space for contemplation. The final area offered reflection on how different religions shape and celebrate time and seasons, and some thoughts about religion in the future. As Philip Sheldrake pointed out, the Millennium Dome was the only truly 'national' building specifically constructed to mark the millennium:

> ... the Dome [was] compared unfavourably to as an expression of human creativity with what our ancestors built in the past. Simply as a construction it has no longterm existence. In terms of content, it is orientated to the present moment only and offers little sense of the history that has brought us to this time and points forward into our future .... The misgivings about the Dome, justified or not, highlight the vital connection between three things: place, memory and human identity ... (2001, p. 1).

Yet that was too subtle and inchoate for some of the Dome's religious critics. Part of the problem for the Spirit Zone in the Dome lay in agreement about the kind of time we lived in, and the focus of time we were celebrating. Some Christians (and representatives of other faiths) appeared to believe in the secularisation thesis more than some sociologists did, who openly espouse the dogma. For this group, the Millennium therefore needed to be (re-)claimed as a Christian event, or at least one that demanded a Christian interpretation and a widespread acknowledgement of this. That is not to say that New Year's Eve that year had any

---

[1]   See my 'The Sacred Canopy: Religion and Time at the Greenwich Millennium Dome' (2000). I was also a Theological Consultant to the Spirit Zone from 1997 to 1999.

liturgical significance. Rather, it is a recognition that, give or take four years, the Millennium celebrated the two thousandth anniversary of the birth of Jesus Christ, and therefore commemorated a particular kind of God-event, which eventually gave birth to the church and Christianity.

A number of Evangelical and 'traditionalist' proponents of such views lobbied hard to 'identify' the Millennium as Jesus' birthday, mainly in order to remind society of its indebtedness to Christian faith, and to use the occasion as an opportunity for evangelism. Many churches and Christian organisations appeared to suggest that the Millennium could only be truly celebrated and understood in a Christian context (e.g., 2000 – © Christianity). Such views were reminiscent of the claims – often seen on wayside pulpits – that it 'isn't a genuine Christmas without the church', 'Christmas – ©', or that 'Christmas without Christ is Xmas'.

Although these claims had some merit, they lacked subtlety. Time, seasons, and the way in which we mark and measure them, are not owned outright by any one group, religious or otherwise. In attempting to 'baptise' the Millennium in an exclusivist way, or monopolise its meaning, some Christian organisations probably missed the opportunity to offer the Millennium to society in a more generous and inclusive manner. Moreover, an entirely Christian interpretation of the Millennium failed to perceive the plurality of ways in which our society has evolved its perception of time.

My own birthday might serve as an example. I was born in the year known as 1962, which counts on (approximately) from the number of years since the birth of Jesus of Nazareth. But I was also born in July, a month named after a Roman god and emperor. I was born on a Thursday, too, a day named after a Norse god. And I was born on the thirty-first day of that month, which is designated as the feast day of St Ignatius of Loyola. So, in spite of an apparently secular drift in society, many of our perceptions of time remain rooted to the sediments of sacred life. In other words, the way in which we tell time and organise our seasons, reflects a 'common spirituality' that is still at work in society.

Some Christians do, of course, bewail the loss of Christian feasts to 'Bank Holidays', holy days to holidays, the observance of Good Friday and Whit Monday and so forth. In such thinking, Christmas and Easter are perceived as being lost to the forces of consumerism, and overtaken by secular interpretations, replete with myths involving bunnies, reindeer and Father Christmas. But this sense of 'Christian time and seasons' somehow being stolen – the sacred being subsumed by the secular – is quite incorrect. Many of the central Christian seasons, particularly Christmas and Easter, were deliberately located within complementary or competitive calendar systems and celebrations that were pagan. The location of Christ's birthday is linked to winter and darkness, and the coming of the light. It is a solar feast that does not move. Easter, in contrast was a Christian 'baptism' of several pagan festivities, and is linked to the lunar calendar, and consequently the date moves just as the earth and the moon rotate. Moreover, its deepest roots lie in another religion: the Passover of Judaism.

This might suggest that the task for the churches in (re-)claiming time is even more complex in a secular and consumer-led world. Yet the size of the problem probably depends on the extent to which one is willing to accept a general secularisation thesis. Jib Fowles' (1995) recent *Advertising and Popular Culture* concludes with some telling remarks about the true meaning of Christmas. Noting that Christmas has a curiously brief social history, he also notes how 'sacred' the season has been for centuries throughout the Northern Hemisphere. At a time when the daylight was weakest, pagan festivals included excessive drinking and eating, the exchange of gifts, normal rules and prohibitions suspended, and even roles reversed (women and men cross-dressing, masters waiting on servants, etc.). The fifth century saw the festival Christianised, but the old customs survived, even if they were reinterpreted.

The censorious attentions of Protestant reformers in the seventeenth century and beyond arrested that, but only to pave the way for the reinvention of the season in the nineteenth century. From this capitalist and industrial base, the scope of Christmas has widened. The season itself lasts much longer. Fowles suggests it runs from Thanksgiving in late November to Superbowl Sunday in mid-January. Yet it remains a curiously 'sacred' and scarce time in a society that is otherwise driven by individualism and competitiveness. In this season, families are more in focus, gifts are exchanged, and our connectedness and interdependence is celebrated. So, contrary to what one might perceive, 'sacred' ideology is usually given a particular voice during this most secular of seasons, and the materialism and consumerism should be seen as an extension of an inborn human and religious instinct. The way we tell time is invariably a weaving together of secular and sacred symbols and seasons that point to the innately spiritual nature of our society. Indeed, the idea of an ecclesial canopy is especially suggestive at this point.

In terms of the relation between culture and religion, we have, of course, been here before. Richard Niebuhr's classic *Christ and Culture* (1951) tries to define culture and the relationality of Christ to it, but independent of the definition. Although an exemplary book, it serves a North American context better than it does a European one, where religion and belief are part of the tapestry of everyday life, even if many of the threads are, at first sight, invisible. The temptation for some groups – to borrow from Niebuhr – is to place Christ against culture, and to remove the notion of sacred time from the secular; in effect, to organise a divorce in the interests of purity. The characteristic liberal response is to locate Christ in culture, and to accept (and perhaps rejoice in) the multiplicity of ambiguity and meaning that flows from this. Another option – favoured by more conservative and dogmatic groups – is to place Christ above culture. As we have already noted, this protects the 'myth' of Christ as the Lord of Time, but it is also alienating rather than participative; it is the logos before and after incarnation. The key to understanding Niebuhr's categorisations is to perceive the end in his meaning; he is chiefly concerned about 'relativism', but also believes that an appeal to Christ can transform culture.

Relating this to time, we might say that Niebuhr's stance on the Millennium would have been to appeal to the God who not only creates, but also enters creation, and accepts constraints; what is assumed can be redeemed. Time, then, becomes a *place*, a sacrament if you will, a pivotal point of instrumentality in which the life of God can meet the life of the world. There can be no guarantees about outcomes, but the offering of the moment itself can be a transforming matrix, holding as it does some insights into the paradox of our freedom and dependence. As Niebuhr notes, the Lord of Time who transforms things does this by 'lifting them up': the image is spatial, not temporal (R. Niebuhr, 1951, p. 195).

Canopies of Space, and Time

The concept of an ecclesial canopy has both a spatial and a temporal dimension. The space creates the sense of place. And the possibility of dwelling in that space, and encountering God, confronting suffering and joy, settling and journeying, all require time. This relationship between space and time has preoccupied anthropologists of religion for a century or more. Durkheim, Hubert, Mauss and Bourdieu have all seen time and space as being mediated by society, or, rather, by the collective representation that is generated by persons that will reflect the social structure of particular societies. Awareness of space and time can only be composed and systematised by a process of division and differentiation, and such structuring has its origin in social life. Thus, there is 'ordinary time', penitential time and celebration in Christian calendars (as in other religions). But these are spaces too. Similarly, there are seasons and their harvests, which are marked not just by changes in climate and productivity, but also by rituals and performance that demarcate boundaries and intervals. Frequently, the social world, or rather its ordering, is a 'map' of the cosmos as it is perceived by a group.

According to Jedrej, Hindu temples generally 'map' the cosmos, with the construction of a temple constituting the re-creation of the universe.[2] The Sanskrit term referring to the temple, *Vimana*, means 'well-measured' or 'well-proportioned'. One could argue that certain Christian liturgical structures attempt the same, moving time through themes of creation, fall, redemption and, finally,

---

[2]   For further discussion, see M. Jedrej's 'Time and Space' (1996).

fulfilment. Even church buildings can reflect the ordering of time and space. Over the centuries they have provided sundials that map the world and the universe, as well as telling the hour of the day. Inside, fonts situated close to the entrance porch signify the start of life's journey, the altar is centre (for the rest of life), and there is often a separate and rarely-used side door leading off into the graveyard. There is space for birth, life and death: space for time.

However, the most common ground of space-time relations remains in festivals and events. Seasonal activities are used to indicate time, even in apparently secular societies. Foods, rituals and stories still play a significant role in Christmas and Easter observation for a large majority of people in Britain, even if they are nominally Christian, and even if they operate more obviously under the sacred canopy of capitalism and consumerism than that of official religion. It is the time that delivers the social space, creating conditions in which gifts can be exchanged, families and friends visited, and some ritual enacted. Thus, a threat to the way in which time is given space (the 'Keep Sunday Special' campaign comes to mind) is normally perceived as a social threat, not just a religious one. Disruptions to time and space can be deeply anti-social; to move with the times, in the social space provided, is to be part of society. Thus, a common socio-theology of time, functioning at a subliminal level in many societies, incorporates two notions: time as linear, and time as repetitive (or cyclical). Modernity, in the interests of progress, favours the first of these: hope lies in the future. Religion, on the other hand, although it may have a future hope, tends to favour cyclical time, as the stories of time are caught up in stories of creation and redemption.

Theology could perhaps operate responsibly here by owning up to the relation between calendars and power. As Alfred Gell notes in his exemplary essay on time, the person who occupies a central position in society is the one who controls the calendar.[3] At the beginning of a new Millennium, society continues to see the sacred and the secular tussle for power over time. In Britain, competitive frames of reference for time are never far below the surface. Broadly, and theologically speaking, we have expressed these as being linear and cyclical; in fact, they are simultaneously episodic and dispositional, with functions of carrying memory and constructing sociality. Both have strong religious roots. Linear time suggests a beginning, middle and end. Behind this may well lie a notion of a God who is Alpha and Omega, of time being part of creation, but as something that will end. The secular version of this has no 'end' as such (save perhaps some unforeseen catastrophe), and places

---

[3] See Alfred Gell (1992). Gell uses the example of the *bangara*, the 'Big man', a dealer in nuts, pigs and shell rings on the Solomon Island of Simbo. The Bangara is a hereditary position within a clan, and the commerce is linked to harvest seasons, which in turn dictates the calendars.

linear time in a modernist framework, in which ever-expansive progress continues to beckon us forward. Cyclical time, on the other hand, speaks of the permanence of return; the seasons, ashes to ashes, dust to dust, dawn and dusk, night and day.

The cycles of time remain those events and public spaces in which society constructs its meaning, weaving together sacred and secular. The outcome is that that neither really wins, and that the process of telling time evolves into something that is wonderfully syncretic. The Dome itself, with its Spirit Zone, inevitably reflected that: pushing us forward in linearity, but drawing us back to the well-springs of ritual that structure the days and the years.[4]

Here, any theology of time must be some kind of teleology; knowledge and hope for a future that is to come. Christianity has traditionally responded to this by offering a God who is both beyond time and yet also deeply enmeshed and enfleshed within. God has made time and redeemed it, and the natural response from within creation is to provide space for the creator, and make time for the One whose gift is time. This is both linear and cyclical. Linear time, in its progressive sphere, is the memory of redemption and the hope of its fulfilment. Cyclical time is the celebration of the movement of God amongst us in the natural ordering of creation and social intercourse. These two ideas of time, which are both secular and sacred, are also sacramental at juncture. That is to say, time is a pivotal point of instrumentality, in which the life of God meets the life of the world. Time is that space where we encounter God; it behoves us to use it wisely. The poet of *Ecclesiastes* (3: 1–4, 6–8) had an especially laconic way of expressing this:

> For everything there is a season,
> and a time for every matter under heaven:
> a time to be born, and a time to die;
> a time to plant, and a time to pluck up what is planted;
> a time to kill, and a time to heal;
> a time to break down, and a time to build up;
> a time to weep, and a time to laugh;
> a time to mourn, and a time to dance;
> a time to seek, and a time to lose;
> a time to keep, and a time to cast away;
> a time to rend, and a time to sew;
> a time to keep silence, and a time to speak;
> a time to love, and a time of hate;
> a time for war, and a time for peace ...

---

[4]   Philip Larkin expresses the competition between sciences and theologies of time in his poem 'Days'. See Roberts (ed.) (1965), *The Faber Book of Modern Verse*, p. 368.

Conclusion

The meditative timbre of *Ecclesiastes*, however, should not be allowed obscure the challenges the churches surely face in the twenty-first century. We might recall that much of the Old Testament, in which *Ecclesiastes* is situated, was written when the Israelites were either oppressed or in exile. Yet the faith, hope and love survived, and flourished. But there needed to be some strong and discerning prophetic stances against those agencies that sought to undermine or destroy the faith, or to simply dilute it. Time and time again, the Israelites have to negotiate their own versions of the challenge of pluralism, materialism and distraction. What emerges from the long sweep of history and God's providence is not a 'pure' faith or church, but rather one that remains capacious and true, but has also been tempered with contextualisation and accommodations, as much as righteous resistance. The same is true of the New Testament church; that through its early diaspora, it had to work through how culture and religion interacted in each given situation, and to balance the local with the catholic. In the same way, any ecclesial canopy that can survive into the twenty-first century will need to be both hospitable and discerning to those alien influences that come from without; and also resistant to those that may in fact be inimical. This is the vocation of the canopy, and the vocation living within the canopy – one of discernment and hospitality, seeking to continue offering a shelter and capacious space within the wider context of modernity.[5]

If the twin towers of consumerism and secularisation represent significant challenges for the future, the churches and theology will need to be more robust in their readings and critiques of culture. The brochure for the Spirit Zone invited attendees to 'take a moment to reflect in a haven of tranquillity (and) explore the values that underpin our society'.[6] The idea of entering a zone that provides both simulation and stimulation is at the heart of both the problem and the opportunity here. It risks clutter and vacuity; emptiness and nothingness; and the offering of forms of nourishment and sustenance that simply cannot feed the soul, nor deeply enrich society for the common good. The emphasis on experience – but abstracted, as it were – is one of the major challenges that churches face today, namely being corralled into providing meaning and experiences that can be consumed, but do not necessarily lead to any longer-term transformations for the individual or wider society.

At the same time, the church, in common with other institutions (politics, education, medicine, social care, etc.) is experiencing a crippling deficit of trust. The very soil upon which civilisation is founded, and in which its virtues

---

[5]   On this, see Dan Hardy (2010).

[6]   See Neil Leach (1999), p. 31.

and social character are rooted, have been steadily bleached and eroded by consumerism and secularisation. But if our culture is to flourish once more, it may now be that virtues have be to be explicitly taught rather than simply left to chance. We cannot assume that faith, hope and charity – or trust, wisdom and honesty, for that matter – will simply get picked up by the emerging generation, or occur without any intentionality on our part. Accountability, democracy and transparency, though important and worthy, are not adequate replacements for such virtues. Institutional, public and political life – rather like ecclesial identity – will not flower if they are constantly uprooted for public inspection. A society that requires unrealistic standards of inspection is actually lacking in trust. It is precisely this sort of negative culture that inhibits rather than enables education, for example. When trust and security are stripped out, only fear enters. And, to reverse 1 John 4: 18, perfect fear drives out love. Without trust in those bodies that bear our values and virtues, we risk corralling institutions and public servants into states of insecurity and neuralgic policy-making. It remains the case that some of the best 'good' we have in the world is the result of long periods of gestation and maturation, and not constant over-bearing inspectional intrusion.

There can be no question that secularisation and consumer culture presents a profound problem for the churches. Malls compete with cathedrals for people, space and attention. Leisure and shopping compete with worship. With consumption now such a dominant social practice, belief systems now also find themselves directed away from traditional practices into new forms of consumption – and perhaps especially individually-centred, therapeutically-attuned forms of spirituality. Self-transformation is often subordinated to consumer choice. Moreover, when consumers do eventually find their own way through to embracing rich religious and faith traditions, they often find them in a fragmented and precarious condition. Or, once again, in an emerging commodified form. Yet, as Vincent Miller argues,

> … consumer culture (also) brings opportunities as well … the doors of the archives have been opened to the masses. People have more access to cultural material than ever … the positive aspect of consumer culture provides the possibility for the tactic of deepening agency. We need not retreat to the monasteries to ride out the new dark ages while the barbarians wreak bricolage. The path lies forward, through this explosion of agency, by embracing and forming it (V. Miller, 2004, pp. 225–6).

Miller concludes his essay by suggesting that theology has three lessons to learn from its struggles with consumer society. First, attend to the structures and practices of faith that connect belief to daily life. Second, attend to the lived and ordinary or operant theology of faith communities. Third, to help churches preserve and sustain faith and tradition in the face of corrosive globalising capitalism. Or, in a single word: adjust. To cultivate theologies and practices that have sufficient malleability to cope with some of the topological distortions we have explored earlier. Indeed, to follow the argument of the preceding volumes in this trilogy, to be faithful and grounded, and also shaped and shaping. As Timothy Gorringe noted in *Furthering Humanity* (2004),

> Can the church be part of culture and yet not culturally assimilated? All Barth's methodological labours were devoted to trying to show that despite the necessary 'Wholly Other', that which is not a member of this or any universe can find speech within (and) engage with human culture without being subsumed by it (Gorringe, 2004, p. 43).

Our culture, then, may well respond positively to fresh initiatives and leadership from the church that lead to a re-setting of social paradigms and horizons within a wider context of faith, hope and charity. The churches could well lead the way here, but by looking outward rather than inward, and having regard for the fate of the world, not only for itself. Henry Scougal, writing almost two centuries ago, opined that charity was a major 'branch' of religion,

> under which all the parts of justice, all the duties we owe to our neighbour, are eminently comprehended: for he that doth truly love the world, will be nearly concerned in the interest of everyone; and so far from wrongdoing or injuring any person, that he will resent all evil that befalls others, as if it happened to himself (Henry Scougal, 1829, p. 16).

The church need not, therefore, fear its immersion in culture. It can and will retain its shape, and its identity. But it cannot afford, at the same time, to presume upon this. It can retain its essential topology, even though the cultural *terroir* it is embedded in may be quite inimical at present. True, there are always risks and threats, as much as there are opportunities and possibilities. The Greenwich Millennium Dome, with its close association to global time (i.e., Greenwich Meantime – GMT), provided a unique, brief window into how sacred and secular struggled for power and social ordering at the end of a century, and again at the beginning of a new millennium. The religious significance of time could not easily be ignored then, even in an apparently secular era. Yet those who designed the Spirit Zone within the Dome were also to discover that time-telling today can now no longer be dominated by a single faith. Thus was it ever so. Ultimately, and at the end of the last Millennium, it was science, not religion, that told the time. And it was now physics, not faith, that determined and measured our space. But it is still the case that faiths, religion and theology continue to interpret our times and spaces, and provide them with the significance, meaning and value by which we measure and weigh our existence.

It is perhaps ironic that Dionysius Exiguus, a largely unknown sixth century monk, was able to set an extraordinary agenda for the world in his calculations on time. In removing the relation of the calendar to the Caesars, and relating it to the birth of Christ, he helped create what we now know as Millennia.[7] And yet we now also know that he was wrong in his calculations for the birth of Jesus; out by four to seven years, depending on which dating theory one subscribes to. Yet the error of Dionysius contains some remarkable forward-looking messages for the Third Millennium, and for the shaping and sustaining of the capacious ecclesial canopy that might still offer a space in a busy world, and a transforming space within modernity. It is a lesson that faith, hope and charity also teaches. Namely, that the church and theology should always be prepared to adjust within the times and places it is given to engage with. To be incarnate: the embodiment of God's love and intention for humanity and creation.

So this ecclesial canopy is ultimately a kind of social skin for the world. Never complete, yet always being replenished, it can sometimes tear, as much as it often stretches. It registers the pain and the pleasure of the world, and can also hold it together in profound and deep ways. Like all bodies, it is distinct and robust in identity. It is open, yet discerning. Yet as a living, breathing and adapting body for the world in which it is set, the ecclesial canopy still offers worldviews and values which still guide a set of common assumptions, and give meaning and order to contemporary life. Yet as we have seen, there are fresh challenges to such a canopy. Our culture is beginning to look for other sources of authority to address the great questions and issues that now face us: the meaning of life, and how we shall live. The task for the church is urgent. In our time – as in all ages – we need a replenished and renewed ecclesial canopy under which all can find identity, meaning, security and comfort. Indeed, nothing less than a kingdom that is come and becoming – transcendent, embodied and capacious – a space in which all can find a home.

---

[7]   Cf. Duncan (1998), pp. 104ff.

Coda

Faith in the Free-market:
A Cautionary Tale for Anglican Adults

The story below is offered as a simple-but-cautionary satirical tale of what the future might hold for a church that unintentionally embraces the gods of our age – growth and success, with its High Priests in corporations and business – and in so doing, evacuates itself of patience, charity, hope and faithfulness. Written and published in the early 1990s, and at the height of free-market ideology in Britain, the story asks what might happen if the church were to adopt the same economic, political and ideological pulses that were also shaping the nation.[1]

There are quirky details that seem quaint now: the invention of the portable fax machine has not come to pass in quite the way one might have envisaged twenty years ago. Technology has developed even faster with mobile phones, tablets and handheld computers. But that is hardly the point. The satire takes its cue from the dominant consumerist and managerial lingua of our age. As church polity is increasingly shaped by the horizon of market forces, and by targets, strategies and plans – all representing a kind of rather inward-looking cluster of concerns that are clothed in apparently missional rhetoric, which it believes itself to be 'out-facing' – the story might serve as a timely, even prophetic caution. The closing parable, although unrelated to the satire, is drawn directly from Bill Countryman's fine *The Truth About Love*, and is a brief reminder that though the church may sometimes seem down, it is never out.[2] Just when secularisation or consumerism seems to have triumphed, spring, buds and new life appear. Winter passes, as it must. The one problem the church always faces never really changes: namely, coping with the overwhelming abundance of God.

---

[1]   This was originally published in *Signs of the Times*, Lent 1992, and in a revised form in *Modern Believing*, July 2011, with the addition of the Postscript.

[2]   Countryman (1993).

The Churchgoer's Charter

The time is set about 25 years In the future. England has become a Republic. The Story is in five parts:

The Present

The bright flashbulbs and camera lights of the nation's press reporters filled the Hall at Church House. The Bishop of Southbury, Michael Talent, blinked. Flanked by Bishops, plus other officials from Church House and Sir Marcus Lloyd from the Church Commissioners, Bishop Michael began his speech

> Ladies and Gentlemen. As you will know, today sees the launch of one of the most important documents the Church of England has produced this Century ... even though we are less than a few decades into a new Millennium. The House of Bishops has felt for some time that the church is too unwieldy in its structure to meet the needs of the people. There has been too much bureaucracy and red tape, and not enough action. Congregations have declined in number: confidence in the Church has dwindled. Today we hope to put the Church of England back on the road to recovery, with the launch of *The Churchgoer's Charter*. This will give power back to the people, and will make clergy and churches more accountable to the parishes they are supposed to be serving ....

Bishop Michael held up the glossy volume; camera motors whirred, and journalists began punching in copy into their portable faxes. 'This will look great in the papers', thought the Bishop to himself. He was right. The headlines and leader columns were fulsome in their praise. *The Times* wrote a lead article under the caption 'Bishop Sees Red (Tape)'; 'Bishop Prunes Vine' reported the *Telegraph*; 'Weeding the Weedy Church' trumpeted the *Sun*, lauding the Bishop in an article on page seven.

The Churchgoer's Charter had all begun after the government had been re-elected in 2014. It was the Prime Minister's Idea. Britain's drift towards becoming a Republic had been sealed with the suspension of the House of Lords, now replaced by a new Upper House of Senators. Key posts, such as 'Archbishop of Canterbury', had become Cabinet positions, the Archbishop now being the 'Minister for Church Affairs'. It was inevitable, really, that the government and church now worked together more closely. Cathedrals had been identified as major tourist attractions and potential income earners as long as thirty years ago.

When the government had stepped in to help rebuild and refurbish some, and then the Church Commissioners had applied for a Euro-loan, it had opened the way for church and state to cooperate at levels unknown since the days of the Reformation. One day, over coffee, the Prime Minister had chatted informally to the Archbishop about 'opening up the church to the ordinary people ... making ministers more accountable to their parishes ... streamlining services, and capitalising on investments and ministries'. The fruit of their dialogue was a Republican commission, chaired by the Bishop of Southbury. And now, today, here was *The Churchgoer's Charter.*

Two Years Later

For the Revd Maurice Green, *The Churchgoer's Charter* had been a Godsend. His flourishing eclectic church in a prosperous university town had been one of the first to opt out of the diocese of Southbury. As a self-governing body, they were now free from many of the diocesan central structures that they felt had held them back from competing effectively with other churches. They had stopped paying their quota. They had always found it uncomfortable supporting a broad church; all those causes, churches and theological outlooks they had never liked could now fend for themselves. Besides this, they had 'rationalised' their giving to charities and outside bodies, in favour of concentrating their resources on the local situation.

The results had been spectacular. Three fizzy new curates had been hired: the duff old one the diocese provided had been made redundant. The new administrator, together with a new full-time accountant, had identified the areas of ministry that were most profitable. Fees for Baptisms, weddings and funerals were set at market rates. A new building programme provided further opportunities for income-bearing outreach. The Church Flower Shop provided all tributes, displays and bouquets for weddings and funerals. The new Church Brasserie (The Cana Wine Bar) did the catering for all special events; it was already featured in the *Michelin Guide.* A local photographer was awarded the exclusive contract for all weddings at the church, after it had been put out to competitive tender. Certain hymns and prayers had attracted sponsorship from local companies. A local building firm was always mentioned when 'The Church is One Foundation' was sung; the local privatised electricity board sponsored the Collect for Evening Prayer, 'Lighten Our Darkness'.

Alas, other parishes had not been nearly so innovative. Some had obviously just not used their talents as wisely. Of the fourteen churches in the town, six had already shut in two years, or been forced to merge. Of course, where possible, the stronger churches had attempted to cover areas that were now no longer served by a Parish Priest. But in some of the poorer estates on the fringe of town this had proved problematic. Providing a spiritual service at a realistic cost was difficult, especially when some of the people living in impoverished urban areas seemed 'to want something for nothing'. The Revd Maurice Green did feel some sadness about this. Yet he comforted himself with the proverb that 'Sheep always go where the grass is'. People would come to church if it offered a good service: it wasn't his fault if some clergy buried their talents.

Three Years Later

Bishop Michael of Southbury sat in his study. The rain poured down outside. 'Ah, where on earth has It all gone wrong?' he sighed. He had some answers, of course; but they were painful to face. For example, there was the share issue in the Church of England, launched in 2020. Called *20–20 Vision: Your Share In the Future*, congregations had been encouraged to buy shares in the national church, which entitled them to discounts for weddings, funerals and baptisms, and a small dividend each year if the Church Commissioners property speculation had gone well. It had been difficult to get off the ground initially, but the message had soon got home. The Share Issue would allow the public a greater say in how the church was run, and in its future direction.

To Bishop Michael, it had seemed the natural follow-up to *The Churchgoer's Charter*, which had already brought sweeping changes. Administrative posts had been cut by a half in his diocese. Education, Welfare and Social Responsibility officers had been pushed into 'private practice', so churches that needed them could purchase their services when they required them. The poorer parishes that had relied on them far too much in the past were now being encouraged to discover their own resources. Parishes had merged, inefficient clergy laid-off, and non-cost-effective areas of ministry identified and re-prioritised. As far as the Bishop was concerned, this was all excellent. However, it had got out of control. The agenda of *The Churchgoer's Charter* seemed like an unstoppable train. Now it looked as though he, the Bishop (of all people), was in danger of losing his job.

The problem had begun six months ago when the more cost-effective parishes in his Diocese had got together with other like-minded churches from neighbouring Dioceses. They had taken a comprehensive look at synodical and ecclesiastical structures. A clergyman from his own Diocese, the Revd Maurice Green, had argued that Bishops were too many and too expensive: 'they confirm some people in your church once a year, ordain you a new Curate every four years and for that they get a hundred grand, a jolly nice house and a chauffeur-driven car! They're simply not worth it.'

Changes soon followed. Quotas were again withheld by wealthy parishes until all Bishops signed up for the 'ERM' – the Episcopal Exchange Rate Mechanism. The idea was to let Bishops 'float', and open up competition. They would no longer get the exclusive contract for a diocese. Those that did good confirmation addresses or retreats would be paid for their services; those that didn't would be gradually laid off. Some Bishops had already gone into 'private practice', specialising in confirmations, ordinations, dedications, after dinner speeches or radio broadcasts. However, for the Bishop of Southbury, the writing was on the wall: he knew he couldn't compete with some of the younger, more dynamic Bishops. His letter of resignation was prepared, and sat on the table. He was going to go on a very long retreat.

Four Years Later

Sitting in the Hall at Church House, Michael Talent, now the former Bishop of Southbury, must have thought he'd seen it all before. Masses of cameramen, journalists, photographers and soundmen lined up six or seven deep waiting for him to speak. He was not flanked by other Bishops this time. The only endorsement he had was a letter from his friend, the former Archbishop of Canterbury, who'd retired early due to ill health.

He began to speak, this time holding aloft a copy of a new book written by him, called *Faith in Society*. Its message, he said, was simple. You cannot place a value on spiritual service. Everyone is entitled to ministry, whether they can afford it or not. The National Church Service must be there for all its people, not just a few. The richer churches must support the poorer ones, even if it cost them so much that it hurts them. An apparently weak and 'broad' church is probably better placed to serve society than a handful of strong eclectic ones. True, the Church is accountable to people, but also to God, the maker and judge of us all.

One journalist asked him where all this fresh vision had come from. In reply, Michael Talent said it was actually quite an old vision. But it hadn't been given a fair hearing. He referred to the Parable of the Talents, pointing out that 'most people thought that this was about wise financial investment'. 'But', he added, 'it is really about people and truth as well: they need to be invested in too, not buried out of fear. And sometimes apparently attractive gains need to be sacrificed; after all, we are called to lose our lives, not win them.' As he was speaking and replying to questions, journalists shuffled, looked irritated, and then began to leave.

'I bet this won't look very good in the newspapers tomorrow', he thought. And he was right. They didn't print a word of it.

Postscript – Ten Years Later

Retirement rather agreed with Bishop Michael. It had given him the chance to reflect on the changes that had come about in recent years, especially as a number of them had been something of surprise. For example, he could not have predicted the fate of the Revd Maurice Green. His church had witnessed enormous growth in the early years of new development. But the constant demands to make the buildings and projects financially viable had led to compromises, and also to divisive and fractious church meetings. The Victorian gallery in the church – a huge space – had been converted into a fitness centre, complete with glass wall that allowed those attending the gym to watch services as they lifted weights, ran on the machines, and exercised on the benches.

It had seemed like a good idea at the time. Come to church and get fit; pay a subscription too, and witness some worship. And why not stay for a Fairtrade chocolate drink in the café after? ('Sweat, Sacrament, Divine', ran the advertisement). But some of the worshippers – even dyed-in-the-wool modernisers – had objected. They did not think that their church was a place for a gym. Some objected that worship was now confused: could people really give their all to God if at the same time they were also thinking about their weight, their fitness, and how they looked? The out-sourcing of the Cana Wine Bar and café to a new catering company who paid good money for the franchise, but sat light to the ethos of the church, had also caused complications.

The church was still making money, and still had many members. But something was missing. Some worshippers felt the soul had gone from the place. Then the economic recession, which hit everyone and everything in its path, bit swiftly and deeply. Suddenly, church meetings were consumed by talks of mergers, redundancies, out-sourcing and rationalisations. Added to which, some worshippers just started to drift off to a local church with far fewer members, and no apparent entrepreneurial outlook at all. But which apparently had something that Maurice's church didn't: a soul. And a sense of awe and wonder, with a priest you could see in the week without going through a plethora of PAs and administrators. The church members were restless for change.

When Maurice's post came up for renewal, everything was basically fine; the recession was weathered; the income streams back on track; the number of worshippers steadied, having stemmed the earlier haemorrhaging. But the Church Council did not renew Maurice's contract. They thanked him for all he had done, but said that they felt God wanted to do something new with the church. To return it to being a place of sacredness and peace; a house of prayer, and an oasis of stillness. People wanted a change of direction; not what Maurice offered.

He left with a handsome pay-off, but somewhat bitter. And also curious. He remembered – from years ago at seminary – another pastor's words. Was it Niemoller, from Germany? He wasn't sure. But the gist of it was this. First the market forces came for the weaker parishes; but I didn't say anything. Then they came for the clergy who were deemed not to be successful or useful; but I didn't say anything. Then they came for the officers and administrators supporting the weaker parishes and clergy; and I didn't say anything. Then they came for the people who had introduced the change-management – for they too were expendable; and I didn't say anything. Then finally they came for me. But there was no-one left to speak for me.

Maurice Green's church had hired a new pastor – a former monk, called Benedict – who had not much in the way of business acumen, and little in the way of charismatic or dynamic leadership. There was not much money about any more, and little in the way of numerical or financial growth. But Benedict prayed for his people, visited faithfully, and was seen about the parish. The Cana Wine Bar was taken back into ownership by the church, and the space used to feed to poor. The gym and fitness centre went out of business, and now housed bunk-beds for the homeless. Had the entrepreneurial church failed? It was hard to say. But the congregation seemed happy enough. There was energy for mission, but no longer the ersatz of chimera-consumerist Christianity. Something earthy and authentic was now coming into existence.

Gone were the aims, objectives, targets and measuring of outcomes. 'Just how do you measure God's activity?', asked Benedict of his congregation, in a sermon one Sunday. 'The church is not competing in a popularity contest, with Christianity hoping to win more customers and consumers in contemporary culture than other activities. Our faith is about sacrifice and service. Who knows, we might find we're at our best when we're faithful, not successful', he argued. It made people think.

And Bishop Michael had watched this all unfold. It gave him just the smallest pang of pleasure to see the pendulum swing back, to a time long before *The Churchgoer's Charter* was launched. But he knew it might swing again. Meanwhile, some lessons had been learnt.

A Parable

There was a woman who lived on her own. She had no neighbours or close friends, but there was an old man who lived half a mile away. The woman had a house and a garden, and at the foot of a garden, she had two apple trees that were her pride and joy. Once she was called away to see a sick relative. She gave the keys of the house to the old man, and asked him to check the house, but he was too infirm to tend the garden. She thought she would be away for a few days, but she was in fact gone for a few years.

From far away she heard of drought and storms, and she feared the worst. But when she did get home, things were pretty well as she had left them. She went into the garden, which was very overgrown. But the apple trees were still there, and in full bloom. She drank it all in, and her heart filled with delight and thanks.

Then she went to the toolshed, got out her pruners, went to the apple trees, and started to cut away at the dead wood. And she thought of the time when there would apples for herself and for her neighbour.[3]

---

[3]   Bill Countryman, 1993, p. 86.

Select Bibliography

Adair, J. and Nelson, J. (2004), *Creative Church Leadership*, Norwich: Canterbury Press.

Aldridge, A. (2000), *Religion in the Contemporary World*, Cambridge: Polity Press.

An-Na'im, A. (1992), *Human Rights in Cross-Cultural Perspective: A Quest for Consensus*, Philadelphia: University of Pennsylvania Press.

Atherton, J. (ed.), (1994), *Social Christianity: A Reader*, London: SPCK.

Audi, R. (2000), *Religious Commitment and Secular Reason*, Cambridge: CUP.

Avis, P. (1992), *Authority, Leadership and Conflict in the Church*, London: Mowbray.

Avis, P. (2001), *Church, State and Establishment*, London: SPCK.

Bagemihl, B. (1999), *Biological Exuberance: Animal Homosexuality and Natural Diversity*, London: Profile Books.

Barber, B. (1995), *Jihad vs McWorld*, New York: Norton and Co.

Barber, B. (2007), *Consumed: How Markets Corrupt Children, Infantilize Adults and Swallow Citizens Whole*, New York: Norton and Co.

Barth, J. Robert (1977), *The Symbolic Imagination: Coleridge and the Romantic tradition*, Princeton: Princeton University Press.

Barth, K. (1954), 'The Christian Community and the Civil Community', *Against the Stream*, London: SCM.

Barth, K. (1958), *Church Dogmatics*, vol 4, part 2, Edinburgh: T&T Clark.

Bauman, Z (2000), *Liquid Modernity*, Cambridge: Polity Press.

Bayne, S. (1964), *An Anglican Turning Point*, New York: Church Publishing.

Bebbington, D. (1989), *Evangelicalism in Modern Britain: A History from the 1730s to the 1980s*, London: Unwin.

Beck, U. (2010), *A God of One's Own*, London: Polity Press.

Beckford, J. (1989), *Religion and Advanced Industrial Society*, London: Unwin.

Beckford, J. and Gilliat-Ray, S. (1998), *Religion in Prison: equal rites in a multi-faith society*, Cambridge: CUP.

Bell, D. (2001), *Liberation Theology After the End of History*, New York: Routledge.

Bellah, R. (1975), *The Broken Covenant: American Civil Religion in a Time of Trial*, New York: Seabury Press.

Bellah, R. (1985), *Habits of the Heart: individualism and commitment in American Life*, Berkeley: University of California Press.

Bendroth, M. (1993), *Fundamentalism and Gender: 1875 to the Present*, New Haven: Yale.

Berger, P. (1963), 'A Market Model for the Analysis of Ecumenicity', *Social Research*, 1963, vol. 30.

Berger, P. (1966) (with T. Luckmann), *The Social Construction of Reality: A Treatise on the Sociology of Knowledge*, New York: Doubleday.

Berger, P. (1967), *The Sacred Canopy: elements of a sociological theory of religion*, New York: Doubleday.

Berger, P. (1974), *The Homeless Mind*, London: Penguin.

Berger, P. (1977), 'Secular Theology and the Rejection of the Supernatural: reflections on recent trends', *Theological Studies*, vol. 38.

Berger, P. (1979), 'Religion and the American Future', in Lipset, S. (ed.), *The Third Century*, Chicago: University of Chicago Press.

Berger, P. (1981), 'New Attack on the Legitimacy of Business', *Harvard Business Review*, October.

Berger, P. (1993), 'Social Sources of Secularisation', in Alexander, J.C. and Seidman, S. (eds), *Culture and Society*, Cambridge: CUP.

Berger, P. (1999), *The Desecularization of the World: resurgent religion in world politics*, Washington DC: Ethics and Public Policy Center.

Berger, P. (2010), *Between Relativism and Fundamentalism: religious resources for a middle position*, Grand Rapids, Il.: Eerdmans.

Berger, P., Davie, G. and Fokas, E. (2008), *Religious America, Secular Europe? A Theme and Variations*, Aldershot: Ashgate.

Bermejo, L (1989), *The Spirit of Life: The Holy Spirit in the Life of the Christian*, Loyola University Press: Chicago.

Bibby, R. (1987), *Fragmented Gods: The Poverty and Potential of Religion in Canada*, Toronto: Stoddart.

Bibby, R. (1993), *Unknown Gods: The Ongoing Story of Religion in Canada*, Toronto: Stoddart.

Birdwell-Pheasant, D. and Lawrence-Zuniga, D. (eds) (1999), *House Life: space, place and family in Europe*, London: Berg.

Blanning, T. (2002), *The Culture of Power and the Power of Culture*, Oxford: OUP.

Bocock, R. (1974), *Ritual in Industrial Society: A Sociological Analysis of Ritualism in Modern England*, London: Allen and Unwin.

Brierley, P. (2010), *God's Questions: Vision, Strategy and Growth*, London: ADBC Publishers.

Brueggemann, W. (1978), *The Prophetic Imagination*, Philadelphia: Fortress Press.

Casanova, J. (1994), *Public Religions in the Modern World*, Chicago: Chicago University Press.

Clark, P. (2000), *British Clubs and Societies 1550–1800: the origin of an associational world*, Oxford: OUP.

Coakley, S. (ed.) (1997), *Religion and the Body*, Cambridge: CUP.

Coleridge, S. (1976), *On the Constitution of Church and State*. London: Routledge, Kegan and Paul (eds). Originally published by Taylor and Hessey, London 1839, London: Taylor & Hessey.

Colson, C. (1984), *Born Again*. London: Hodder & Stoughton.

Collins, S. (2000), 'Spirituality and Youth', in M. Percy (ed.), *Calling Time: religion and change at the turn of the millennium*, Sheffield: Sheffield Academic Press, pp. 221–37.

Countryman, B. (1993), *The Truth About Love: Reintroducing the Good News*, London: SPCK.

Davie, G. (1994), *Religion in Britain Since 1945: believing without belonging*, Oxford: Blackwell.

Davie, G. (2007), *The Sociology of Religion*, London: Sage.

Dawson, C. (1936), *Religion and the Modern State*, London: Sheed and Ward.

Drane, J. (1999), *The McDonaldization of the Church: spirituality, creativity and the future*, London: DLT.

Dulles, D. (1974), *Models of the Church*, New York: Doubleday.

Duncan, D.E. (1998), *The Calendar: the 5000 year struggle to align the clock and the heavens*, London: Fourth Estate.

Edge, P. and Harvey, G. (eds) (2000), *Law and Religion in Contemporary Society*, Aldershot: Ashgate.

Ehrenreich, B. (2009), *Smile or Die: How Positive Thinking Fooled America and the World*, London: Granta Books.

Eliot, T.S. (1939), *The Idea of a Christian Society*, London: Faber.

Esposito J. and Watson, M. (2000), *Religion and Global Order*, Cardiff: University of Wales Press.

Featherstone, M. (1991), *Postmodernism and Consumer Culture*, London: Sage.

Ferguson, K. (1999), *Measuring the Universe: the historical quest to quantify space*, London: Headline.

Figgis, J. (1913), *Churches in the Modern State*, London: Longmans Green & Co.

Foster, C., Dahill, L., Golemon L. and Wang Tolentino, B. (2006), *Educating Clergy: Teaching Practices and Pastoral Imagination*, San Francisco: Jossey-Bass.

Fowles, J. (1995), *Advertising and Popular Culture*, New York: Free Press.

Fromm, E. (1941), *Escape from Freedom*, New York: Henry Holt Publishers.

Fromm, E. (1956), *The Art of Loving*, New York: Harper.

Fulkerson, M.M. (2008), *Places of Redemption*, Oxford: OUP.

Furbey, R. (1999), 'Urban Regeneration', in *Critical Social Policy: a journal of theory and practice in social welfare*, issue 61, vol. 19 (4), November 1999, London: Sage Publications, pp. 419–45.

Gell, A. (1992), *The Anthropology of Time*, London: Berg.

Gerhardt, S. (2006), *Why Love Matters*, London: Simon and Schuster.

Ghanea-Hercock, N. (2000), 'Faith in Human Rights: Human Rights in Faith', in J. Thierstein and Y. Kamalipour (eds), *Religion, Law and Freedom: A Global Perspective*, Westport, Conn.: Praeger Press.

Giles, R. (1999), *Re-pitching the Tent: re-ordering the church building for worship and mission*, Norwich: Canterbury Press.

Giles, R. (2005), *Always Open: Being an Anglican Today*, New York: Cowley Publications.

Gilliat-Ray, S. (2001), *Religion in Higher Education: the politics of a multi-faith campus*, Hampshire: Sheffield Academic Press.

Gillingham, J. and Griffiths, R. (2001), *Medieval Britain*, Oxford: OUP.

Gorringe, T. (2004), *Futhering Humanity: a theology of culture*, Aldershot: Ashgate.

Gould, S.J. (1997), *Questioning the Millennium: a rationalist's guide to a precisely arbitrary countdown*, London: Jonathan Cape.

Friedrich Graf (2004), *Die Wiederker der Gotter*, Munich: Beck.

Grierson, D. (1984), *Transforming a People of God*, Melbourne, Joint Board of Christian Education of Australia and New Zealand.

Gribbin, J. (1998), *The Birth of Time: how we measured the age of the universe*, London: Weidenfeld & Nicholson.

Guitierrez, G. (1973), *A Theology of Liberation*, New York: Orbis Books.

Haight, R. (2004), *Christian Community in History: Historical Ecclesiology* vol. 1, New York: Continuum.

Haight, R. (2005), *Christian Community in History: comparative ecclesiology* vol. 2, New York: Continuum.

Haight, R. (2008), *Ecclesial Existence: Christian Community in History*, vol. 3 New York: Continuum.

Hardy, D. (2002), *Finding the Church: the dynamic truth of Anglicanism*, London: SCM Press.

Hardy, D. (2010), *Wording a Radiance: Parting Conversations of God and the Church*, London: SCM Press.

Hardy, D.W. (1989) (with Colin Gunton) (eds), *On Being the Church: Essays on the Christian Community*, Edinburgh: T & T Clark.

Hardt, M. and Negri, A. (2000), *Empire*, Boston: Harvard University Press.

Hare, D. (2009), *The Power of Yes*, London: Faber.

Harris, M. (1998), *Organizing God's Work: challenges for churches and synagogues*, London: Macmillan.

Hastings, A. (1997), 'The Case for Retaining Establishment', in Modood (ed.), *Church, State and Religious Minorities*, London: Policy Studies Institute.

Haynes, J. (1998), *Religion in Global Politics*, London: Longman.

Haynes, J. (2000), 'The End of Tolerance: engaging cultural differences', in *Daedalus*, vol. 129, no. 4, Fall 2000.

Hauerwas, S. (1988) *Christian Existence Today*: essays on church, world and living in-between, Durham: The Labyrinth Press.

Healy, N. (2000), *Church, World and Christian Life: Practical-Prophetic Ecclesiology*, Cambridge: CUP.

Heard, J. (2008), *Inside Alpha: explorations in evangelism*, Carlisle: Paternoster Press.

Herbert, D. (2001), *Religion and Civil Society: Multiculturalism, Democracy and Spirituality*, Aldershot: Ashgate.

Herbert, George (1633), 'The Temple', in (1857) *The Poetical Works of George Herbert*, New York: D. Appleton & Co.

Hervieu-Leger, D. (2000), *Religion as a Chain of Memory*, Oxford: Polity.

Hill, M. (1999), 'Church Autonomy in the United Kingdom', a paper presented to the Second European/American Conference on Religious Freedom, '*Church Autonomy and Religious Liberty*', University of Trier, Germany, 27–30 May 1999.

Hooker, R. (1907), *The Laws of Ecclesiastical Polity*, London: J.M. Dent (Everyman Edition).

Hopewell, J. (1987), *Congregation: Stories and Structures*, London: SCM.

Hunt, S. (2001), *Anyone for Alpha?: evangelism and nurture in contemporary Britain*, London: DLT.

Hunt, S. (2004), *The Alpha Enterprise: evangelism in a post-Christian culture*, Aldershot: Ashgate.

Hyde, L. (1983), *The Gift*, New York: Random House.

Inge, J. (2003), *A Christian Theology of Place*, Aldershot: Ashgate.

Izuzquiza, D. (2009), *Rooted in Jesus Christ: toward a radical ecclesiology*, Grand Rapids, Il.: Eerdmans.

Jedrej, M. (1996), 'Time and Space', in Barnard, A. and Spencer, J. (eds), *Encyclopaedia of Social and Cultural Anthropology*, London: Routledge.

Jellinek, G. (1979), *The Declaration of the Rights of Man and of the Citizen*, Westport, Conn.: Hyperion Press.

Jones, Lawrence E. (1965), *The Observer Book of Churches*, London: Frederick Warne & Co.

Kepel, G. (1994), *Revenge of God*, Cambridge: Polity Press.

King, M.L. (1963), *Strength to Love*, Cleveland: Collins.

Kirk, Kenneth (1946), *The Apostolic Ministry: essays on the history and doctrine of episcopacy*, London: Hodder & Stoughton.

Kleist, J. (ed.) (1948), 'Epistle to Diognetus', *The Ancient Christian Writers*, no. 6, New York: Newman Press.

Kwint, M., Breward, C. and Anysley, J. (1999), *Material Memories*, London: Berg.

Kwong, P (2011), *Identity in Community: Toward a theological Agenda for the Hong Kong SAR* (Explorations in Intercultural Theology, vol. 9), New Jersey: Rutgers University/Transaction Publishers.

Lacey, R. and Danzinger, D. (1999), *The Year 1000*, London: Little, Brown.

Larkin, P. (2001), *Collected Poems*, London: Faber and Faber.

Leach, N. (1999), *Millennium Culture*, London: Ellipsis Books.

Lee, R. (1960), *The Social Sources of Church Unity*, New York: Abingdon Press.

Locke, K.A. (2009), *The Church in Anglican Theology: A Historical, Theological and Ecumenical Exploration*, Farnham: Ashgate.

Lodge, D. (1980), *How Far Can You Go?*, London: Penguin.

Lynch, Thomas (1998), *The Undertaking: life studies from the dismal trade*, New York: Penguin.

Lyon, D. (2000), *Jesus in Disneyland: Religion in Post-modern Times*, Cambridge: Polity Press.

March, A. (2009), *Islam and Liberal Citizenship: the search for an overlapping consensus*, Oxford: OUP.

Markham, I. (1999, 2nd edition), *Plurality and Christian Ethics*, New York: Seven Bridges Press.

Martin, D., (1980), *The Breaking of the Image*, Oxford, Blackwell.

Marty, M.E. (1985), 'Hell Disappeared. No-one Noticed: a civic argument', *Harvard Theological Review*, vol. 78, 00. pp. 19–31.

Mauss, Marcel, *The Gift: Forms of Exchange in Archaic Society* (1924; transl. 1967), New York: Norton and Co.

McCutcheon, R. (1997), *Manufacturing Religion*, Oxford: Oxford University Press.

Medhurst, K. and Moyser, G. (1988), *Church and Politics in a Secular Age*, Oxford: Clarendon Press.

Menon, U. (2000), 'Does Feminism Have Universal Relevance? The challenges posed by Oriya Hindu family practices', in *Daedalus*, vol. 120, issue 4, pp. 31–54.

Micklethwait, J. and Woolbridge, A. (2009), *God is Back: how the global rise of faith is changing the world*, London: Allen Lane.

Milbank, J. (1990), *Theology and Social Theory: beyond secular reason*, Oxford: Blackwell.

Milbank, J. (1997), *The Word Made Strange: theology, language, culture*, Oxford: Blackwell.

Miller, D. (1987), *Material Culture and Mass Consumption*, Oxford: Blackwell.

Miller, D. (1997), *Capitalism: An Ethnographic Approach*, Oxford: Berg.

Miller. D. (1998), *A Theory of Shopping*, Cambridge: Polity.

Miller, V.J. (2004), *Consuming Religion: Christian Faith and Practice in a Consumer Culture*, New York: Continuum.

Modood, T. (1997), 'Introduction: establishment, reform and multiculturalism', in Modood, T. (ed.), *Church, State and Religious Minorities*, London: Policy Studies Institute.

Moore, R.L. (1994) *Selling God: American religion in the marketplace of culture*, Oxford: OUP.

Morgan, D. (1999), *Protestants and Pictures: Visual Culture, and the Age of American Mass Production*, Oxford: OUP.

Murphey, N. (1996), *Beyond Liberalism and Fundamentalism*, Valley Forge, PA: Trinity Press International.

Nekola, Anna (2001), 'US Evangelicals and the Re-definition of Worship Music', in M. Bailey and G. Redden (eds), *Mediating Faiths*, Aldershot: Ashgate.

Neuhaus, R. (1984), *The Naked Public Square: Religion and Democracy in America*, Grand Rapids, Il.: Eerdmans.

Newbigin, L. (1953), *The Household of God*, Grand Rapids, Il: Eerdmans.

Newbigin, L. (1978), *The Open Secret*, Grand Rapids, Il: Eerdmans.

Newbigin, L. (1988), 'On being the church for the world', in Ecclestone, G. (ed.) *The Parish Church?* London: Mowbray.

Newbigin, L. (1986), *Foolishness to the Greeks*, London: SPCK.

Nicholls, D. (1967), *Church and State in Britain Since 1820*, London: Routledge.

Nicholls, D. (1988), *Deity and Domination: images of God and the state in the nineteenth and twentieth centuries*, London: Routledge.

Niebuhr, R. (1941), *The Nature and Destiny of Man*, London: Nisbet.

Niebuhr, R. (1951), *Christ and Culture*, New York: Harper.

Niebuhr, R. (1963), *Moral Man and Immoral Society*, London, SCM.

Noddings, Nel (1984), *Caring: a feminine approach to ethics and moral education*, Berkeley, California: University of California Press.

Noddings, Nel (1998), *Philosophy of Education*, Boulder, Colorado: Westview Press.

Noddings, Nel (2002), *Educating Moral People*, New York: Teachers College / Columbia University Press.

Noddings, Nel and Shore, Paul (1984), *Awakening the Inner Eye: intuition in education*, New York: Teachers College / Columbia University Press.

Norman, E. (1979), *Christianity and the World Order*, Oxford: OUP.

The Ecclesial Canopy

Oates, S. (1982), *Let the Trumpet Sound: A Life of Martin Luther King*, New York: HarperCollins.

O'Donovan, L.L. (1998), 'Historical Prolegomena to a Theological Review of Human Rights', *Studies in Christian Ethics*, vol. 9, no. 2, pp. 52–65.

O'Donovan, O. (1996), *The Desire of Nations: rediscovering the roots of political theology*, Cambridge: CUP.

O'Donovan, O. (2008), *The Church in Crisis: the Gay Controversy and the Anglican Communion*, Eugene, Oregon: Cascade Books.

Ogilvy, D. (1985), *Ogilvy on Advertising*, New York: Vintage Books.

Orchard, H. (2000), *Hospital Chaplaincy: modern, dependable?*, Sheffield: Sheffield Academic Press.

Paley (1785), *The Principles of Moral and Political Philosophy*, Foreword by D.L. Le Mahieu (2002), Indianapolis: Liberty Fund.

Parekh, B. (1997), 'When Religion Meets Politics', in *Keeping the Faiths: The New Covenant Between Religious Belief and Secular Power*, London: Demos, no. 11.

Paulhus, F.D. and Bradstock, A. (2007), *Moral, But No Compass: Government, Church and the Future of Welfare*, Cambridge: Von Hügel Institute and Matthew James Publishing.

Parsons, T. (1963), 'Christianity and Modern Industrialised Society', in E. Tiryakian (ed.), *Sociological Theory, Values and Sociological Change*, London: Collier-Macmillan.

Percy, M. (1998), *Power and the Church: Ecclesiology in an Age of Transition*, London: Cassell.

Percy, M. (2000), 'The Sacred Canopy: Religion and Time at the Greenwich Millennium Dome', in *Religion, Time and Change*, M. Percy (ed.) (2000), Sheffield: Sheffield Academic Press.

Percy, M. (2001), 'A Place at High Table? Charismatic Renewal in Perspective', in L. Woodhead and G. Davie, *Predicting Religion*, Aldershot: Ashgate.

Percy, M. (2005), *Engaging Contemporary Culture: Christianity, Theology and the Concrete Church*, Aldershot: Ashgate.

Percy, M. (2006), *Clergy: The Origin of Species*, London: Continuum.

Percy, M. (2008), 'Sacred Sagacity: Formation and Training for Ministry in a Church of England Seminary', *The Anglican Theological Review*, vol. 90, pp. 285–96.

Percy, M. (2010), *Shaping the Church: The Promise of Implicit Theology*. Farnham: Ashgate.

Peterson, E. (2006), *Eat this Book: A Conversation in the Art of Spiritual Reading*, London: Hodder and Stoughton.

Pickard, S. (2009), 'Church of the In-between God: recovering an ecclesial sense of place down-under', in *Journal of Anglican Studies*, vol. 7, issue 1, May 2009.

Podmore, C. (2005), *Aspects of Anglican Identity*, London: Church House Publishing.

Podmore, C. (2011), 'Two Streams Mingling: The American Episcopal Church in the Anglican Communion', *Journal of Anglican Studies*, vol. 9.1.

Pratt-Ewing, K. (2000), 'Legislating Religious Freedom: Muslim challenges to "Church" and "State" in Germany and France', in *Daedalus*, vol. 120, issue 4, pp. 31–54.

Radner, E. and Philip Turner (2006), *The Fate of Communion: The Agony of Anglicanism and the Future of a Global Church*, Grand Rapids, Il.: Eerdmans.

Rauschenbusch, W. (1912), *Christianizing the Social Order*, New York: Macmillan.

Reed, B. (1978), *The Dynamics of Religion: Process and Movement in Christian Churches*, London: DLT.

Richards, E.G. (1998), *Mapping Time: the calendar and its history*, Oxford: OUP.

Richardson, Ann (ed.) (2009), *Through the Eyes of Children*, London: Church House Publishing.

Ritzer, G. (1993), *The McDonaldization of Society*, Thousand Oaks, CA.: Pine Forge Press.

Roberts, Michael (ed.) (1965), *The Faber Book of Modern Verse*, London: Faber.

Robertson, R. (2000), 'The Globalisation of "Traditional Religion"', in M. Stackhouse and P. Paris, *God and Globalisation (vol. 1): Religion and the Powers of Common Life*, Harrisburgy, Penn.: Trinity Press International.

Robinson, G. (2008), *In the Eye of the Storm*, London: SCM-Canterbury Press.

Rogers, L. (1999), *Sexing the Brain*, London: Weidenfeld & Nicholson.

Roof, W.C. (1993), *A Generation of Seekers: The Spiritual Journey of the Baby Boomers*, New York: HarperCollins.

Roof, W.C. (1999), *Spiritual Marketplace: Baby Boomers and Re-Making of American Religion*, Princeton: Princeton University Press.

Roof W.C. and McKinney, W. (1987), *American Mainline Religion: Its Changing Shape and Future*, New Brunswick: Rutgers University Press.

Roszak, T. (2000), *The Making of a Counter Culture*, London: Faber.

Rousseau, J. (1973), *The Social Contract and Discourses*, London: Dent.

Rudge, P. (1968), *Ministry and Management: the Study of Ecclesiastical Administration*, London: Tavistock Publications.

Sachs, W. (2009), *Homosexuality and the Crisis of Anglicanism*, Cambridge: Cambridge University Press.

Sager, L. (2000), 'The Free Exercise of Culture: some doubts and distinctions,' *Daedalus*, vol. 129, issue 4, pp. 193–208.

Sandel, M. (2009), *Justice*, London: Allen Lane.

Schmiechen, P. (2005), *Saving Power: theories of atonement and forms of the church*, Michigan: Eerdmans.

Schoffeleers, J.M. (1999), *In Search of Truth and Justice: confrontations between church and state in Malawi 1960–1994*, Blantyre: Christian Literature Association.

Scougal, H. (1829), *The Life of God in the Soul of Man*, New York: C. & F. Rivington.

Selznick, P. (1957), *Leadership in Administration: A Sociological Interpretation*, New York: Harper.

Sen, A. (2009), *The Idea of Justice*, London: Allen Lane.

Shanks, A. (1990), *Civil Religion, Civil Society*, Oxford: Blackwell.

Sheldrake, P. (2001), *Spaces for the Sacred*, London: SCM.

Shweder, R. (2000), 'What About Female Genital Mutilation? Why understanding culture matters', in *Daedalus*, vol. 120, issue 4, pp. 209–33.

Spohn, W. (1999), *Go and Do Likewise*, New York: Continuum.

Stackhouse, M. (1988), *Apologia: contextualisation, globalisation and mission in theological education*, Grand Rapids, Il.: Eerdmans.

Stackhouse, M. and Paris, P. (eds) (2000), *God and Globalisation*, vol. 1, Harrisburg, Penn.: Trinity Press International.

Stark, R. and Bainbridge, S. (1987), *A Theory of Religion*, New York: Peter Lang.

Stark, W. (1966), *The Sociology of Religion: a study*, London: Routledge.

Sterrett, J. and Thomas P. (eds) (2011), *Sacred Text-Sacred Space: Architectural, Spiritual and Literary Convergences in England and Wales*, Leiden: Brill.

Stoppard. T. (1974), *Jumpers*, London: Faber.

Stout, J. (1988), *Ethics After Babel*, Cambridge, Mass.: James Clarke.

Swatos, W. jr and Wellman, J. jr (1999), *The Power of Religious Publics: staking claims in American society*, Westport, Conn.: Praeger Publishing.

Tawney, R.H. (1922), *Religion and the Rise of Capitalism*, London: John Murray.

Taylor, C. (2007), *A Secular Age*, Harvard MA: Harvard University Press.

Temple, W. (1942), *Christianity and Social Order*, Harmondsworth: Penguin.

Thomas, K. (1971), *Religion and the Decline of Magic*, Oxford: Oxford University Press.

Thompson, D. (1997), *The End of Time? Faith and Fear in the Shadow of the Millennium*, London: Sinclair.

Tomasi, J. (2001), *Liberalism Beyond Justice: Citizens, Societies and the Boundaries –a Political Theory*, Princeton: Princeton University Press.

Torry, M. (2005), *Managing God's Business: religious and faith-based organizations and their management*, Aldershot: Ashgate.

Troeltsch, E. (1966), *Protestantism and Progress: A Historical Study of the Relations of Protestantism to the Modern World*, Boston: Beacon Press.

Tuck, R. (1993), *Philosophy and Government: 1572–1650*, Cambridge: CUP.

Tweed, T. (2006), *Crossing and Dwelling*, Cambridge, MA: Harvard University Press.

Van der Ven, J. (1996), *Ecclesiology in Context*, Grand Rapids, Il.: Eerdmans.

Wadell, P., Gregory Jones, L. and Paulsell, S. (eds), (2002), *The Scope of our Art: The Vocation of the Theological Teacher*, Grand Rapids, Il.: Eerdmans.

Walter (1994), *The Revival of Death*, London: Routledge.

Ward, P. (1999), 'Alpha – the McDonaldization of Religion', in *Anvil*, vol. 1, no. 4, pp. 279–86.

Warner, R. (2011), 'How Congregations are Becoming Consumers', in M. Bailey and G. Redden (eds), *Mediating Faiths*, Farnham: Ashgate.

Warren, R. (1995), *The Purpose-Driven Church: Growth Without Compromising Your Message and Mission*, Grand Rapids, Il.: Zondervan.

Warren, R. (2002), *The Purpose-Driven Life*, Grand Rapids, Il.: Zondervan.

Watson, D. (1980), *Jesus Then and Now*, Tring: Lion Publishing.

Weil, S. (1973), *Waiting For God*, New York, Harper.

Wenger, E. (1998), *Communities of Practice: Learning, Meaning and Identity*, Cambridge: Cambridge University Press.

Wenger, E., McDermot, R., and Snyder, W. (2002), *Cultivating Communities of Practice*, Boston MA: Harvard University Press.

Westerhoff, John H. (ed.) (1972), *A Colloquy on Christian Education*, Philadelphia: United Church Press.

Westerlund, D. (ed.) (1996), *Questioning the Secular State: the worldwide resurgence of religion in politics*, London: Hurst & Company.

Williams, R. (May 2004), 'The Christian Priest Today', Lecture, 28 May 2004.

Williams, R. (2004), *Anglican Identities*, London: DLT.

Willimon, W (2000), *Calling and Character: Virtues of the Ordained Life*, Nashville: Abingdon Press.

Winter, G. (1961), *The Suburban Captivity of the Churches*, New York: Macmillan.

Woodhead, L. (2010), 'Implicit Understandings of Religion in Sociological Study and in the Work of Hugh McLeod', in Brown, C. and Snape, M. (eds), *Secularisation in the Christian World*, Farnham: Ashgate.

Wright, T. (1992), *The New Testament and the People of God: Christian Origins and the Question of God*, London: SPCK.

Wuthnow, R. (1988), *After Heaven: Spirituality in America Since the 1950s*, Berkeley, CA: University of California Press.

Wuthnow, R., Hunter, J., Bergesen, A. and Kurzwell, E. (eds) (1984), *Cultural Analysis: the work of Peter Berger, Mary Douglas, Michael Foucault and Jurgen Habermas*, London: Routledge.

Yingqiang, Hu (2010), 'Protestant Christianity and Chinese Religions: an ecumenical perspective', in *Chinese Theological Review*, Vol. 22, pp. 25–41.

Index